REAL LIFE, REAL LOVE

7 Paths to a Strong & Lasting Relationship

BERKLEY BOOKS, NEW YORK

REAL LIFE,
REAL LOVE

✦

Father Albert Cutié

W

306.73
CUT
DISCARDED

Most Berkley Books are available at special quantity discounts for bulk purchases for sales promotions, premiums, fund-raising or educational use. Special books, or book excerpts, can also be created to fit specific needs.

For details, write: Special Markets, The Berkley Publishing Group, 375 Hudson Street, New York, New York 10014.

THE BERKLEY PUBLISHING GROUP
Published by the Penguin Group
Penguin Group (USA) Inc.
375 Hudson Street, New York, New York 10014, USA
Penguin Group (Canada), 90 Eglinton Avenue East, Suite 700, Toronto, Ontario M4P 2Y3, Canada
(a division of Pearson Penguin Canada Inc.)
Penguin Books Ltd., 80 Strand London WC2R 0RL, England
Penguin Group Ireland, 25 St. Stephen's Green, Dublin 2, Ireland (a division of Penguin Books Ltd.)
Penguin Group (Australia), 250 Camberwell Road, Camberwell, Victoria 3124, Australia
(a division of Pearson Australia Group Pty. Ltd.)
Penguin Books India Pvt. Ltd., 11 Community Centre, Panchsheel Park, New Delhi—110 017, India
Penguin Group (NZ), Cnr. Airborne and Rosedale Roads, Albany, Auckland 1310, New Zealand
(a division of Pearson New Zealand Ltd.)
Penguin Books (South Africa) (Pty.) Ltd., 24 Sturdee Avenue, Rosebank, Johannesburg 2196, South Africa

Penguin Books Ltd., Registered Offices: 80 Strand, London WC2R 0RL, England

This book is an original publication of The Berkley Publishing Group.

The events described in this book are the real experiences of real people. However, the author has altered their identities and, in some instances, created composite characters. Any resemblance between a character in this book and a real person, therefore, is entirely accidental.

While the author has made every effort to provide accurate telephone numbers and Internet addresses at the time of publication, neither the publisher nor the author assumes any responsibility for errors, or for changes that occur after publication. Further, the publisher does not have any control over and does not assume any responsibility for author or third-party websites or their content.

First edition: January 2006

Berkley hardcover ISBN: 0-425-20542-8

This book has been catalogued with the Library of Congress

PRINTED IN THE UNITED STATES OF AMERICA

10 9 8 7 6 5 4 3 2 1

This book is dedicated to the countless people who have opened their hearts and lives to me through my work in television, radio, and the written press, asking for advice about their troubled relationships, or at times, simply looking for someone who will listen to their pain . . .

This book is for all of you, especially those who have insisted that I "put it on paper." Here it is!

Acknowledgments

In 1998, I received a phone call from an international television network, asking me to host a talk show—something one never expects to do as a Catholic priest. It was there that I discovered what I consider the real "mission territory" of the twenty-first century—the media.

I want to acknowledge Nely Galan, the creator and mastermind of my first television program, and Rafael Bello, my first executive producer, for getting me started in the media world. I also want to express my deepest appreciation to those who put up with me on a daily basis at Pax Catholic Communications (Radio Paz and Radio Peace in Miami, where I serve as general director), Enrique Duprat of EWTN "El Canal Catolico" and Servio Tulio Mateo, my executive producer at channel 48 in Honduras. The staff at *El Nuevo Herald* in Miami, where my column originated, helped me to reach people all around the world with what I hope is inspirational and practical advice.

My special gratitude also goes to my literary agents, Johanna Castillo and Jennifer Cayea, who believed in this project and have pushed me every step of the way. I thank Denise Silvestro and Ed Myers for their editorial expertise and great skills.

Finally, a special word of gratitude goes out to my spiritual family at the various communities where I have served. Namely; Saint Francis de Sales and St. Patrick's (on Miami Beach), San Isidro (in Pompano), St. Clement (in Fort Lauderdale), and St. Mary Star of the Sea (in Key West), as well as my God-given family who have given me so much love and support in my ministry through the years.

May God bless you all! Ad Multos Annos!

Contents

Introduction

One evening not long ago, I sat resting and thinking at a beach near the parish house where I live in Miami Beach. The time was just before sunset. The beach was almost empty; the water was calm. I'd come there to pray the Evening Prayer (Vespers) in this serene place. It only takes about ten minutes to pray the Evening Prayer, so I knew I had plenty of time before the light faded. I couldn't have wanted a more prayerful setting.

The few people present there went about their business—couples walking, joggers jogging, a middle-aged man playing fetch with his dog. I felt comfortable being alone yet also content to have others around me. These folks ignored what at least some of them must have considered a slightly odd sight: a priest in clerical garb sitting there on the beach.

Gradually, though, I became aware of one particular passerby—a young woman in shorts and T-shirt—who had walked past me several times. Each time she passed, she came a little closer. I continued saying my prayers without looking up, as I really just wanted to be there on my own. But soon I heard a question I'm often asked: "Are you the priest I see on television?"

"I guess I am," I replied.

"Could I talk with you a moment?"

"Sure." I try to be available to people whenever they need me, so I changed my plans right then and there to hear what was on her mind.

It turned out there was quite a lot. "I'm in a relationship with someone I care about," this woman told me, "but being in love seems so much harder than I expected. Ari and I argue over everything! We want things to work out. We try to *make* it work. But it's so . . . *difficult*!" This young woman, whose name was Daniela, then explained her concerns in great detail. Now in her early thirties, she had experienced ups and downs in other relationships. She felt a growing urgency about finding a man with whom she could build a marriage, have a family, and share her life. She felt confident that she was in love, yet she still wasn't totally sure if her boyfriend was the man she could count on for a long-term commitment.

Daniela and I proceeded to have a long conversation about the meaning of relationships and the best way to attain personal happiness. Mostly I listened to her concerns. I also offered Daniela my own reflections on what she said and my impressions of how she might strengthen her relationship with Ari. We talked for a long time, then parted company. I felt glad to have helped her, and she seemed content to have crossed paths with a priest in the middle of a public beach.

I hope I gave her some good advice. The details of what I said aren't really so important in what I'm telling you now. My point is simply that incidents like this conversation happen to me often, and they show me time after time how confused and needy so many people are as they struggle with the many issues that couples encounter.

A BOOK ABOUT RELATIONSHIPS

This brings us to the matter at hand: the book you're holding.

As a parish priest, as the host of TV and radio advice shows, and as the author of a newspaper advice column, I constantly hear about the difficulties that men and women face in relating to each other. Sometimes these difficulties are the ordinary, day-to-day interactions that cause stress or confusion. Sometimes the difficulties are more serious conflicts and misunderstandings. It's no secret that relationships take a lot of time, energy, and attention. The situation is clear to me in my several roles: the greatest struggle that most people face on a daily basis comes from dealing with the person they've chosen as a mate. In fact, almost everyone struggles with the difficulties and the differences of opinion that arise from their relationships.

- ∞ How can you bridge the gap between our culture's romantic expectations about love and the reality of everyday domestic life together?

- ∞ How do you live with the differences that occur in a relationship where two totally different people must interact, compromise, and live together?

- ∞ How can you communicate effectively as a couple?

- ∞ How can you come to terms with the different cultural, familial, and individual expectations that you and your partner may hold?

- ∞ How can you solve the problems and resolve the conflicts that occur in even the happiest marriages?

- ∞ How can you nurture love over the years of a long relationship—especially given the demands that work and parenting exert on a couple?

These are just a few of the fundamental issues that give rise to relationship troubles. In my work as a priest, I see signs of these troubles on a daily (sometimes even hourly!) basis. Almost all of the questions that people ask me concern the struggle to figure out the roles, changes, habits, decisions, expectations, and daily events that constitute a marriage. In a happy relationship, the partners must still come to terms with all these issues. In a conflicted relationship, the partners often feel frustration or pain because they can't "get a handle" on the issues well enough to live in peace together. This holds true for couples that are just getting started together, as well as those in longer-term relationships. Even the best marriage in the world will present the spouses with issues that require adjustments, compromise, accommodations, and soul-searching.

As a priest, I could write a book about many issues that concern theology or spiritual issues. These are certainly matters I think about a lot. However, I believe that the issues that affect all of us most often and most intensely at every level of our daily life—including at the level of spirituality—are those concerning our relationships. I also believe that when people come to their priest, or when they seek advice from a member of the helping professions, it's usually to ask for help with relationships. This is why I've written *Real Life, Real Love: Seven Paths to a Strong and Lasting Relationship*.

WHY A RELATIONSHIP BOOK BY A *PRIEST*?

When people know a little about my background, they often ask me, "How on earth did a deejay become a priest?"

I always answer by saying, "Maybe you should ask God that question. If I were God, I wouldn't have called *me* to be a priest!"

But the truth is, God *did* call, and I heard Him loud and clear despite all the noise on the dance floor. I knew I loved Him above all things. I loved people, too. So a life as a parish priest seemed the natural choice—serving God and serving His people. Great idea, right? Within a short while, this drastic shift in my "career plans" put me in the middle of a seminary.

Then, three years after I was ordained a priest, God surprised me again. A Spanish-language national TV network asked me to host a television talk show that would be seen all over the United States and Latin

America. I'd never expected to be on television, and I don't think I'd seen one full television program in the ten-years-plus between the start of my seminary studies and my invitation to be on TV. But the surprises kept coming. Television then led me to radio, first when my archbishop asked me to run day-to-day operations for the Church's own stations in Miami, then later when I began to appear in the mainstream media, sending a message to millions of listeners. And then the press came after me, asking me to become a kind of "Dear Abby with a spiritual twist." I now write six advice columns every week.

As for the other question some people ask me . . . it's this one: "What does a celibate priest know about relationships and marriage?"

This is a reasonable question, and I'm happy to answer it.

First off: I wasn't born a priest. I didn't grow up on another planet and get beamed down to earth like something out of *Star Trek*. I grew up in an ordinary family. I've spent my whole life interacting with relatives, friends, and acquaintances, and throughout my whole life I've been observing and understanding what goes on in relationships of many sorts.

Second, I come from a family in which I was surrounded by three wonderful marriages. My maternal grandparents were married fifty-eight years before my grandfather passed away. My paternal grandparents were married fifty-four years. And my parents were married until my father was diagnosed with cancer and died as a relatively young man. I'm the product of those three marriages, and I lived in the context of family life and married life for so many years that I came to understand the good, the bad, and the ugly in marriage.

Third, my preparation for the priesthood included a certain component in pastoral counseling, and much of that training focuses on helping couples through the various stages of their relationships. Just as a marital therapist can be thoughtful and effective as a counselor even if he or she isn't married, I believe that a priest can help couples despite being celibate and single. (Ironically, it's possible that priests see marriage *more* clearly—or at least with a different kind of clarity—than people do when they're "on the inside" of a marriage. We priests may appreciate married life a lot more than some people do precisely *because* we are celibate.) I don't think that you have to be in the middle of a specific condition to help people who are coping with it. For instance, a psychologist or psychiatrist doesn't have to have personal experience of mental health problems to offer helpful insights to those who suffer from them. In fact, it's precisely the therapist's *distance* from these problems that makes his or her insights objective, clear-sighted, and useful.

Fourth, at least 70 or 80 percent of my pastoral ministry has been directly involved with couples at every stage of the marital experience—preparing to be married, getting married, being married, struggling with personal differences, and sometimes finding themselves thinking separation and divorce are the only solution. So a large portion of my day-to-day work involves helping people with a wide variety of relationship issues.

So how does this all add up?

I realize, of course, that I have both personal and professional limitations, and I'm aware that I can counsel people only to a certain degree. But I've devoted my life to helping people cope with all kinds of challenges and crises, including the crises they face in their relationships. I have a lot of insights based on my personal experience and perceptions working with thousands of couples. And I find that most people who ask a priest's advice do, in fact, take that advice. So I'm hoping that, as they look to solve their relationship problems, people who come to this book will find the same type of help.

SEVEN PATHS

Here's how I see the situation:

I believe that all human beings have an innate drive to be happy and fulfilled, and relationships are one of the primary ways that all of us express that drive. Unfortunately, our society and some of our own misunderstandings about life tend to make us ignore our innermost needs and the needs of the people we care about. Countless people these days express deep unhappiness with themselves and with their most significant relationships. I hear from many of these people in my work—people who voice worries, anxieties, and fears about problems that burden their hearts. Most of the people I counsel don't come to me with great theological questions about the nature of God, humanity, or the universe. Instead, what troubles them most are dilemmas of the heart: How can they find real love? Why are good intentions sometimes unable to keep a relationship alive? What can I do to build a strong, long-lasting marriage? What can spouses do to get along better—to support each other and help each other? How can partners solve their problems when they disagree or find themselves in conflict? These are the sorts of questions that weigh on the men and women who come to me for advice.

I would never, ever say that I have all the answers to these questions. I would never claim to have simple solutions to what are, after all, some of the most intense and complex dilemmas that human beings face. At the same time, I've learned a thing or two from my work helping couples. I've written this book as my own contribution to helping men and women solve their "relationship troubles" and find happiness together.

Here's what I want to offer in this book: the seven "paths" that I believe can help lead couples toward better relationships. These aren't cure-alls. They aren't definitive solutions to all the difficulties that couples face. I do believe, however, that these Seven Paths are useful guidelines to help you explore the "terrain" of your own relationship.

These are the Seven Paths:

- ❧ Path One: Build Solid Foundations

- ❧ Path Two: Respect Each Other

∾ Path Three: Clarify Your Expectations

∾ Path Four: Be Honest

∾ Path Five: Communicate

∾ Path Six: Learn to Accept Your Differences

∾ Path Seven: Make a Commitment to Growth and Maturity

I will explain these paths in more detail as I come to it in the book. But for now, I'll say simply that *relationship trouble* is a real condition. It's what happens when people don't pay attention to the basic rules, boundaries, and norms for interacting with those they care about. My hope is that each of the Seven Paths that I offer in this book will help you deal with relationship trouble in your life.

This book is designed to provide the same straightforward, no-nonsense approach to couples' relationships that I've tried to provide in my parish work and in my involvement in the media. I've written this book with the conviction that men and women can overcome the many frustrations and difficulties that complicate their interactions. It's true that relationships can be challenging. Relationships can cause great stress. Relationships always involve some degree of risk. As human beings, we're all more vulnerable when we relate to other people than when we hold back and keep to ourselves. But by opening up and accepting each other fully and openly, the partners in a couple make a calculated gamble that can provide the most profound satisfactions in our earthly life.

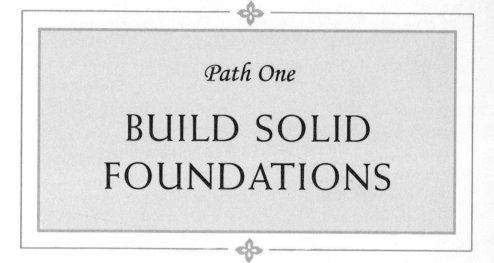

Path One

BUILD SOLID FOUNDATIONS

To live is to relate.

There's really no way around it. From the moment you leave your mother's womb, you have to interact with other human beings. Babies are so dependent that they can't survive even a few hours without the care and nurturance of other people. And from the moment of birth to the moment of death, you deal with people in all sorts of relationships. Relating is as much a part of the human condition as breathing.

How has this profound *relatedness* come about? I'm not a biologist or a psychologist, but I believe it's clear that we human beings have a natural drive toward connection with others. Each of us has an inborn desire to reach out toward someone else. And I believe that this experience of reaching out, of connecting with others, is what ultimately makes us human. We don't live on an island by ourselves. We have to relate in order to develop and discover ourselves. As many psychologists, philosophers, and theologians have stated in many different ways, being human is a matter of how we relate—how we share ourselves with other people. We need to love and feel loved. This doesn't mean interacting superficially—it means getting to know other people on deeper levels and building meaningful, lasting relationships.

For these reasons, the first path I want to discuss is Path One—Build Solid Foundations. Building solid foundations means focusing on the perceptions, decisions, values, and actions that support and strengthen caring relationships over the long term.

It's true that during adulthood you're much more autonomous than you were when younger. You can function on your own, live alone, work alone, and play alone. But it's safe to say that despite your adult autonomy, you probably continue to feel a great craving for relatedness with others. You have a desire to connect with someone who will be a lifetime partner—someone who will be there through thick and thin, who will share your dreams, who will give you a sense of meaning, the person who will share the gift of parenthood during the child-rearing years. Like most people, you long for that special person who is out there somewhere. Or else you've found that person already, and you're now trying to make the relationship strong enough to last for a long, long time.

So how, then, can you build the solid foundations that your relationship will need? That's what this path will explain.

Chapter 1

Complications, Complications!

Jenny is a pretty typical member of her generation. At the age of twenty-four she is bright, ambitious, attractive, and eager to explore all that life has to offer. Her job as a marketing rep for a pharmaceutical firm provides many professional and social opportunities. In addition to offering good career advancement, Jenny's work puts her in contact with many interesting single, young men. She also meets guys at the local gym, through an online dating service she joined, and through friends' efforts to play matchmaker. This wide range of "romantic options," as Jenny calls them, is important to her: in addition to pursuing a career, she wants to get married and have a family.

Yet at times she finds the situation frustrating. "I meet lots of guys," Jenny explains, "and I go out a lot. But sometimes I wonder where it's all heading. I put so much time and energy into getting to know someone, and then usually nothing comes of it. A lot of these guys are just looking for sex. Or else we have major compatibility issues. There are also misunderstandings about what's supposed to happen because there don't seem to be any clear-cut rules nowadays. Everybody has different expectations, and this leads to a lot of hard feelings. I'm looking for a soul mate, not just a bed partner. But it's hard to make a commitment when you can't even agree with the other person on what you're making a commitment *to*."

It used to be that institutions and rituals in our society simplified the process of finding a lifetime partner. Growing up in a town or neighborhood, you met prospective mates in your village or parish. Well-established courtship rituals provided some degree of stability for how young men and women got to know each other. But obviously much has changed over the past several decades. There's much more freedom now for how couples meet, get acquainted, get married, and settle down together. All to the good? Maybe, maybe not. Even if there's more freedom, there's also much less predictability and less stability than in the past. As we abandon so many of the traditional aspects of our society, we risk discarding the customs, institutions, and rituals that helped people find and build the relationships they wanted. Yet human beings still have the same emotional needs as in the past. People still want to meet the right person—"my life partner," "my other half," "my soul mate"—someone who can be a lifelong traveling companion on their earthly journey.

I have to admit that when I hear people speak longingly of "my other half" or "my soul mate," these words often sound very idealistic. But believe me—underneath the idealism is the genuine, basic human need to connect with someone for the long term. The words people say may suggest a starry-eyed attitude, but they reflect an important truth. People are searching. People are longing for connectedness—for a relationship with "the other." The English poet John Donne wrote, "No man is an island, sufficient unto himself." Well, there may be a *few* people who are completely self-sufficient, but there aren't many, and frankly, a lot of them are out of touch with their own needs, desires, and feelings. Everyone else needs someone. But now the search for a soul mate is, I believe, more complicated than ever.

Here are some significant complications that may challenge your efforts to build solid foundations for your relationship.

COMPLICATION #1: CONFUSION AND ANXIETY OVER NEW METHODS TO SEARCH FOR LOVE

People say, "I want to find my soul mate," or "I want a partner I can share my life with." But *how*? How do you find this person in a world where so many longstanding social structures have dissolved?

It's true that we have new methods to help people find each other. There may be no village matchmakers nowadays, but we have many new ways for people to meet and get to know each other. Men and women meet through social clubs, online dating services, singles ads, parties, singles bars, and sports events, to name just a few ways. Some of these arrangements work better than others. All of us probably know of a few strong relationships that have emerged from a computerized dating service, a chance encounter at a party, or some other nontraditional "match." Are these methods for finding a partner more effective at fostering good relationships than traditional arrangements used to be? Well, yes and no. I'm certainly not suggesting that we return to the days of arranged marriages! That method had its own drawbacks and produced its own quota of dissatisfactions and even outright misery. But I often hear people complain about the unpredictability of their quest for love—a feeling that there are no ground rules left, no set patterns, no clear sequence of steps to take. This sense of unpredictability leads to a lot of anxiety and confusion over the issues that couples have always faced.

- ❧ What's the best way to meet potential partners?

- ❧ Once you meet someone, what's appropriate behavior during the early phases of a relationship?

- ❧ How do you judge the proper timing for increased emotional and physical intimacy as you get to know someone?

ॐ What is the best timing for a transition from a "casual" relationship to a "serious" relationship?

ॐ When—and how—should a couple explore the possibilities of marriage?

ॐ How can couples reach an agreement about whether to start a family, how many children to have, and how to raise them?

It's now harder than ever to answer these questions definitively. And, lacking a clearer source of information or authority, it's no wonder that people resort to horoscopes, magazine checklists, and online questionnaires as they search for love. Are those sources of guidance better than nothing? Sometimes I wonder. I certainly wouldn't advise basing your future on articles with titles like "Ten Hot Tips to Help You Catch Mr. Right." When I see the mixed results and dissatisfactions that can result from reliance on these methods, I often feel that they complicate rather than simplify the task of finding and building good relationships. But I'm aware that many men and women are groping for answers, and I'm certainly sympathetic to their plight. I worry, though, that our society is just making up the courtship dance as we go. Without rules, we stumble, so it's no wonder that people will grab at anything that will keep them on their feet.

Here's an example of one of the issues that concern me: Internet matchmaking.

Maybe it's no surprise that people turn to these services. It's easy to post a notice stating, "Mr. Handsome Young Professional Seeks Beautiful Miss So-and-So," or a variation on that theme, and then hope for the best. It's practical and convenient to find someone who meets certain criteria you've specified. And, yes, the Internet provides a much bigger "pond" in which to cast your net. You can flag any features you want— age, height, weight, hair color, ethnic background, profession, hobbies, taste in music, you name it. Does that mean that you'll catch the person you've gone fishing for? Does it mean that you'll actually be able to exclaim, "This is my soul mate!"? Well, I think you rarely find the person you're looking for simply by specifying so many criteria. Why? There are lots of reasons, but one is that the vision in your mind of your ideal mate may not translate into reality.

To complicate the situation further, many people who post their information on the Internet turn out to be far different in real life than they appear on the computer screen. Some potential partners present themselves in ways that can only be called (to give them the benefit of the doubt) wishful thinking. Some people lie outright. Jessie, for example— a twenty-six-year-old nurse in the Boston area—has carried on several "digital relationships" with prospective partners she has met on the Web; she has felt intrigued by the seemingly attractive personalities that take shape on-screen. But she has discovered more than once that the men in question aren't as attractive, as interesting, or even as well-intentioned in person as they seemed in cyberspace. Several of these "young singles" were neither young nor single!

So what, then, is the moral of the story? I'm not saying that people shouldn't consider using recent innovations, including Internet dating services, as they search for love. What I *am* saying is that these methods for finding a partner don't necessarily work very well. They may even complicate the task. In any case, you should use them with caution—and with your eyes wide open.

COMPLICATION #2:
IMAGES OF WHAT WE WANT

Another complication is that the images in people's minds aren't shaped just by their own inner needs, but also by Hollywood, the media, and the fashion industry. When I ask couples what each of them is looking for in a husband or wife, I hear amazingly precise "specs" for the ideal mate.

One guy told me, "My ideal wife should be slim, five-six, blond, and blue-eyed—and she should have a really great figure." A young woman said, "The man I'm looking for needs to be dark-haired, really buff, kind of rugged-looking, and at least six-foot-two." Another man said, "My dream woman needs to be athletic, good at dancing, no taller than five-foot-four, pretty, ambitious but not *too* ambitious, and no heavier than a hundred and ten pounds." And another woman told me, "I want my husband to be athletic, a good dresser, and a great provider—either a lawyer, a doctor, or a successful businessman." The "shopping list" of must-have features can get even more specific! Sometimes I wonder: Are people looking for a mate or going on a shopping trip?

I also wonder where all these precise expectations come from. Do they well up from deep inside us? Or are they images we've picked up from the culture around us? Who knows? I'm sure each person has personal inclinations and preferences for possible relationships. That's fair enough. But I'm concerned that the detailed, picky specifications that people express about ideal mates can become obstacles that prevent them from connecting with reality. You won't build a strong relationship based on someone's *image*—at least not for the long term. You may be attracted to someone at the start of your relationship for these reasons, but attraction doesn't always translate into a long-lasting or profound relationship. You don't find your lifetime partner as a result of *only* an initial attraction. As a matter of fact, that initial attraction usually gets brought down a few notches when we listen or speak to people as we get to know them.

In our society, we have a tendency to judge a book by its cover. We don't really look inside. We've lost some of our ability to reflect, analyze, and go into issues in depth with others. This tendency to stay on the surface affects and even impairs our ability to get to know someone on a deeper level. I'd venture to say that many of the people who enter a serious relationship with marriage as the goal—or who enter into marriage itself—become disappointed or disheartened at some point because they haven't looked beyond the other person's surface. I hear this all the time.

People tell me things like, "I'm sleeping with a stranger," "I don't know this person anymore," "This isn't the person I married," or "This isn't the person I wanted to spend my life with." Why do they find themselves in this situation? Generally it's because they fell into the trap of knowing someone only on a superficial level.

Here's a story that reveals a different attitude. Al, who had been blind since birth, recently lost Sally, his beloved wife of forty years, following her long battle with cancer. At a reception for family and friends after the funeral, someone asked Al if he'd ever wondered about his wife's physical appearance. Al had, in fact, never seen Sally in the conventional, visual sense of the word. But his answer showed that he knew more about her than anyone else. "My wife's beauty was her soul," Al told the person who'd asked the question. "Her soul was filled with love and generosity. I know all about her—not because I saw her, but because I loved her. And believe me, by knowing her this way, I knew her beauty better than anyone who could see her."

That's real love. That's the real "stuff" that relationships should be made of: to see into another person's heart and to find the treasure that lies within.

I believe that too many people form relationships based on external qualities that have little or nothing to do with what the person really yearns for and needs for the long term. This is an area in which our society has failed us—by encouraging us to base our choices on externals. The woman falls in love with a guy because he has a certain type of hair or looks like someone who can just sweep her off of her feet. The man falls in love with a woman because of her great figure or her sexy style of dressing. But maybe the outside image doesn't really reflect what's underneath. Maybe the guy isn't someone who will affirm her, meet her emotional needs, and support her aspirations. Maybe the woman isn't considerate or patient or loyal. Maybe this couple can't truly build a long-lasting commitment and a real sense of fidelity. Basing a relationship on images isn't a great way to build strong foundations.

COMPLICATION #3: IMAGES OF PERFECTION

Sometimes the issue of image goes even further—all the way to a fixation on perfection.

One day a young man named Patrick ran into Jake, a friend from his childhood years. After a few moments of small talk, the inevitable question came up when Jake asked: "So, Patrick, are you married yet?"

Patrick replied, "No, I'm not—I haven't found the perfect woman yet."

Jake responded with laughter, "Well, hey, the perfect woman doesn't even exist, right?"

To which Patrick responded, "Yes she does—I dated her for three years!"

Jack seemed intrigued: "Well, then, if she was so perfect, why didn't you marry her?"

Patrick sighed, "Because she left me. She went off to go find the perfect man!"

Let's face it: perfect human relationships don't exist. Some may be wonderful, but even those require lots of hard work, and they're far from perfect. The very definition of perfection—"to be without flaw" or "free from error"—contradicts a basic truth: we are all ultimately flawed. We're far from perfect. For this reason, our relationships are also flawed and imperfect. Fair enough—that's just part of the human condition.

But here again we're all under societal pressure to chase after perfection. We hear from many sources, for example, that younger is better—better for looks, for jobs, for image, for everything. A multimillion-dollar industry tells you if you take this or that pill your skin will be more elastic and smooth, you'll be less wrinkled, and life will be wonderful. A lot of people constantly strive for external youth. Some even undergo cosmetic surgery because they figure if they get Botox, a tummy tuck, or a face-lift, they'll be better off. Others go on rigorous, expensive diets to lose weight in the hopes that a slim figure will guarantee a great love life.

Do these external changes really make a difference? Will they give us the inner satisfactions we crave? Frankly, I think we're being misled. We're being misled by our image-oriented society, which tells us that you're worth what you look like. You're worth what others *see*. Now, appearance may be part of what makes us who we are, but it's only one part. And if you look only at what's outside, you'll never discover the treasure inside. So part of a rich relationship is to constantly go past the outside and discover what lies within.

You'll probably experience a great deal of needless strife and anxiety by imagining you'll find perfection in relating with other people. This expectation often leads to disappointment and frustration—so much so that some people even begin to think about giving up on relationships altogether. Believe me, pursuing perfection in relationships doesn't lead to happiness. On the contrary, you can become more and more miserable by seeking the impossible. My suggestion: accept what is real and truly attainable instead. Accepting imperfect human reality rather than striving for perfection is the only way to build strong foundations for a relationship.

COMPLICATION #4: RUSH RUSH RUSH

A lot of people I hear from want a relationship *right now*! Well, I understand that many men and women are lonely, and relationships are unquestionably important. But at times the urgency people feel seems a little too frantic, and it can lead to situations that resemble ordering goods through the Internet—or sending away for a mail-order mate! *I don't have time to get out and face the whole dating scene. I have so much to do!* People really feel pressured to get into a meaningful relationship *fast*.

Here's a troubling example of this phenomenon: men and women sometimes "interview" each other with incredibly numerous, specific questions—even on their first dates—as if they were screening applicants for a job. I'm not referring to the necessary, appropriate process of people getting to know each other. I'm talking about a process that approaches interrogation. One guy I heard about actually used a detailed checklist so he could systematically size up this prospective partner's "strengths and weaknesses"! ("How much time do you spend cooking dinner each night? Do you use fresh ingredients or processed foods? What kinds of cuisine do you favor? Do you use cookbooks or just 'wing it'?")

Another rush-rush-rush approach called "speed dating" has become popular in Manhattan and other large U.S. cities. In speed dating, a group of twenty or thirty singles meet at a predetermined location; the men and women pair off in a room furnished with sets of chairs facing each other; and each male-female pair then spends five precisely timed minutes getting to know each other. After the designated five-minute period ends, the men get up and rotate to the next "station" to interview the woman seated there. The process continues until each woman has had a chance to meet and converse with each man. Proponents of this method claim that although it maybe be imperfect, even a hasty five minutes of face-to-face communication reveals a lot more than interactions by e-mail. That's probably true. But this approach, like so many other experiences in our speed-obsessed culture, also risks snap judgments based primarily on appearance and other external attributes.

There's another risk. Whether by means of speed dating, Internet dating, matchmaking services, the bar scene, or even more traditional ways of meeting people, it's hard to explore another person and his or her place in your life when your efforts are so *focused on finding a mate.* You're in such a rush to move the relationship along that you never really get to know the person. Instead of perceiving the other person fully in his or her own terms, the pressure you feel may tend to force your vision. You may not be as open to the other person in all of his or her own complexity, richness, and contradiction. You may pay attention only (or mostly) to beauty, "coolness," and attributes of wealth and social status. How can that sense of haste lead to building good, solid foundations in your relationship? Unfortunately, it can't.

Here are some of the problems I often see in couples who resort to rushing:

- ❧ Rushing means that you get into the relationship too fast, which can lead to one or both parties feeling hurt, deceived, or confused about the nature or "terms" of the relationship.

- ❧ Rushing means that you're more likely to get deeply involved before you really know if the other person is what you're looking for.

- ❧ Rushing risks the situation you face when ordering goods "on impulse" (either at a store, from a catalogue, or through the Internet): you may commit yourself, then discover that what you've "ordered" isn't what you bargained for.

- ❧ Rushing makes it harder for you and the other person to get to know each other beyond an initial, superficial level, which can lead in the short term to misunderstandings, disillusionment, and resentment, and in the longer term to unstable marriages and even divorce.

COMPLICATION #5: THE RUSH TO INTIMACY

For some people, the fast pace of establishing relationships may also rush a specific aspect of this important process: the physical expression of intimacy. Don't get me wrong. Physical intimacy, including genital intimacy, is an important, beautiful part of a marital relationship, but it should be the result of closeness with someone on other levels first. In our society, however, many people connect in a very intimate physical way with partners they haven't even gotten to know. This doesn't lead to good foundations for the relationship.

Some of the risks of rushing intimacy are:

∽ Mistaking your *physical* relationship for your *entire* relationship, or at least focusing on physical intimacy at the expense of more profound forms of intimacy

∽ Neglecting to learn about each other's nonphysical attributes—your mutual interests, your differences, your habits and quirks, your abilities and eccentricities, your talents and delights

∽ Delaying the establishment of deep trust and close communication of the sort that should precede rather than follow physical intimacy

∽ Feeling vulnerable to misunderstandings or hurt feelings that can occur as a couple experiences the passions and explores the complexities of a sexual relationship

My experience as a counselor to many people tells me that your relationship will be much richer, much better, and much more profound if you connect with your partner on the more fundamental, nonphysical levels before you delve into physical intimacy. Get to know your partner well before you begin something as special and as exclusive as an intimate relationship. The rush to intimacy can complicate—even burden—a relationship rather than strengthening it. I feel that a couple's physical relationship—a relationship between spouses who love, trust, and feel connected to each other emotionally and spiritually—is a wonderful thing. But getting to know the other person and developing your special relationship takes time, and physical intimacy that starts too early can cloud your judgment and damage the subtle process of getting to know each other.

COMPLICATION #6: DELAYS, THEN HASTE

I feel concerned about many young women today. So many are delaying marriage until later and later in life. Sometimes they have good reasons—finishing their education or getting established in a profession. Other people just take longer to decide to get married. But there's certainly a feeling of pressure that can build as a result of delays, and many women then start to worry about their sense of timing. Some tell me, "My biological clock is ticking. I'd like to have children, but now I'm getting older, and my doctor tells me I shouldn't wait much longer." One of the side effects of such delays is that some people feel pressured into relationships. To some degree there's pressure from society, and often there's family pressure, too.

I also think many people pressure themselves because they feel they may not find fulfillment if they don't get going and start a family. Many people feel incomplete. I know lots of women in their thirties who are far along in establishing themselves in their professions. Unfortunately, they often lack an important element that they want in their lives—a relationship that will provide them with children and a family. The frustration even translates to the point where some women are beginning to explore the option of having children without a mate. They're looking for an immediate gratification of their maternal instincts without the whole process of building a family.

But there are some big risks inherent in this approach.

First off, you shouldn't rush a set of decisions as crucial and personal as starting a family. The birth of a child should be the result of a carefully considered sequence of choices—choices made within the context of a stable, loving marriage—not as a goal to achieve at all costs. Many women understand what's at stake, but the sense of urgency they feel prompts them to scramble to find a relationship (and sometimes to settle for a less-than-ideal relationship) that will make motherhood possible.

Sometimes the situation works out all right; often it doesn't. There's a real hazard of putting the cart before the horse.

Second, this situation ignores the reality that it's okay to be single. Some single people find deep fulfillment in their work and their relationships, and they may choose to stay single over the long term. Others may find a life partner after some years of being single. Is there any way of knowing definitively what's right for you? If your goals include marriage and parenthood, is there any sure way of attaining them? Well, life is too unpredictable for that kind of certainty. Even so, I think it's a mistake to assume that delay is so deadly that you'd better rush to find a mate, settle down, and have a baby. My advice: proceed carefully and thoughtfully. By all means strive to attain fulfillment as a spouse and as a parent, but don't be so hasty that you jeopardize your long-term happiness—and that of your child—by regarding parenthood as your goal even in what could be less-than-ideal circumstances.

COMPLICATION #7: THE "UNDECIDED MALE"

Another complication I see in couples more and more often is what I call the "undecided male"—the male who's afraid of making a commitment. His girlfriend or fiancée has invited him to make the marriage commitment. The young man may even have responded to her eagerness by proposing to her. It's not as if he's digging in his feet. But somehow the groom isn't *emotionally* ready. This is a very common situation. The woman is emotionally ready to build a life with another person, but the male is reluctant or undecided—he's not sure about making the commitment.

Why does this happen so often?

One partial explanation may be changing attitudes within our culture regarding premarital sex. The male has already gained some gratification, so perhaps—if that's his primary goal—he figures he doesn't have to worry so much about making the commitment. In the past, couples went out, courted, got married, and only then began their sexual relationship. That's not necessarily how it goes these days, is it? A large percentage of couples become intimate early in the process of getting acquainted—and sometimes before they know much about each other at all! Since many men consider sex as a primary goal of getting involved—often *the* primary goal—early-phase sexual intimacy "delivers the goods" without much emotional investment.

Another explanation for the frequent occurrence of the "undecided male" phenomenon is that many young women have reached a clear understanding of what they need and what their life goals are, while young men are often still unsure. To put it bluntly: the young men are less mature. In dealing with some couples, I see people from two different worlds. The woman wants to be a partner, a wife, and a mother. The man may or may not have a clear idea of what he wants or what marriage is like. So developmental issues may be a big part of the picture.

The type of fathering men have experienced also contributes to the problem. Our society has a huge generation that is essentially fatherless. So many single mothers are raising their boys without any paternal assistance at all! If the boys lack a male mentor, what concept of fathering will these men have as they grow up? Little or none. When they get married, who's going to be their role model for what the marriage experience is supposed to be? They never saw it at home, so they don't have good images of fatherly responsibility or loyalty. Instead, all they know is the Hollywood image of the dashing macho guy who's out conquering the world. How do you promote the values of fatherhood and fidelity in someone who has never experienced them?

All of these various complications influence couples' ability to build strong foundations. Maybe you're affected by some or all of these complications; maybe not. But they're worth thinking over. If you know what can complicate your choices and decisions, you're better prepared to create the relationship you truly want.

Now let's examine the nature of relationships, how they affect us, and what the different kinds of relationships tell us about the nature of real love.

Chapter 2

The Two Basic Kinds of Relationships—and Why They Matter

So where dose this situation leave you? If modern life complicates the quest for love so severely, how are you supposed to find someone to love—someone with whom you can build a strong, satisfying, lifelong relationship?

That's a question I'll use this whole book to answer. Before we move on to the specifics, though, I want to address two topics that I consider crucial. One is the importance of recognizing two kinds of relationships—*inherited* and *acquired*—and also recognizing the differences between them. I'll address this issue in just a moment. In addition, I want to discuss the issue of the sacred center. Both of these topics will help us understand what makes a good relationship.

INHERITED AND ACQUIRED RELATIONSHIPS

Inherited relationships are the ones you're born into—mostly family relationships—which are meaningful in part because of their primal nature. These are the relationships that often carry a powerful sense of bonding and fundamental commitment or obligation. "Blood ties," we call them. By contrast, *acquired relationships* may lack the primordial sense of an unbreakable bond, but they tend to be meaningful precisely because they are volitional—relationships you *choose*. The very fact that you've chosen them raises the stakes. You may have to work harder to maintain them. You have to think more clearly about why you chose them in the first place. You have to shape and energize them. They're the result of decisions, not just the consequence of events beyond your control, such as being born into a particular family.

INHERITED RELATIONSHIPS

We don't choose our parents, grandparents, siblings, aunts and uncles, or other relatives. Yet these are the first relationships we experience, and often the most important, since they create intense emotional bonds between us. These relationships become part of our lives through what we call "family," and they deeply affect how we relate to the rest of the world. This is where we first learn about otherness. You could even say that family is the first "school of relationships"—a concept that modern psychology confirms. We know, for instance, that how we relate to our mothers and fathers will have a lasting effect on how we deal with a future spouse and with other people as well. For this reason, inherited relationships have a lasting impact on our relationships throughout life.

Does this situation mean that our personalities, our behaviors, and our choices are completely determined by these inherited relationships? No—because as human beings we are capable of change. It's true that many people spend years in therapy trying to figure out how their inherited relationships (chiefly with their family of origin) have confused or frustrated or messed up their lives. But it's also true that adults are capable of deep insight and change. Even though inherited relationships affect us in many ways, they don't seal our fate. We are capable of making decisions and exercising our free will. We can overcome our origins.

ACQUIRED RELATIONSHIPS

By contrast, *acquired relationships* are the ones we select and cultivate freely, with no strings or bloodlines attached. These acquired relationships are the ones we develop throughout our lives. This is where friendships or life partners come in—the people we *choose* to share life with. This book focuses strongly on acquired relationships.

The affection you feel in acquired relationships may be as intense, or even more intense, than what you feel toward your family. Why? Because it's more spontaneous and chosen, while inherited relationships include more of a sense of duty. For example, consider the difference between being kind to your mother and choosing to be kind to an elderly, lonely neighbor. The first interaction is based on an expectation (your ties through a blood relationship), while the other is something that you give freely and choose because of an attraction between different personalities or even a sense of compassion. I'm not claiming that acquired relationships are stronger, better, or more special than inherited relationships. The bonds between you and your parents, siblings, and other blood relatives are intensely powerful and important. Your inherited relationships shape you, influence you, and help to build your foundations as a human being—your personality, your character, your interests. If you have strong, positive inherited relationships, you'll be more confident and creative as you grow up and move out into the world. If you have troubled, negative inherited relationships, you'll be more hesitant and self-doubting as you cope with life's challenges and opportunities. Either way, it's likely that your inherited relationships will remain a significant influence on you throughout the rest of your life. So, yes, inherited relationships are immensely powerful.

Rather, what I'm saying is simply that precisely because we can choose them, acquired relationships have a special kind of power and a special kind of significance. You can't decide who your parents, siblings, or other blood relatives will be; you just have to deal with the ones you've got. Your friends and romantic partners are present in your life because you've decided that they are important to you. This situation gives you a lot more freedom. But with freedom comes responsibility. Precisely because you can choose, you need to be careful as you make your choices.

Why does the difference between inherited and acquired relationships matter to our discussion? It's true that *all* relationships matter. I certainly urge you to honor and nurture your inherited relationships—your ties to your parents, your siblings, and your other relatives. But precisely because acquired relationships are volitional—something you choose—they're central to our discussion of couples' relationships and to the task of building strong foundations.

And this in turn leads us to an important issue at the heart of what I recommend regarding couples' relationships.

THE IMPORTANCE OF THE SACRED CENTER

We human beings have a sacred center—the innermost core of our being. The sacred center is a deep well containing what we feel most strongly, believe most intensely, and hold dearest in life: our fears, hopes, dreams, wishes, and vulnerabilities. It's the place where love truly lives, and it's the dwelling place of intimate relationships. And because it's so personal and profound a part of our being, the sacred center is, ideally, a place we should safeguard, a place that only the people we most fully trust should enter—only those persons who we feel most completely merit our innermost thoughts and emotions. The sacred center is the part of our being that we try to protect from the twists and turns of life, including betrayals, lies, and other hurtful situations. Sometimes we make the mistake of prematurely letting others into the sacred center. If we do so, and if someone takes advantage of us or betrays our trust, we may feel psychologically or spiritually damaged or wounded. For this reason, we should protect this sacred center, precisely because we have often experienced pain at the hands of people who are careless with our feelings and emotions. But of course all relationships require an element of risk. How, then, do we decide whom to let into this sacred center—this core of our being?

This question isn't easy to answer. Throughout life, we develop different relationships—relationships that vary in their intensity and significance. We relate to others at first in relatively superficial ways—not letting them into our sacred center—until we feel safe and able to allow them to enter. Each person has a different sense of timing in this process. Some people are more guarded and thus slower to be vulnerable. Others are quicker to let down their guard. (All of us probably know someone who says, "I wear my heart on my sleeve.") How do we decide when (and how much) to open up? I'd say that for each person the answer to this question is partly a result of temperament and partly a result of past experience. But both for people who take their time and for people who are more impulsive, feeling betrayed by our choices often prompts us to blame the other party. We're rarely ready to take responsibility for our own actions. However, we are the only ones ultimately responsible for our choices and for how these relationships develop.

I see two risky extremes in the situation I'm describing.

One extreme is the person who is indiscriminate in allowing others into the sacred center. Typical of what I'm describing are men or women who are so hungry for affection, so desperate for a relationship, or so vulnerable to others' pressure, that they lower their defenses too quickly. This state of mind is often characteristic of people with low self esteem or a profound sense of loneliness. It's true that opening up quickly isn't a guarantee of "getting burned"; sometimes other people honor this kind of vulnerability and don't take advantage of it. But I believe it's still hazardous to allow access to the sacred center without carefully sizing up who's coming in.

The other extreme is evident in the person who builds a fortress around his or her sacred center and rarely or never allows anyone else to enter. People of this sort often have a deep fear of getting hurt, or else they have an extreme need to be self-sufficient. Men and women who live so guardedly have often experienced frequent, severe interpersonal conflicts in the past. It's not uncommon to hear such people make statements like "I've been burned too much already, and I'm not going to get burned again." In some ways, this attitude is understandable—they don't want to be hurt any more. But this extreme guardedness is an unfortunate situation. Without a sense of real emotional healing, these people find it hard to open up to others and begin new meaningful relationships. For some, the sacred center even becomes almost impenetrable, a barrier against any possible future attacks. Such people may be aloof, emotionally cold, or altogether incapable of intimacy. This situation is unfortunate. Trust and love go hand in hand. The person who can't trust others will never be truly free to love—free to open himself or herself to someone else at this profound level. Trust is one of the fundamental gambles in human experience. We must let ourselves take certain calculated risks to allow others into the most private areas of our lives. This gamble requires faith and trust in the other—and it also requires openness to the possibility of failure.

Where does this leave us? Simply put, it leaves us needing to be careful yet also willing to be open to other people.

WHOM DO WE LET IN?

Relationships are truly central to the human experience. Building a relationship benefits and fulfills many of your fundamental needs. That same relationship also helps to benefit and fulfill the other person, too, so there are mutual advantages in what you're building together.

But at once some questions arise. Whom do you let into the sacred center? And how do you decide who is safe and worthy of permission to enter? No doubt you meet people at work, at social occasions, or at large in the world. That's the external process. But what's the *internal* process of making contact with others? How do you decide who is really right to let into that level of emotional and physical intimacy? How do you decide who is right for you—and right to let into your sacred center?

Well, that's a crucial question. On the most basic level, the person has to be someone you trust. Does he or she respect you? Listen to you with an open mind and open heart? Value your opinions? Honor your feelings? If this person's response to you over time justifies your trust, then he or she is probably someone you can allow into your sacred center. He or she must be a person who hasn't been severely damaged or hurt by life, who doesn't feel major self-esteem issues, who doesn't have a deeply guarded sense of self-security—someone who's not going to have a hard time letting you in. In turn, your behavior and attitudes—your respect toward the other person, your openness, your valuing of opinions and honoring of feelings—will be the evidence that he or she can trust you and allow you into his or her sacred center.

I believe that most of us make these choices carefully. Most of us spend a lot of time interacting with people before we allow them into the sacred center. Many couples will circle around each other, trying to decide. They're fond of each other, but they wonder, *Is this my soul mate? We have good times together, we share many values. We think we'd both like to start a family together. But is he [or she] the right person?* There's still a guardedness about whether to let down all the barriers and be completely vulnerable and trusting to this person.

So is it appropriate to be a little cautious about this process? If you're going to build a relationship strong enough to last forty, fifty, sixty years, shouldn't you be careful about whether your future spouse is honest? Whether he or she is likely to honor the commitment to your marriage? Is that caution appropriate?

It is. If you're going to let someone into your sacred center, you have to be sure that person has the qualities listed below that will enable him or her to meet your most fundamental needs.

- ∽ This person shows a pattern of respecting me as a human being.

- ∽ This person also shows a pattern of respecting others.

- ∽ This person shares my fundamental values and morals.

- ∽ This person is authentically affectionate—not indifferent, dismissive, or abusive toward me—and the affection stems from a lasting mutual commitment, not just a passing whim.

- ∽ This person tries to understand me and my needs, and he or she knows that selfishness has no place in the relationship.

- ∽ This person is honest and truthful, and he or she has a strong sense of integrity.

How do you determine whether these attributes are present? Well, there's no fail-safe test. It's easy to say, "Trust your intuition," but intuition, though certainly valuable, isn't always adequate for judging others' intentions or character. (It's not uncommon, for instance, for people to get involved repeatedly with romantic partners who seem charming and well-intentioned but turn out to be dismissive, demeaning, or even abusive.) I recommend that in addition to evaluating potential mates with a mental checklist like the one above, you keep an eye out for danger signs like these:

- ✎ Lack of respect for you, your beliefs, and your feelings

- ✎ Selfish behavior rather than generosity and a sense of common endeavor

- ✎ Lying or evasiveness

- ✎ Manipulative behavior

- ✎ Emotional coldness or withholding of affection

- ✎ A pattern of impatience or dismissive attitudes or behavior toward what you value or toward you as a person

- ✎ Verbal or physical abuse of any sort

In addition, I urge you to take the following steps to safeguard your physical, emotional, and spiritual safety:

Don't be too hasty. I've touched on this subject before, but I'll mention it again. If you rush the process of getting to know the other person, you run the risk of making snap judgments and leaving yourself vulnerable to getting hurt. Take your time. You have little to lose and much to gain by moving thoughtfully and carefully.

Avoid wishful thinking. Out of a desire to find love, it's tempting to overlook the other person's shortcomings or the incompatibilities between you. It's also tempting to compromise on crucial issues, deceive yourself about the nature of the relationship, or view your prospective partner as someone whose habits or character you can change or reform.

Stick to your principles, values, and morals. Be honest, straightforward, and true to your deeply held beliefs. Finding love is important, but not at the expense of what you value most.

Communicate. To get to know another person—and, especially, to allow him or her into your sacred center—you need to discuss what matters to you openly and fully. To reach an understanding of basic issues, you need to talk about them together.

Again, there are no shortcuts and no easy answers in dealing with these issues. If you can follow these principles, however, proceeding carefully and letting each other into your sacred centers will be much more likely to work out to your satisfaction.

WHAT IF THERE'S EMOTIONAL DAMAGE?

People who feel damaged by how they've been treated in the past—either in their family of origin or by others—often isolate themselves, or else they hold other people at arm's length. They are reluctant to let other people into their sacred center. They are hesitant to *relate*.

My immediate instinct in these situations is to believe that there's a crucial need for emotional and spiritual healing. If you've been hurt by your fundamental relationships, and if you're unable to heal that hurt, you won't be able to move on. If you don't face the demons from your past, you can't live in an emotionally healthy way in the present and future.

However, there is something you can do, and I believe it applies to any faith, tradition, or culture. If you believe in a higher power—and if you believe in the ability of God to intervene in your life—you're much more able to experience healing and to feel comfortable with it. If you have a relationship with God and there's a real sense of spirituality in your life, you'll be more likely to accept the gift of healing for yourself—to believe that you don't have to carry this burden with you forever. Many people live with the burden of their past. They don't know how to let go. They need someone else to come in and cut the rope and say, *Let go of that. You can move on.* That can make a huge difference in learning to be open to others once again.

But what if despite your faith in the possibility of redemption, you have gone through such trauma that experiencing forgiveness alone isn't enough? What if you feel violated, betrayed, or unappreciated in profound ways? Then what?

Although faith is an ongoing relationship that can develop throughout life (depending on the person's openness and spirituality), you may also need therapeutic care. Many people need both spiritual care *and* psychological care. These approaches aren't an either/or situation; on the contrary, they complement each other. Therapeutic care can be crucial. Both of these elements can help you live your life as fully as possible. The most important element here when you're trying to heal the past and move on is your decision to heal your past. You need to accept a sense of forgiveness and move on. A good psychotherapist or counselor can contribute to that process.

LETTING WISE PEOPLE INTO THE SACRED CENTER

All of us need people in our lives who are guiding lights in moments of darkness. We all need people who are wiser than we are—people who can be our mentors, who can give us advice when we struggle with problems or concerns about what to do next. The person can be a minister, a priest, or a rabbi. It can be a good therapist. It can be a professor at the local university. It can be a mentor at work. The more objective these people are, the better. For some people, it may be a parent—but keep in mind that a parent is often too close to you to provide objective insights. Sometimes you need someone who is outside the immediate picture.

We have many wise people around us already. We just don't necessarily notice them, and we don't rely on them enough. There may be elders who are willing to help and guide you. They may be trained professionals. And they have lots of experience. You just need to identify them and say, "Hey, can you give me a hand?"

Here are some brief examples of when and how you might turn to one of these people for help or insight:

Life transition. Change is inevitable and often difficult. Events such as starting a job, losing a job, getting married, having children, moving, and suffering personal losses all present you with new experiences and significant challenges. No one can go through these transitions for you—but that doesn't mean that you have to face such experiences alone. For instance, Jeb felt more and more anxious as his wedding day approached. He loved his fiancée, Celeste, but worried that he'd "let her down" because he might not "prove good enough" for her. But conversations with his favorite uncle, Alan, gave him a safe place to express his fears of inadequacy and to hear an older man's perspective. Alan's opinion: Jeb was feeling little more than ordinary jitters—nothing that would prevent him from becoming a terrific husband.

Confusion over relationships. Many women seek their girlfriends' and female relatives' opinions when they feel confused about family conflicts, boyfriend troubles, and other kinds of relationship issues. I sure wish men had the good sense to seek counsel in a similar way—but that's not often the case. Women are also much more likely than men to seek professional help, such as discussing relationships with their priest, minister, rabbi, or counselor. Typical of this situation is Emilia, who felt growing concern about how her husband, Beto, had been treating her. She had known for years that Beto was possessive and moody, and she'd married him with full knowledge of his personality; however, in recent years his moodiness had shifted into unpredictable, abusive outbursts. Eventually Emilia sought the advice of her priest, who persuaded her that the couple urgently needed counseling to avert an even worse interpersonal catastrophe.

Stress and anxiety. Life is difficult—that's no secret. It's unfortunate, though, how many people compound their struggles and intensify their hardships by suffering in silence. Do they really believe that no one cares? The opposite is true: we're often in the company of many people who would eagerly offer assistance if they only knew we needed help. You can ease the stress and anxiety of day-to-day life by confiding in a trusted mentor. An example: when feeling overwhelmed by work and family issues, Lillian periodically seeks out Marie—a now-retired former teacher who's also a close friend—as an advisor and "sounding board." Conversations with Marie help Lillian let off steam, gain insights into her situation, and feel less burdened than she would otherwise.

Personal crisis. A wise friend can provide guidance and stability when you face a personal crisis of almost any sort. Following her mother's sudden death, for instance, Angie, age twenty-five, felt overwhelmed by the intensity and persistence of her grief. Dora, a middle-aged coworker at the office where Angie worked, reassured the younger woman that her intense grieving was normal and would eventually ease. Dora's greater breadth of life experience provided a sense of perspective that Angie found consoling. Other people find similar solace through guidance from a thoughtful relative, counselor, or member of the clergy.

I should mention that it's possible to misuse or rely too much on relationships of this sort. First of all, you need to be just as careful with relationships of this sort as you would be any other kind. Make sure that the person you seek for counsel and insight is worthy of your trust. How?

By getting to know him or her over a period of time and by observing his or her behavior for integrity and signs of good character. Also remember that you're not looking for someone to tell you what to do. You're not abdicating responsibility for your choices. Rather, you're seeking another person's "reality check" and his or her clarity of mind when you're coping with situations that seem too complex or emotionally charged for you to make clearsighted decisions. If you step carefully, though, letting a wise person into your sacred center can be a huge help as you navigate through life.

WHAT'S LOVE GOT TO DO WITH IT?

Love is the foundation of any meaningful and authentic relationship between the partners in a couple. There are, of course, many other important kinds of relationships, and love of many different sorts is present within each of them. The love between parent and child, between siblings, and between friends are just three of the most obvious examples. My point here is simply that whatever other relationships may require, a couple's relationship will stand or fall according to the strength of the love between the partners. And I'm convinced that too many couples get hurt because they enter relationships without true love as the foundation. For instance, how do we explain to people in our over-eroticized society that lust isn't really love? Strong physical attraction and compatibility are certainly important aspects of a good sexual relationship, but they shouldn't be confused with a long-term loving, unconditional relationship. I see this situation all the time, especially in people who don't make good choices as to who they let into their lives. Solid, good, lasting relationships must be based first and foremost on love.

So defining love is our first problem, since the word has lost its clear definition. What is love, ultimately?

I'd like to suggest a simple way to comprehend what I mean when I use the word *love*. Here's what I feel real love is meant to do:

- Real love prompts you to give your heart in a radically committed way—not timidly or cautiously, but fully—with a profound concern for the other person's well-being.

- Real love grants you the potential for seeing beyond superficial aspects to the deeper aspects of personhood (kindness, loyalty, patience, strength of character, and capacity to love).

- Real love gives you strength to maintain this commitment in both good times and bad.

- Real love inspires you to share your entire being without counting the cost.

- Real love teaches you to take the long-term view of your relationship rather than just focusing on short-term satisfactions.

- Real love challenges you to go beyond yourself—to transcend yourself, to become more than you thought you were—and it leaves no room for selfishness.

When you think over these several points, what image does it create in your mind? I'm sure you can think of couples you know—I *hope* you know at least one such couple—in which the partners' love for each other seems deep, durable, patient, and thoughtful, with each person concerned primarily about the other rather than himself or herself. Similarly, I'm sure you can think of couples in which the partners' love for each other seems shallow, fragile, impatient, and inconsiderate, with each person concerned primarily about himself or herself. No outsider can truly know or understand what's in another person's heart or mind, and the same holds true for what we know about another couple. Still, it's also true that you can sometimes get to know a couple whose love seems particularly powerful and selfless. And couples of this sort tell us a lot about the nature of real love.

Here's an example—drawn from my own experience—of what real love can be.

When I was a seminarian, I often took my grandparents out to the supermarket, and what I witnessed while with them affected me greatly. They had been married fifty-eight years before my grandfather died, but they looked like a couple of teenagers in love. They were in their eighties—and they still held hands! You don't see that closeness too often. And I still often ask myself the question: Why *don't* we see that too often? Is it because not many couples start out that way? I don't think so—because lots of couples are head-over-heels in love at the start of their relationships. Is it because people get caught up in so many other things that they fall out of love? Maybe so. Is it because the partners think too much about themselves and not enough about the other person? I think that's closer to the mark. When I'd watch my grandparents, I'd see them in the cereal aisle, for instance, and my grandfather would ask my grandmother, "Oh, honey, which one do you want?" And my grandmother would say, "Oh, whichever *you* want." And they'd go back and forth. This grocery store incident is just one example. There and everywhere else, each of them showed a constant desire to satisfy the other. Many couples would be much happier, much more satisfied in their marriages, if they had this focus on the other person—what in Spanish we call *entrega*, or self-giving, selflessness. How do I satisfy *you*?

Love is all about self-giving—the ability to sacrifice for your beloved. It's not expecting anything from that person in return. Now, I'd be the first to say that there can be unhealthy expressions of self-sacrifice. If someone has suffered psychological trauma—such as abuse at the hands of a parent, some other relative, or a spouse—that person will have suffered damage to his or her sense of self and feel worthless as a person, and the sacrificing that grows out of this isn't part of real love. What I'm describing isn't a desire to give to the other person because you feel empty but, on the contrary, to give because you feel full. You give out of choice, not out of compulsion.

This is the most important question we have to face when dealing with human relationships: Are they, or are they not, based on authentic love? Is love truly part of the equation in your relationship? How much of what your do in your most significant relationships speaks clearly about love, free of any trace of selfishness?

TOWARD A MATURE VISION OF LOVE

You see, we often ask the wrong questions. If the fundamental question in marriage is, "How can *I* be satisfied, and how do I get what I want?" then it's flawed. This situation suggests dependence and a self-centered orientation. It's possible that someone with this basic attitude may feel some sort of love, but it isn't mature love. A mature vision of love is about *giving*. And if both people in the relationship feel the same way— if they both act upon this desire to give and love—there's a constant, mutual flow of generosity, goodness, and kindness. There's a constant desire to please the other. That works well in many aspects of a marriage—in conversations, in the bedroom, in the time you spend with your children. You'll be able to share all kinds of issues. There will be true intimacy in the couple.

This kind of giving *generates* energy rather than *draining* energy. Why? Because if you give to your partner freely, spontaneously, and generously, he or she will be aware of your good deeds, your acts of kindness, and your expression of love; your partner will feel boosted, strengthened, and energized by your generosity; and he or she will then proceed to give back to you in further good deeds, acts of kindness, and expressions of love. Your partner's generous, open, and loving acts will further strength and energize you in turn, which will prompt you to further acts of generosity and love. There is a definite dynamic there, a circle of giving that doesn't stop. This is the ideal for a couple's loving relationship. Perhaps you've been around couples like this—couples in which the partners almost effortlessly look after each other. Even being in their company can be a positive experience, full of good humor and warmth.

So here's what I see as the big question. To understand whether love is going to be long-term, mature, and based on a deep understanding of commitment, the first question you should ask yourself is, *How much of myself am I willing to invest in this relationship?*

For many years, I've heard people comment that marriage is a fifty-fifty arrangement. I believe that this statement is one of the biggest lies in our society. Marriage can't be fifty-fifty. When you say fifty-fifty, you're saying that you'll give of yourself up to the halfway point, but you're not willing to go beyond that. If that's what you're saying, you're not really talking about love. You're talking about a business deal. You're saying, "I'll give you this much *if* you give me the same amount back." This isn't an accurate understanding of real love. For love to be genuine, you have to give yourself *totally*. Real love is about giving yourself totally to the other person without counting the cost—without expecting a specific payback. It's fine to have certain expectations. All of us, on entering into a relationship, want to know that the commitment is stable and honorable and will be reciprocated. But it's not valid to say, "I'll only give myself up to here." If the relationship involves a true commitment to lasting love, you're willing to give it your all. Real love isn't fifty-fifty—its one hundred–one hundred.

So how should you distinguish between superficial love and a deep type of love? The short answer is: by determining how much you're willing to invest in the relationship. Are you willing to give it your all?

Chapter 3

How to Build Strong Foundations

So far we've discussed a lot of the issues that couples face as they start and maintain their relationships. I've commented along the way about how you can build strong foundations that will help both you and your partner in the long and short term. Now I'd like to extend and expand this process in a more systematic way.

NINE TASKS TO HELP YOU BUILD STRONG FOUNDATIONS

Can a series of suggestions guarantee the durability of your love relationship? Of course not. There are no certainties in love. But here are nine tasks that will strengthen the relationship you're building.

Task #1
Strive for Balance

What kind of balance can you achieve in your life? People often tell me they have no time to exercise. They're working long hours, they have a bad commute, they're tired—they have all sorts of excuses. Well, people who say they don't have time to exercise are basically telling me they don't organize their time very well. How long does it take to get a little exercise? This is a pretty fundamental human need—just one of the basic things you need to stay healthy.

And one of the other needs is for satisfying relationships. You have to find time—or make time—to discover friendship and love, and to nurture those relationships. If you ignore your need for relating to other people, you risk becoming incomplete. You become a human *doing* rather than a human being.

For this reason, you need to set aside the time and make the effort to gain a sense of who you are. If you feel unable to build the relationships you'd find satisfying, you have to ask yourself these and other questions:

- What do you want from this life?

- What are your emotional and interpersonal needs?

- What do you need from others—and what are you capable of offering to others?

- How much are you willing to exert yourself to attain what you're looking for?

- How do close, long-term relationships fit into your life?

- If relationships of this sort are important to you, have you taken specific, thoughtful steps to find someone who is compatible—someone with whom you can build a life together?

∾ If you have taken steps, do they seem to heading in the right direction?

∾ If you haven't taken any steps, why not?

∾ Specifically, what is it in your life that's not allowing you to make a connection with someone who could share your life with you?

The issue of relationships is fundamental. For most people they're not just a luxury; they're a necessity. And if you feel you're getting nowhere—you're blocked or stalled in your search—the complaint about having no time is probably just an excuse. *Nobody* has enough time these days! The lack of time is something we all face. So I believe that this issue is really more a matter of priorities and self-discipline.

Task #2
Slow Down the Process

Earlier, I mentioned that too many couples rush the process of getting to know each other, and they rush the process of becoming intimate. This sense of haste does a lot of damage. How can you proceed more slowly, thoughtfully, and carefully?

I believe that it all comes down to the issue of reflection. It's important to reflect, look at your life, and look at the big picture. It's important to clarify what your goals are and what you're spending your resources on. If your entire goal is to be a successful professional, it's probably going to affect your personal life. If your entire goal is to make a lot of money, it's probably going to affect your relationships. If your entire focus is to have the ideal apartment or the ideal sports car or the toys that you want most, it's going to affect your relationship.

When you're young and ambitious, it's easy to forget that this life is a big journey. There will come a day when you're not going to have all this energy—and when you won't want to expend all of what you have on achieving at work or acquiring material possessions—when you won't be the best professional in the world, when you won't be able to keep up with the Joneses. What happens when you don't have so many material possessions—or youth, or energy, or even health? What is your long-term plan for your life, a plan that meets not just your material needs, but your emotional and spiritual needs as well? You need to size up your priorities, think about what you'll need and want twenty, thirty, forty years from now, and plan certain aspects of your life. Here are some questions that I recommend you ask yourself:

- ❧ Do you feel that you're being loved sufficiently to meet your emotional needs?

- ❧ Are you able to love someone in return?

- ❧ Do you have a meaningful person to share your life with?

- ❧ If so, are you "going with the flow" or working to build the relationship you need and want?

- ❧ If you don't have someone to share your life with, are you seeking out that person?

- ❧ Are you putting as much emphasis on the personal/emotional aspects of life (as opposed to work/leisure aspects) as you feel is appropriate?

- ❧ If not, what does the "shortfall" on the personal/emotional side mean, and what should you be thinking about and doing?

- ❧ Where should you be directing your energy, your gifts, your talents?

- ❧ Do you have a long-term plan for achieving your personal and emotional fulfillment?

    ~ If not, what will you do to think through such a plan?

    ~ What specific steps will you need to take to achieve the fulfillment
       you envision?

By asking yourself these questions, you can clarify your fundamental
goals and work toward them at a clearheaded pace rather than in impulsive haste.

Task #3
Nurture Love and Commitment for the Long Term

A lot of young couples I know are very attentive to each other at the start
of their relationship—almost to the point of being joined to each other!
But after a while they get testy and easily annoyed by their partners.
I hear young women, especially, complaining about their husbands: "He
really doesn't pay attention to me anymore" or "He used to tell me I'm
very pretty, but now he doesn't say anything" or "He takes me for
granted." I remember a letter from one of my readers, a woman who had
dated her fiancé for three years and had now been married for only a year.
She felt totally frustrated because her husband no longer showed the
same type of affection that he showed before they got married. Her question to me was "Father, why did he change so much once we got
married?"

    Here's my issue with this couple—and with many others I hear from.
In the beginning, what was their understanding—or, more accurately,
what was the husband's understanding—of the nature of their relationship, their love, and their affection toward each other over time? Did he
understand all those beautiful things that he'd said to his bride—about
seeing their children and their children's children, and being together
forever? If you listen carefully to the rites in a religious marriage cere-

mony, you'll notice that the words speak about your descendants and about growing old together. Did the young man have a sense that the relationship was ever going to change?

Many unmarried couples believe that just because they are physically intimate, they must be emotionally close and fully committed to each other. They think that having a sexual relationship means that they know each other and that they've taken their relationship as far as it can ever go. The relationship is one big, exciting adventure. But then, following the wedding, the situation changes. Suddenly the sense of adventure wanes—and often vanishes completely. The partners are in a committed relationship now, a relationship characterized less by candlelight dinners and romantic outings than by paying the bills, washing the dishes, doing the laundry, and taking care of a hundred other ordinary tasks. Even if the couple lived together before marriage, something shifts. A realization eventually dawns on the spouses—either gradually or all once—that their relationship is no longer just fun and games. Now there's responsibility. There are bad times as well as good. There's sickness as well as health. There are lean times as well as flush times. This is a long-term relationship now, not just playing house. This is committed love.

So what changed for the man whose wife wrote me that letter? Maybe he didn't understand that he was making a lasting commitment—that it was no longer just a game. Now it was real life. How did that affect him? Well, it affected him in what is obviously a negative way. He wasn't able to translate the dynamism, the joy, and the love that he and his partner felt before the marriage to the actual marriage. Now they've been married a year, and his wife asks, "Why has he has changed? Why is he cold?"

There's something else going on here that I find interesting. The woman seemed able to communicate her needs and her desires effectively in her letter to me, but I wonder if she was able to communicate as well with her husband. The husband may not even understand that he's gotten cold. As a matter of fact, I wouldn't be surprised if, when she eventually confronts him about it, he says that he doesn't see any difference.

So perhaps there is also a communication problem in this marriage as a two-way street. (Later on in this book, we'll focus closely on communication issues.)

When a couple first gets together, everything is new and wonderful—it's the honeymoon stage. But eventually, as time goes on, the honeymoon ends and reality sets in. At this point, many people panic at the magnitude of their commitment. Fear and anxiety overshadow the excitement of the earlier time, and the couple doesn't really know how to keep things exciting and new. They don't know how to nurture the love that they felt initially. This is precisely why love is much more than just "Hey, we're living together!" That part is easy. The problem is the other part. How do you nurture each other? How do you keep things new and fresh? Some couples do this very well, while others have no idea how to do it.

Love isn't based only on a first reaction or love at first sight. That's great for the beginning—for the initial spark—but it's not going to keep you together for the long term. What will keep you together for the long term is learning to grow in your appreciation of the other person—really getting to know his or her qualities and gifts. If you pay attention, you'll discover new things every day. You'll discover that there's something about this person that you didn't know before, and now you're realizing it's there. Look at your partner, look at your relationship, and value the love you share—and the person you share it with.

Task #4
Look Ahead—A Reality Check

It's revealing to speak with couples during premarital counseling. When I listen to them—and I have to tell you, 90 percent of the comments usually come from the bride—almost everything I hear has to do with details about the wedding. Not the *marriage* the *wed-*

ding. Their focus is the one-hour ceremony, not the decades of married life that follow. Very few couples are willing to talk about the marriage!

They're simply not addressing the real issues. The groom usually sits there across from me, quiet and unresponsive. Sometimes I'll try to engage him and try to get him to speak, but many times he'll say, "Oh, just ask her. She's got all the answers." But she doesn't. She's not talking about the important things. What about the long term? I want to say, "Forget the ceremony for just a moment! What about the twenty, thirty, forty, fifty years of married life that follow?" How can you walk together into the future if you've never talked about where you're going? How can you really know someone if you haven't discussed your goals? Many young couples spend more time considering their options for napkins at the wedding reception than they spend discussing what they need, what they want, and what they expect from the long-term commitment of marriage.

For this reason, Task #3 is a reality check—a series of questions to help you clarify your long-term view of your relationship. I use a similar exercise with the couples I counsel. Here are some questions that may start the process:

- ❧ What are you going to be like when you're thirty? Forty? Fifty? Older?

- ❧ What do you expect your spouse to be like at these ages?

- ❧ In what ways do you expect your appearance to change? Are you going to be just as slim as you are now? As handsome? As physically fit?

- ❧ In what way will your spouse's appearance change?

- ❧ What will be the foundation of your relationship as the two of you age, change, and grow older?

ᴥ What are the values on which you're building your relationship?

ᴥ How do you feel that your love will change—and how will it stay the same—as the years pass and you grow older?

You need to fast-forward and imagine what issues will matter to you at forty, fifty, sixty years of age. I don't mean to sound negative, but you have to understand that almost everything about your physical condition will change, and that many life circumstances will also change. Difficulties—even crises—will come up: illnesses, job loss, sick kids. So many things can happen. Are you willing to love your spouse through all of this?

In Path Seven of this book—Make a Commitment to Growth and Maturity—we'll examine specific ways that you can explore the long-term aspects of marriage. For now, it's important simply to perform this reality check and look ahead.

Task #5
Build a Sexual Relationship Based on Respect and Understanding

In the past, couples began to experience sexual intimacy only after getting married. Today, though, people often engage in sexual relationships and live together before marriage. I'd venture to say that most young people nowadays are sexually active from their teenage years.

As a result of this situation, I find that many young couples already consider themselves experts on sexuality. They've been having sexual intimacy for some years, and they don't really want advice on any aspect of this subject. But often the attitudes they hold regarding sex within a long-term, committed relationship aren't very realistic. They may be captive to Hollywood's image of what a sexual relationship is like. They may not be patient regarding the long process involved in building a good sexual relationship. Their expectations may simply be too high. Or maybe the spouses aren't compassionate toward each other or aren't understanding about each other's needs. The result of this "disconnect" between their expectations and reality is a dissatisfying physical relationship. The whole fantasy-driven media image of sexuality that our culture promotes—and that young couples often accept without question—isn't very well suited to the reality of married life.

It's difficult to explain to couples how important *foundations* are as they prepare for marriage. When you go through courtship, you're building what in Spanish we call *cimientos*—the foundation that a building stands upon. Establishing your *cimiento*s helps you build something that's strong and destined to last. But if you don't know what you're building, or if you don't build a strong base, you can't feel secure and confident later on as you build the rest of the relationship.

How does this situation affect a couple's sexual relationship? A couple that faces later difficulties—whether physical, emotional, or both—will be better off if they've built a strong foundation for their relationship in general. They'll be better able to solve their difficulties if they care deeply for each other. If you need to overcome any dysfunction, repression, or frustration in the sexual aspects of your relationship, your deep love and concern for the other person will be the basis for understanding, helping, and working with him or her. You can work through problems and crises far better if you've already built a strong foundation of love and mutual acceptance.

I believe that you should enter your relationship with the understanding that your sexual relationship with your spouse exists just as much (or more) on the emotional and spiritual levels as on the level of physical intimacy. Physical intimacy is wonderful, but first and foremost it's the result of good spiritual and emotional intimacy. Why? Because every human being has been created not just with a body but also with a mind and a soul. If you focus only on physical intimacy, you attend to the body's needs but ignore the mind's and the soul's needs. This imbalance can't help but lead eventually to imbalance in your relationship.

But if you have reached a state of balance between your physical, psychological, and spiritual needs in the context of a committed, lasting relationship, then giving yourself to your spouse in a sexual act creates more than just physiological pleasure. You're also strengthening a long-term, unifying relationship that's based on consideration and affection. You are renewing your love for each other every time sexual intimacy occurs between you.

Here are some steps I urge you to take that can help you build a strong foundation for your sexual relationship.

✤ *Step 1:* CLARIFY YOUR ATTITUDES

As is true for everyone, your attitudes are partly the result of the values and messages you received growing up. We all receive our attitudes about sexuality primarily from our families of origin. But because many families are uneasy dealing with issues of sexuality, many people enter a marriage with "baggage" about sex. If you were taught during childhood to speak freely about sexuality as a normal part of life, you'll probably deal with this aspect of life much better than if you lived in a home where your parents told you that sex is dirty and bad. I hear from many people who feel uneasy, ashamed, or tense about themselves as sexual beings. I also hear more and more often from people who say that they were sexually abused at some point during their childhood or adolescence. Perhaps an uncle or a neighbor acted inappropriately, or perhaps a classmate took advantage of them. As a result of these and other negative experiences, people often bring great pain into their otherwise positive marital relationships, and the lack of healing can become a burden for a couple during courtship and marriage.

What's the result of this situation? Well, if you have conflicted feelings about sexual behavior, or if your feelings are downright negative, those issues will unfortunately influence your marriage. They may well become problems and obstacles in relating with your spouse. Statistically, this situation is very common.

In any case, it's important to clarify your attitudes about sexuality. And it's important for your spouse to understand his or her own attitudes as well. By clarifying these issues, both individually and as a couple, you'll take a crucial step toward building a strong relationship.

Here are some specific questions that will help you clarify your basic attitudes about sexuality:

- ∾ What is your overall reaction to yourself as a sexual being? Do you feel comfortable, uncomfortable, pleased, displeased, etc., with your own sexuality?

- ∾ What have you heard about sexuality from your mother, your father, your teachers, or other people who have been closest to you? Are the messages you've heard about sexuality positive, negative, or mixed?

- ∾ What are the images you have of sexual intimacy, and how do those images prompt you to feel? That is, are you delighted, restless, uneasy, or even disgusted by these images?

- ∾ Are the images typical of what occurs in real relationships between men and women or are they more exotic, illicit, aggressive, violent, adulterous, or "forbidden" than what takes place in everyday, caring relationships?

- ∾ What are the aspects of sexuality that you value most?

- ∾ Can you see sexuality as not just physical expression but also emotional and spiritual?

Answering these questions can provide a good starting point to the process of clarifying your values about sexuality. And this process of clarification can in turn help you understand the images and expectations you bring to your relationship.

✤ *Step 2:* SEPARATE FANTASY FROM REALITY

Another step I recommend is to think through the many ways that our culture influences your perceptions of sexuality. Then, to the degree possible, try to separate fantasy from reality.

We're all influenced by images created by the media. Many people I speak with believe that their sexual relationships should resemble the images of what they see routinely on the silver screen or the TV set. Or else they strive (consciously or unconsciously) to emulate the love lives of rock stars, supermodels, or other celebrities. Imitation of this sort is unfortunate in many ways. First of all, it's hard—if not impossible—for ordinary people to emulate the lifestyles of the rich and famous. In addition, there are issues of content. Movies and TV shows highlight promiscuous behavior that is unlikely to foster happiness or fulfillment in anyone's life. Popular music, for instance, often includes lyrics that express violent emotions, hostility toward women, and other negative attitudes. Most of the media present an unrealistic picture of what real sexual intimacy is about. TV, the movies, rock videos, and the music industry all present sexuality as something that is casual and often self-centered rather than focused on a lifetime commitment to another human being. The result? Many young people enter marriage thinking that sexuality is just a game—a game with an edgy, forbidden, aggressive tone.

Under these circumstances, why are we surprised when long-term problems crop up in real-life relationships?

Here's a more realistic assessment of the situation.

When you live with someone and commit yourself to that person for the long haul, there's a genuine and legitimate need for sexual attraction and mutual desire. That's a normal, good part of being human. It's also part of what can strengthen and deepen a relationship. But it's a mistake to rely on the exotic, forbidden aspects of sex to sustain a committed marriage. If you and your spouse love each other, grow accustomed to each other, and support each other as partners, your sexual relationship can be so much more powerful and intense than a superficial encounter.

However, you do have to work on your sexual relationship to make it better as your marriage develops and changes. You need to accept that your sexual relationship isn't about your earlier, fantasy-based images of sex. What you've seen in movie theaters or on TV, and what you've heard in rock songs and other kinds of music, is an alternate reality that doesn't bear much resemblance to real life.

Here are some of the unrealistic "scenarios" I see couples conjure up—scenarios that complicate their tasks of building a strong sexual relationship:

The "Happily-Ever-After" Scenario. This is an age-old fantasy that affects many people—a belief that once you cross the threshold into married life, all your relationship problems will be solved forever. You'll live in perfect wedded bliss. Your sex life will be wonderful all the time, and keeping it that way will require no attention or effort.

The "You're-My-Trophy" Scenario. The media also popularize another scenario, one in which a spouse is essentially another possession or accessory among all the other consumer goods that you acquire to live the high life. My description may sound harsh, but the attitude I'm describing is lamentably common. You see it in the behavior of many middle-aged men, for instance, who divorce their first wife to marry a younger "trophy wife." You also see it in the behavior of some women who "marry money" in order to acquire a certain lifestyle.

The "You're-My-'Ho' " Scenario. In a lot of popular music—some genres more than others—there's an enormous amount of hostility toward women and an emphasis on the subjugation of women. This view presents women as little more than objects for male pleasure—objects that a man uses rather than a person he shares his life with. Unfortunately, a lot of young men these days are influenced by this set of attitudes.

Regarding these and other unrealistic scenarios about relationships and sexuality, I urge you to set aside the media-driven images that surround us and, instead, view sex as a mutually satisfying, mutually respectful expression of love. It's not about you simply getting pleasure or achieving certain goals in the bedroom. It's a deep form of intimacy that is integral to a marriage. It's another block in the foundation of a solid marriage.

✦ *Step 3:* DON'T USE SEXUALITY AS A PUNISHMENT OR A REWARD

In building a strong foundation for your sexual relationship, it's important to respond always to your spouse out of love and respect, never out of manipulation. The basis of a good relationship is mutual sensitivity, concern, and compromise. Manipulative behavior has no place in a loving sexual relationship.

Unfortunately, some spouses tend to use sex as a punishment or as a reward. The partners may not be aware of what they're doing, but sometimes they do it anyway. Others intentionally use sex as part of a system of "payoff" or retribution. I've heard some couples actually speak outright in these terms: "Well, he hasn't been very nice to me lately, so he's sure not getting any tonight." When you hear statements like that, you realize the couple has set up a reward/punishment system—a kind of economy in which sexual affection is a "currency" that can be bestowed or withheld. I find this attitude disturbing and damaging. Rather than sexual affection being an integral part of a caring relationship—a form of love that is freely given—these couples treat it like a commodity that the other partner has to earn. People may speak of the situation in a joking, funny way, but the reality is the same. If you behave right, you "get some." If you don't behave right, you "don't get any." When a couple resorts to this kind of reward/punishment system, they've reached a point in their relationship where there's almost certainly some other problem at work.

My recommendation: reject this attitude altogether. Don't treat physical intimacy as if it's a gold star on your spouse's good behavior chart. If you feel love and delight in your spouse, express it with all your heart. If you feel frustration, anger, or unease, discuss the issues *as a couple* to identify the cause of your negative emotions, then solve your problems together. Keep your sexual feelings out of the process—unless, of course, sexual feelings *are* the issue, in which case you should discuss those problems in the same spirit of openness and mutual generosity.

There are, of course, many other important aspects of sexuality that contribute to a couple's marital relationship. Precisely because these aspects are so important, we'll explore them in more detail elsewhere in this book—especially in Path Four and Path Seven.

Task #6
Accept Your Own—and the Other Person's—Shortcomings

You have to understand the other person's limitations. Don't underestimate or overestimate your partner. Many people have a tendency to create a false image of who the other person is—or to project their own desires for what they want this person to be. But that may not be the person at all! It's important to be realistic. At a minimum, ask these questions—and be open to having your partner ask them about you, as well:

- How much is this person able to meet your needs?

- How much are you able to meet his or her needs?

- What is your "vision" of the ideal partner or spouse?

∾ In what ways does this vision alter or distort your expectations about the actual human being you intend to spend your life with?

∾ How much of the imperfection of the other person are you willing to accept?

∾ In what ways do you expect the other person to accept your own imperfections?

Acceptance is a big issue, because it's really a question of whether you can love this person truly as he or she is, or if you love the image you have in your mind of what this person should be. A lot of disappointment and grief occurs when people fall in love with an *image* of someone and not the real person.

Task #7
Assess Your Values and Goals

I always ask couples how they met. I've heard all sorts of answers: at a bar, through the Internet, on the job, while doing sports—you name it. I find all those experiences fascinating, because obviously the couple found some sort of a connection there. But my greater concern is, *What happened after the initial connection?* Now, I believe that from a spiritual perspective, God put that initial attraction in us—that desire for the other person—so that other, deeper things could happen. Attraction jump-starts the relationship. The man looks and sees the woman of his dreams, and he thinks, *Wow, this woman is just right for me.* Or the woman meets a man and decides, *He's the guy I've been waiting for.* And so they pursue a relationship and if there's something more than that initial spark, then they get to know each other, begin to understand each other, and go deeper.

Unfortunately, some people *don't* go deeper. Some people don't relate except on the most superficial level. If you look at the divorce statistics, one gets the feeling that it's more and more common.

So I begin to ask some fundamental questions: "Tell me about the dreams you have in common. Tell me about your goals."

Couples usually want a relationship that is lasting, loving, caring, faithful, and exclusive. However, they often fail to ask the fundamental questions. So one of my goals in providing counseling during the marriage preparation phase is to try to help them address those issues. What are your goals as a couple? What values do you share? What values are different—or even in conflict?

These are tough questions to ask! I'm aware that examining these issues can be stressful, challenging, even threatening. A lot of couples worry that if they explore what they believe, they may uncover disagreements that could stress their relationship. I won't pretend that's not a possibility. Soul-searching is hard. It's worrisome to discover differences you didn't even know existed. But here's the truth: these differences will show up eventually. Whatever is a problem now will be amplified after the marriage. It's far better to face these issues now than to pretend they don't exist and then get surprised by them later.

If the groom feels fine about living in a mobile home but the bride wants to live in a mansion, they have a problem. If the groom wants to have six children but the bride wants only two, there's a problem. If she wants to drive a Lexus and he's satisfied with a used Toyota, they have a problem. So part of the process is getting each member the couple to put his or her cards on the table. What really matters to them? What are their real dreams, their real goals, their real ambitions? Because even if you love each other, you intend to be faithful, and you want to spend your lives together, all kinds of issues can push you apart if you don't talk about what matters to you most. You need to connect to your own realities. What is it that you really want from this life?

Task #8
Be Realistic About Stages and Changes in Your Relationship

People often feel dissatisfied with the changes that affect them in their marriage, but here's the truth: all marriages go through different stages. Couples will be happier if they can accept the changes that come over time—and if they grow as a result of those changes. Happy couples are the ones that can accept that everything in life has a season. Some stages are easy; some are difficult. You're not going to be on your honeymoon forever. But just because you're not on your honeymoon doesn't mean you'll live in a state of spiritual and emotional drought. If you can take a broader view of the life cycle and a broader view of your own life, your life will be fuller, not more limited.

Perhaps you're dissatisfied with some aspect of your relationship. Well, dissatisfactions can certainly happen. But you need to ask *why*. And you need to ask what you'll do about your dissatisfaction.

Specifically, I urge you to ask yourself these questions—and for you to discuss them openly with your partner:

- What are your expectations and attitudes about change in your relationship, especially change throughout the course of a potentially long marriage?

- Do you expect that the nature of your relationship will stay more or less the same, or will there be developments, events, and even crises that require you and your spouse to adjust to circumstances over time?

- Are you willing to alter your expectations, behaviors, and attitudes over the years if circumstances require?

- Do you expect married life to be easy and fun all the time?

∾ Whether your answer is yes or no, how much difficulty, challenge, and even hardship are you willing to accept throughout the course of your marriage?

∾ If your spouse were to become ill, disabled, or unemployed, or if he or she suffered some other hardship, would you be able and willing to put your own happiness aside to help your spouse through hard times?

∾ To what degree are you able and willing to discuss situations with your spouse as a way of dealing with challenges, difficulties, and hardships?

∾ Would you be willing to seek outside help (such as from a counselor, priest, minister, or rabbi) to help you and your spouse deal with challenging circumstances?

∾ What other steps are you willing to take that would help address issues or solve problems you encounter throughout the course of married life?

∾ If something in your marriage isn't right, or if something isn't right with this stage of your life, what are you doing to make it better?

∾ What are you doing physically, emotionally, and spiritually to make your marriage more meaningful?

Task #9
Consider Getting Guidance

Some couples are able to tackle their problems and issues alone—including some issues that are very complicated, such as parenthood, job transition, or marital conflict. Other couples aren't as effective in solving problems on their own. They have a greater need for outside help. Fair enough. There's nothing wrong with obtaining help. In fact, it's a sign of maturity and flexibility. Many marriages would benefit from the couple being more open-minded to seeking assistance.

When a couple experiences a crisis in their relationship—sadness, tension, a sense of distance from each other, or anything else—it's appropriate to seek help. But many couples *don't* seek help. Why? Because admitting that you have a problem is such a big step. It's scary. Right away people think: *divorce*. But in reality, facing a problem doesn't inevitably lead to divorce. However, *not* facing a problem often does. When you don't address your problems head-on, the marriage stays miserable for a long time before anyone tries to find help. As a result of this hesitance to get assistance, the damage gets worse and worse. It's like knowing you need to change the oil in your car, but you don't. You let the car go. Eventually there's major damage. It's the same sort of issue. You know there's a problem. You see the symptoms. You feel frustrated and you don't know exactly what you need to do. But if you're really committed to this other person, if you're really in love, you have to do what you have to do to make things better. And the first step of doing that is admitting that there's a problem.

(For information about counseling and guidance, see this book's Appendix—Resource Guide.)

TREASURE HUNTING

Throughout this section, we've explored the issues of building strong foundations. This issue is just what it seems: constructing the base for everything else in your relationship. But for a moment I want to switch images to something a little less practical, a little more exotic.

Relationships are like hidden treasures waiting to be discovered. But treasures don't just turn up out of nowhere. To find them requires pa tience, clear sight, and hard work. The partners must each put aside their prejudices, stay open to each other, and reach out with profound generosity. To build a strong relationship, we must ignore many of our own selfish impulses and focus instead on the other person. But the work involved doesn't deplete you. On the contrary, nothing can make you richer—more abundantly blessed—than your ability to discover the treasures that a good relationship will offer you.

Thales of Miletus, the Greek thinker from the fifth century before the Christian Era (B.C.), was considered one of the seven wise men of ancient Greece. Someone once asked him what he considered the most difficult task in human life. He answered, "To know yourself." Self-knowledge is indeed a difficult task. But if this level of awareness is hard to attain—and I agree that it is—then surely it's also difficult to know another person. To know another person truly—to accept him or her without preconceptions and to value the treasure that this person offers—we must be willing to open the doors of our minds and hearts. Those persons who you let into the sacred center of your being will challenge you but will also give you the greatest gifts of your earthly life

The human desire to love and be loved is essential, and the sooner we all learn this and apply it to our everyday relationships, the happier we will be. That is why love should be the true foundation of any significant human relationship. Love needs to be at the foundation of our lives and the core of our being. We will only be complete when we learn to find love and share love—when we learn to go beyond ourselves.

Path Two

RESPECT EACH OTHER

Listen to these four statements, each of them spoken by one member of a couple to his or her spouse:

> *"I'm not sure I understand what you're feeling, but I'll take your word that you're upset. Can you tell me more about what's going on? I'm listening, believe me. I'm going to try to see things your way. I can't guarantee I'll get the whole picture, but I'll try."*

> *"What's the point of asking you for help? It's more trouble than if I do it all myself! Can't I even trust you to buy a few groceries? Half the stuff you bought isn't even on the list! I bet you didn't even read the list!"*

> *"I disagree with you. If we buy the car now rather than waiting a year, we'll end up paying less money down but a higher payment month after month. That's just not a good idea. Let's check around for a lower interest rate, discuss the situation, and see if we can reach some sort of compromise."*

"You just don't get it, do you? Well, that's so typical! You never did work too hard at understanding what I'm trying to tell you. Seems a big waste of my time even trying to explain!"

These quotes come from four couples discussing an issue they're facing. Each husband-and-wife pair is in disagreement. The speakers in quotes 1 and 4 are the husbands in their respective marriages; the speakers in quotes 2 and 3 are the wives in their respective marriages. But I'm not quoting these couples to point out the male/female issues. Rather, what interests me is the differences in *tone*. Even though all four couples are in a state of disagreement, quotations 1 and 3 reveal a sense of basic respect—a state in which the partners honor each other even when disagreeing. In quotations 2 and 4, though—what a difference! These partners belittle or demean each other. The implications of these two different tones—and of their two fundamentally different attitudes—brings us to a discussion of Path Two—Respect Each Other.

Chapter 4

The Primacy of Respect

Respect is a necessary component in your relationships with the people you allow into your sacred center—that crucial place where serious relationships develop and grow over time. When you open your heart to someone and that person opens up equally to you, it's impossible for the relationship to flourish and bring you happiness without a deep sense of mutual respect. In fact, the absence of respect can make a marriage eventually turn bitter and sour, even disastrous.

So what, exactly, is respect? For a couple, respect in a relationship is the ability and willingness to accept and understand each other. It's being able to see both the good and the bad in each other's personal qualities but still accept the balance. It's being able to understand fundamental differences between you—not only male/female differences, but also individual personality differences, and the commitment to validate each other for who you are, rather than force each other to be someone you're not.

AT THE HEART OF RESPECT: COMPASSION

Certain attitudes and behaviors are necessary to foster respect within a relationship. Some of these attitudes are simply the result of common sense and good manners. Others are virtues that require more attention to create and maintain. At the heart of these virtues—at the vital core of the mutual respect within a couple's relationship—is compassion.

Compassion is one of those words we all toss around without considering it closely. When we are compassionate (Latin root: "to feel with"), we are able to get inside someone else's feelings. Have you ever found yourself questioning your spouse's behavior? Have you ever felt frustrated and unable to understand why he or she refuses to make choices that seem perfectly sensible to you? Well, if you can start to see with the other person's eyes and feel with that person's heart, you may discover the reasons for otherwise strange-seeming, even incomprehensible behavior. With a little compassion, you can begin to grasp your spouse's real situation. And doing so is often a moving experience. This is where compassion and respect go hand in hand.

The biggest lesson to learn about respect is simply this: you're marrying someone who is radically different than you. You are giving yourself to someone who is a separate being with a separate consciousness. Throughout life, that person will experience struggles, emotional ups and downs, and challenges. Your job as a good mate is to try to figure out and understand what this person is going through. That's where compassion and respect come together. You're trying to be open to the other person's needs.

How can you accomplish the difficult task of seeing life as if through someone else's eyes? How can you think as if with someone else's mind? How can you feel as if with someone else's heart? To understand certain behaviors, it's vital to put yourself in the other person's shoes—to attempt to feel what the other person feels and to enter the mysterious world of his or her innermost thoughts. I have no doubt that compassion is the key to this task. Through compassion, you can begin to see the other person's truth and connect with his or her reality. Compassion helps you to "read" people at a deeper level and understand what they are really made of. But how can you attain a higher level of compassion? How can you achieve the insights that lead to greater respect for other people, including your spouse?

There's no easy answer to this question. However, I feel that certain steps you can take will foster compassion and make it a greater part of your life. Here are some suggestions:

Avoid judgmental attitudes. We are all full of opinions and certainties. We're all tempted to pass judgment on other people. As a result of these tendencies, it's easy to tune out what others think and feel, and to focus instead only on our own "take" on reality. But doing so makes it hard to be compassionate. My recommendation: rather than judging others and their actions, try to be more open-minded and open-hearted.

Listen and observe closely. Being open-minded and open-hearted is partly a consequence of perception. It's amazing how little we truly listen to and observe the people around us—including the people we're closest to! We often concentrate more on the inner "chatter" going through our heads than on whoever is right in front of us. It's far more constructive to listen closely to what that person is telling you and watch for clues about his or her experience. Attentive perception of others is one of the keys to compassion.

Communicate. In addition, it's crucial to communicate with the people we're close to. This is an absolutely central task for spouses. How can you truly understand what your partner is going through without a direct, open dialogue? Asking open questions and giving honest answers is the most crucial way for a husband and wife to grasp what each is experiencing. (The issue of communication is so crucial and complex that I've devoted all of Path Five to it later in this book.)

Will taking these steps guarantee compassion? Of course not—there's no sure bet for attaining this goal. But striving for compassion is crucial. Without at least making the effort to understand your spouse's experience, you're unlikely to see things or feel things from his or her point of view. And by making this effort, it's far more probable that you'll develop deeper compassion as a skill and as a habit.

Here's an example of a couple whose different approaches to life led to serious misunderstandings—and whose growing compassion helped them to avoid a major marital rift.

Marissa, age thirty, often felt frustrated by her husband's workaholic tendencies. She knew that her husband, Jerry, age thirty-two, loved her and felt devoted to her. But he often spent more time at the office than seemed necessary, and, after four or five years of marriage, Marissa wondered if her husband might be avoiding her. If that were the case, she felt slighted and even rejected. If not, then his behavior still seemed inconsiderate—a thoughtless, excessive focus on business issues to the exclusion of her emotional needs.

Eventually Marissa confronted Jerry about this situation and told him, "I think you actually prefer the office to your own home, and you prefer your coworkers to me."

Jerry was stunned. "I can't even believe you're saying this!" he exclaimed.

A difficult, emotionally wrenching discussion followed—a major crisis point in their marriage. But their soul-baring conversation helped them understand what was truly at the heart of Jerry's workaholism. It turned out that Jerry's father had been a poor provider for his wife and family; Jerry, his siblings, and his mother had suffered a great deal as a result of the dad's many vocational failures, and Jerry's mother had often berated her husband for his incompetence. You can imagine the impact this had on Jerry throughout his boyhood. One of Jerry's deepest worries as a young husband was that he'd follow in his father's footsteps as a ne'er-do-well. His intense hope was that he would never let down his wife and future children in the ways that his own father had let down his family. In fact, Jerry was a gifted and hardworking businessman. But his thriving career wasn't sufficient to ease his fears. This state of mind—not lack of love or consideration for Marissa—was what drove him to work such long hours.

Once Marissa understood the situation, she could feel compassion for her husband's worries and help to ease them. And once Jerry reached insights about his own behavior and Marissa's frustrations, he could start to relax, strive for a better work/life balance, and respond more fully to his wife's need for attention and affection.

Some people are naturally compassionate. All of us have probably known children who, even as preschoolers or school-age kids, were unusually kind, generous, and concerned about others. (One friend reports, for instance, that his four-year-old daughter, on hearing an infant cry—even at the supermarket or at the mall—will often ask, "Can we go help that baby?") You've probably also known adults who are "do-gooders," "mother hens," or "saintly types" who make themselves available to other people and offer insight, support, and solace. If you're lucky, you have friends or relatives—and, if you're truly blessed, a spouse—who are fundamentally kind, supportive, and nonjudgmental. Why are these people so compassionate—and, it seems, innately so? Perhaps their attitudes and behaviors are partly a result of their inborn personalities. Perhaps such compassion comes from the quality of parenting these people received from babyhood onward. I can't really answer this question, as I'm not a psychologist. I suppose what's most important is that we recognize such people, value them, and learn from them.

It's worth noting that even naturally compassionate people sometimes overlook certain things in the rush of day-to-day life. Fatigue, stress, multiple demands, and busy schedules all take their toll. Do-gooders and mother hens can have a bad day just like everyone else. (In fairness, the same probably holds true for saints!) And because compassion is a process we learn over time, not something we attain fully once and for all, everyone has shortcomings in response to other people's needs. The most generous husband may get grouchy at times; the most supportive wife may feel emotionally depleted. We're only human, right? We're fallible creatures. In marriage, as in other aspects of life, even compassionate people can make mistakes or succumb to selfish impulses. Sometimes previously devoted spouses experience a kind of gradual wear and tear on their compassion, too, that affects their marriage over time. I've known couples who started out as mutually loving and considerate partners but grew impatient and irritable with each other as the years passed. Why? That's hard to say. It's tempting to invoke the cliché that "familiarity breeds contempt," and sometimes that's true. But sometimes familiarity breeds deeper and deeper respect—I've seen that often in couples, too. Unfortunately, even partners who care for each other may get lazy and each forget to notice (or value) what the other partner is experiencing. The waning of compassion doesn't mean that these spouses don't love each other. It's just all too easy to get worn down by stress, to become entangled in your own needs, and to take things for granted.

For most people, mastering the art of compassion is a lifelong task. Here are some issues that I recommend specifically for couples to keep in mind as they strive to build and maintain respect within their relationship:

Pay attention. Half of compassion is simply maintaining an awareness of others. In marriage, especially, it's easy to grow so accustomed to your spouse's presence in your life that you stop paying attention to him or her. Try to stay aware of your partner—his or her thoughts, feelings, needs, and concerns.

Remember your differences. No matter how close you and your spouse may be, you are two separate human beings. You are different in many ways. If you can remember that your spouse has different needs than you do, you can be more perceptive and compassionate in your responses to those needs, which will help your relationship thrive and grow.

Remember your common ground. Just as you have differences, you have common interests, commitments, and endeavors. By reminding yourself of what you share and what you're working toward as a couple, you can strengthen your sense of compassion toward your spouse.

Be aware that time may influence your compassion. Many people become more compassionate over the years, for they gain more experience and learn more about human fallibility, which can lead to a less judgmental, more forgiving attitude toward others. However, I sense that some spouses grow more impatient and *less* compassionate toward each other as time passes. Maybe it's just a consequence of cumulative wear and tear. Or perhaps it's easier to be compassionate early on because the partners are working harder on the relationship. My suggestion: as the years pass, work actively not to take each other for granted.

Slow down. Compassion takes time—time to observe, time to listen, time to consider what you're seeing and hearing, time to perceive the other person clearly. If you live your life in a constant rush, you'll have few opportunities and less energy to understand your spouse and share the thoughts and feelings that make compassion possible.

WHAT ABOUT MALE-FEMALE DIFFERENCES?

A wise old priest once told me, "You know, Albert, God must have a great sense of humor. First he created man and woman—and he made them radically different. And then to liven up the show, he made them live together."

I spend hours listening to couples' issues and problems, and the concerns I hear about often have to do with men's and women's different needs and perspectives. The male perspective and the female perspective can differ radically on so many things! As our society becomes more complex, and as we deal with many issues of gender equality, we tend to ignore some fundamental aspects of who we are. Men are still men and women are still women. Couples are still dealing with the same problems that have arisen for decades (or even centuries)—issues such as division of labor, life priorities, and communication. Are the differences between men and women biological? Are they the result of cultural influences? Or are they, as seems most likely, a mix of biology *and* culture? I'm not a biologist, a psychologist, or an anthropologist, so I'm not in a position to answer these challenging questions. But whatever the big picture may be regarding males and females, I'm sure we all agree that there *are* some differences between individual men and women. And for our purposes, what's most important is to recognize that spouses must acknowledge and deal with their own differences if they are to respect each other.

Ultimately, the crucial issue within a couple isn't the differences between men and women. What really matters is the differences between *an individual man* and *an individual woman*—a specific husband and a specific wife. Above all, what matters is how this couple *copes* with their differences.

Here's how I see it:

A wise husband should do everything he can to understand his wife's perspective on life. That perspective may or may not include traditional "feminine" attitudes and approaches to many issues—work, family/work balance, communication, domestic tasks, and many other topics—that often differ from traditional "masculine" attitudes and approaches. Does understanding his wife's view mean that a husband needs to agree with her on everything? Of course not. But he should express his respect by staying open-minded to her insights; he should discuss the issues good-heartedly; and he should stay open to compromise. Different people have different perspectives on many issues. Your family of origin, your ethnic background, your education, and your personal talents and interests will all influence your goals and means of accomplishing those goals—career, family, leisure, material comfort, and so forth. The same holds true for your spouse. If a husband wants to understand his wife, then the key is for him to listen closely to her *as a person.*

In the same way, a wife should try to understand her husband regardless of what she may consider to be "the male perspective." It's true that men experience the world in ways that women often find baffling. Consider, for instance, the issues of pride and work. Men frequently feel anxious about what their work—either its success or its failure—implies about them. A man's sense of his accomplishments in work can be either devastating or very sustaining. Many men also obtain a lot of self-worth from the income they earn. Despite all the talk in our culture about changing family roles—including men's greater participation in parenting duties—the truth is that most men seem to want a traditional role as chief wage earner and head of the household. Does this situation mean that all couples should fall into the man-as-breadwinner/wife-as-homemaker model? No. Couples should sort through the issues openly and find the arrangement that works best for them. But if the wife can be aware of her husband's perceptions of these issues, she'll better understand where he's coming from, and her compassion will contribute greatly to the marriage.

The best move you can both make in this regard is to accept that *you're different even though you're together.* How does compassion fit into modern life and its shifting gender roles? Well, the answer is that compassion is more important than ever as male-female dynamics change. As more and more women have entered and excelled in the workplace, for instance, many wives are now the primary breadwinners in their families. At the same time, more and more men are heavily involved parents. Many spouses take on multiple roles. The result? It's less and less feasible to fall back on gender stereotypes. It's more and more crucial for each spouse to perceive the other as an individual, not just as a typecast husband or wife, each with a predetermined role. As a result, spouses must work harder to perceive each other's reality in its own terms. Who you are as a husband or wife isn't "carved in stone" just because you're male or female.

Compassion is also crucial as a couple moves through the life cycle. The stages a couple goes through aren't as clear as they were in the past. A man in midlife may be looking forward to retirement, while a woman the same age may anticipate this time as an opportunity to get a job, go back to school, reinvent herself, now that her parenting duties are over. These and other differences will almost invariably challenge the spouses' ability to see each other clearly and respond imaginatively to their different needs. For instance, a man or woman's retirement often alters the dynamic with his or her spouse. Let's say that a husband has reached sixty-five and decides to retire. His wife may see this event as an opportunity for the couple to spend more time together and regain an earlier level of closeness. But the husband may have a different vision of this life event; perhaps he sees it as a chance to have more time to himself, to "do his thing." In this and many similar situations, spouses need to be compassionate with each other, to work toward a better understanding of each other's needs at new stages in life, and to help both partners meet those needs, satisfy their desires, fulfill their expectations, and ease their fears as the years pass and the relationship develops.

So if respect and compassion are so important, how can a couple work to increase their skills in these areas? Do you just hope for the best? Or are there some specific ways to improve your contribution to your relationship in this regard? The path of fostering respect includes many different steps you can take, and we'll discuss those steps in the next chapter. But before we move on, we should explore the importance of boundaries and how establishing and honoring each other's boundaries is essential to fostering respect within a healthy marital relationship.

THE IMPORTANCE OF GOOD BOUNDARIES

In any couple's relationship, it's crucial that they establish and maintain sensible boundaries. Having these boundaries—and honoring them—makes it far less likely that either you or your spouse will violate the respect that's so crucial to your long-term happiness. Mutual respect will strengthen these boundaries, and the boundaries will strengthen your respect. Why? Because without clear boundaries, it's difficult for you and your spouse to clarify your expectations as you interact with each other.

WHAT ARE BOUNDARIES?

The word *boundaries* means different things under different circumstances. Here are some examples to help clarify.

When we were children, we all heard our parents say these words: "Don't talk to strangers." This simple statement provided a boundary because it set up expectations for our behavior. The guidelines were direct and clear. I'm sure all of us understood what we were hearing. This parental statement is one of the best examples of a serious, explicit boundary. It served primarily to protect us from harm during childhood. However, it also contained an embedded message: *Not everyone out there in the world is going to be good. You need to be careful.* Our parents protected us from potentially harmful people by creating clear boundaries—lines that we weren't supposed to cross.

As an adult, you may not think you're surrounded by boundaries, but you are. Social expectations are one example. Some of these expectations are crucial, while others are more trivial. You know most of these rules without thinking about them. For instance, you know that you're supposed to stop your car at a sign that says STOP. You also know that you're supposed to eat soup with a spoon, not with your bare hands. One set of boundaries prevents serious car accidents; the other simply designates polite behavior. Both, however, are ways that our society shapes our behavior for the common good. (Running a stop sign could cause a fatal car accident. Eating soup with your hands won't kill anyone, but I guarantee it'll upset your dinner companions.)

In our relationships, we pay attention to boundaries because they help us maintain the behavior that's appropriate to our closeness to or distance from each person in our lives. A simple example: we're supposed to shake hands with business associates, but it's okay to hug relatives and probably some friends as well. If you hug someone at a business meeting, you're probably asking for trouble. Paying attention to these and other boundaries helps us to protect ourselves from trouble in all our relationships.

WHAT ARE GOOD BOUNDARIES?

We all enter relationships knowing that there are some fundamental unwritten rules. These rules are present whether the relationships are with family members, friends, or people beyond our immediate social circle. And some of the rules have to do with boundaries.

A lot of boundary issues for couples have to do with respect for each other and for the relationship. What are your expectations of the other person? What is acceptable? What is unacceptable? Some boundaries are obvious and almost universally agreed upon. For example, most couples define their relationship in terms of an exclusive sexual bond. Fidelity is a given. Why? Because it's almost universally agreed upon that sexual relations with persons outside the marriage will damage the marital relationship. However, some nonsexual relationships are feasible or even desirable for each spouse to maintain. For instance, the wife may have friends at work or at school, and these relationships may be an important source of emotional support. The husband may have a similar set of friends. In addition, the spouses may have friends in common—other couples they know, single friends they're close to, and so forth. Marital counselors feel that most marriages actually *benefit* from having a supportive circle of relationships. If the spouses agree, it's fine for each of them to spend time with friends. The key is for these other relationships to be mutually agreed upon, fair, balanced, and able to nurture the marriage rather than hurt it.

One of the big issues I see with couples who marry early is that the partners may not have outgrown certain life stages or the activities typical of those stages. The wife may think, for example, that it's normal to go out to nightclubs with her friends on Saturday night. Well, it's not. If you're married, you've entered a new relationship—and you should be in your husband's company, not someone else's, at a place like a nightclub. Or the husband may think that it's okay to go drinking with his buddies at a singles' bar a couple of nights a week. Well, that's not the case. He's not in college anymore. He's not a free spirit. The boundaries change once you're married. Partly it's an issue of knowing what is an appropriate venue for socializing—which isn't the case when a married man hangs out at a singles bar—but above all it's an issue of needing to concentrate on your spouse as the center of your life. Sometimes the situation is clear-cut; sometimes it isn't. For instance, the boys' night out at the singles bar is out of the question. There's just too much about this scenario that's risky for this couple's well-being. By contrast, the husband's having an occasional golf outing with his pals seems like good, clean fun. But even something as innocent as golf could violate a boundary. How? Well, if the husband spends so much time playing golf with the guys that his wife feels isolated, neglected, and lonely, he's gone too far.

It's important for you and your spouse to ask yourselves and each other questions about many issues that will define the boundaries in your marriage—questions about the time you spend together, the balance between work and home activities, the role of in-laws, the role of other relatives, and other matters. What kind of "white picket fence" are you going to build around the protected area of your marriage? How do you create the right boundaries for yourselves? Here are some of the questions that you and your partner should ask and discuss as you establish good boundaries:

- Do you believe that all boundaries are clear-cut and inviolable, or are some of them flexible and negotiable?

- Which issues are completely clear-cut?

- Which are flexible and negotiable?

- Is it acceptable for you (or your partner) to be friends with an ex-boyfriend/girlfriend (that is, in a platonic friendship)?

- Is it acceptable for you (or your partner) to have friends of the opposite sex?

- When should you negotiate boundaries on these and other issues, and when should you simply concede to your partner's wishes?

- If you need to negotiate with each other on these issues, how will you do so (on your own, with advice from a friend, with intervention from a pastor or counselor, and so forth)?

- How will you respond if one of you feels upset about a difference of opinion over boundaries (for example, if one spouse feels that a certain friendship is unacceptable, while the other feels that the friendship shouldn't be considered problematic)?

- Is the most important thing to respect your spouse's wishes, even if his or her preference is unreasonable?

HOW DO YOU CLARIFY BOUNDARIES?

Boundaries are so essential that you and your partner should clarify them as fully as possible. We know that we all need a certain amount of respect and space for ourselves, but we don't make clear distinctions to define how much space or what kind of respect. We don't clearly establish the *criteria* for what we expect from the other person. We don't define what would be bad for us or what would be hurtful for our relationship.

Clarity about boundaries is something we all struggle with, especially in a society where customs and expectations are constantly changing. In many situations, though, uncertainty about boundaries can lead to mis-understandings, disagreements, even conflict. Our society is now much less traditional than in the past, when expectations were more clear-cut. Social interactions during much of American history—and to this day in many parts of the world—used to focus on same-sex interactions based on work outside the home (for men) or within the domestic setting (for women). Now men and women interact in a multitude of settings and through an expanded web of relationships. As a result, there's a great need for a couple to clarify boundaries for their mutual benefit.

It's also true that boundaries change and develop as the relationship changes and develops. That's natural and inevitable. Within most mar-riages, many boundaries are unwritten and even undiscussed. (How many spouses have talked over exactly what sorts of nonmarital friendships are acceptable?) And it's not uncommon for these boundaries to shift to some degree as time passes. This is understandable, and often it's not a problem. But I believe that if the boundaries change in any radical way—and if the boundaries become unclear—the spouses need to be in agree-ment about the nature and degree of the changes. If not, the situation will cause a lot of tension. You don't want to ignore the fundamental rules you've established. Anything that pulls you and your spouse apart, that causes disagreement, tension, lack of peace, or lack of stability in your home, isn't good for you.

This brings us back once again to the issues of communication. You and your spouse should actively—and on a regular basis—clarify your boundaries together. You should help each other understand what's good for you both *individually* and *together*, and also what's not so good for you individually and together. With experience and maturity, you'll begin to understand what can nurture you and what can push you apart.

For a relationship to be strong, you should take two steps regarding boundaries: first, clarify your boundaries; and second, protect the boundaries.

✤ *Step 1:* CLARIFY YOUR BOUNDARIES

Here are some questions for you to help you clarify your boundaries:

- How much leeway do I need (for independent activities, hobbies, social activities, etc.)?

- How much leeway does my spouse need?

- What is an appropriate amount of "downtime" for each of us?

- What activities can we enjoy together?

- What activities can we or should we do separately?

- How much free time should a spouse be able to have with his or her friends?

- What are the expectations we each have about boundaries?

As you answer and discuss these questions, it's important to distinguish between *marriage-nurturing* situations and *non-nurturing* situations. If a relationship or activity outside of the marriage nurtures the unity of marriage, you know it's healthy, and it will help you in the long term. If an external relationship or activity crosses boundaries in a way that *doesn't* nurture the marriage—or if it depletes, burdens, or causes tension in the marriage—then it's not a healthy relationship or activity. (Admittedly, some situations may be neutral. The situation I mentioned earlier—in which a husband plays golf with his buddies—would be neu-

tral if his wife doesn't mind his occasional outing; there's neither a positive nor a negative effect on the marriage. But if the man is out golfing
so often that his absence leaves his wife feeling miffed and lonely, then
this same outwardly harmless activity could create a negative situation for
the marriage.)

How do you determine which is which? Well, I think it's rather simple. When someone or something enters your relationship in a way
that's not welcome, you know there's a problem. Sometimes the situation is a traditional "intrusion" into the marriage. For instance, a husband who devotes romantic attention to a woman other than his wife
is engaged in a relationship that will harm rather than nurture his marriage. The same would hold true for a wife who has a romantic relationship with a man other than her husband. But sometimes the situation
is harder to define.

For instance, Jonathan spends many hours a week playing an online
fantasy game. For a while his wife, Stela, reassured herself that this computer game wasn't illicit—her husband wasn't visiting porno sites or others that she would find deeply offensive. But Jonathan still showed far
more interest in the orcs, elves, and warriors on-screen than he showed
toward his real, live wife. Jonathan's online fantasy world distracted him,
displaced his wife from the center of his attention, hurt Stela's feelings,
and stressed the couple's marriage.

Only you and your spouse can determine what activities nurture and
which are harmful to your relationship. You need to talk—and, more im-
portantly, you need to listen—to learn how each other feels. If you feel
that a pastime you pursue or a friendship you value is harmless but your
spouse has negative feelings about it, you need to take those feelings seriously. Exploring the situation is crucial. Find out what bothers your
spouse about what you're doing. What's at the root of your partner's
feelings? Is it the actions that you are taking (such as spending time with
a friend that your spouse finds threatening)? Or is the issue something in
your spouse's own experience (such as having been slighted or ignored

by his or her parents, previous partners, or someone else)? Getting to the crux of the matter is of paramount importance.

What if your partner's objections seem unreasonable? That's a frustrating situation, but it's all the more reason to delve deeper and find out what the problem is. Talk, talk, and talk some more.

Here's an example. Julio, a court stenographer, devotes his Saturdays to outings with a local bicycle club. After spending five days of every week cooped up in the local courthouse, he feels an intense need to be outdoors and get some strenuous exercise. But his wife, Anna, feels miffed that Julio doesn't stay home with her instead. Tensions over this issue have smoldered for months. During a big argument, Anna accused Julio of not being attentive to her, while Julio accused Anna of not understanding how desperately he needs to "let off some steam" after his long, boring workweek. Their discussion led to a new arrangement: Julio will spend Saturday mornings with his bike buddies; then the couple will have a regular Saturday-evening date and a quiet Sunday morning together.

❖ *Step 2:* PROTECT YOUR BOUNDARIES

I always tell couples that marriage makes the home into a temple. Your home becomes a sacred place, a place where you can nurture and protect what's most valuable in your life together—your love for each other, your closeness, your values and morals, your future. You have to be cautious of what you allow into your home. And when I say "be cautious," I don't mean just cautious about obvious threats, such as intruders. I also mean cautious about disturbing media (certain television programs, videos, or Web sites) and disruptive persons (manipulative or ill-intentioned "friends," inappropriate relationships). The new family unit you've established is subject to damage if you let harmful influences come into the place in which marital and parental growth occurs. Relatives, friends, neighbors, coworkers, and other people who help to nurture the union between you and your spouse—who nurture the love between you—are more than welcome in this sacred space. But the people who negatively influence your marriage—who limit or damage the love between you and your spouse—shouldn't be welcome.

Here's an example. Martin, age twenty-eight, recently married Jacqueline, who is twenty-seven. They love each other deeply and are both delighted with their marriage. But Jacqueline feels frustrated by frequent visits from Nick and Ernie, two of Martin's longtime buddies. These guys aren't bad people, but they show up too often, stay too long, and influence Martin in annoying ways. Usually what happens is that Nick and Ernie arrive unannounced, set a couple of six-packs down on the kitchen counter, pop open a few beers, raid the fridge, turn on the TV, and cheerfully disrupt whatever has been going on in the household. Jacqueline knows that Martin isn't too thrilled to have these guys settle in yet again, but he's reluctant to throw them out—after all, he's been friends with them since boyhood. And once Nick and Ernie start watching a ball game and yukking it up, Martin joins in. Jacqueline feels sidelined and ignored. Is there something immoral about her husband's hanging out with the guys? No. But Jacqueline is right to feel that these uninvited guests violate some sort of boundary within her marriage. Martin should be more forthright in protecting the couple's privacy. Getting together with Nick and Ernie now and then might not be a problem, but allowing them to invade the newlyweds' home and disrupt the couple's focus on each other could, if allowed to continue, do real damage to this marriage.

This is what boundaries are for: to protect the marriage from outside influences that may weaken, exhaust, or damage the couple's growth and intimacy. Establishing boundaries is all well and good. In addition, though, you have to protect them. You have to draw the line and say, "This space is ours," and then let only certain people into your private haven. By carefully choosing the people you allow to enter, you'll protect your boundaries and foster intimacy and respect within your relationship.

What are some ways in which you can protect your boundaries? Here are some suggestions:

- ∾ **Be fair.** Make sure that your boundaries apply to both of you. Double standards will backfire and lead to resentment.

- ∾ **Trust each other.** A spirit of mutual trust will lead to more, not less, respect between spouses.

- ∾ **Be alert.** At the same time, be aware when either of you inadvertently violates a boundary—most likely as the result of misjudgment, but still risking damage to your relationship.

- ∾ **Communicate, communicate!** Nothing replaces honest, direct communication about these issues.

In this chapter, we've discussed the primacy of respect and how good boundaries help a couple establish and maintain it. Some spouses are "naturals" in respecting each other—husbands and wives who have an easy, almost intuitive ability to honor each other. Others have to learn respect and practice it before they understand its importance. I believe that all couples encounter some respect problems sooner or later, whether as a result of misunderstandings, differences of temperament, day-to-day fatigue, external pressure, or other influences. So if you experience one or more of these problems in your relationship, how should you deal with it?

That's the subject we'll turn to next.

Chapter 5

How to Solve
Respect Problems

Respect isn't just an attitude, though your attitude is a crucial part of it. Respect is also a modus operandi—a way of operating. It's the acts you do and the words you say. It's also what you *don't* do and *don't* say. If you say exactly what's on your mind when you're exhausted or angry, it's easy to disrespect your spouse. If you submit to every impulse you feel, it's easy to ignore your spouse's need for respect. Impulsiveness can also lead to verbal abuse, which takes place when a spouse is so unhappy with himself or herself that the one spouse willfully humiliates and denigrates the other. At its most extreme, this kind of anger and emotional misery can lead to domestic violence. Domestic violence is, in fact, the ultimate violation of respect—someone physically hurting a mate because that person can't control his or her own impulses. Another extreme violation of respect happens when someone submits to a state of addiction—whether it's drugs, alcohol, or something else. That usually leads to losing balance, losing sight of priorities, losing a sense of your commitment to your spouse. So that, too, expresses a profound lack of respect.

So if respect involves not just *what you feel* but *what you do*, are there practices or habits that can help you solve problems with respect? The short answer: absolutely! There are, in fact, all kinds of techniques for solving respect problems. Let's look at some of those techniques and how they can help your relationship.

Task #1
Rebalance Respect When It's Out of Kilter

Sometimes both partners are at fault in allowing respect to deteriorate. But often there's an imbalance in the behavior—and one spouse may be more at fault than the other. For instance, one husband I know habitually treats his wife in a bossy, demeaning way, almost as if she's his personal maid rather than his life partner. He didn't used to act this way, but somehow his respect for his supportive, affectionate wife has diminished over the years to this deplorable state. Another example is Sally, who used to treat her husband respectfully but now nags him, constantly criticizes him, and publicly belittles him. Why? That's hard to determine. But both of these marriages are clearly in trouble because of imbalanced respect.

Regarding these and similar instances, I want to state outright that such behavior is inappropriate. Expressions of disrespect, contempt, and impatience all violate what your marriage is meant to be. A couple whose mutual respect has deteriorated should face the situation together and figure out what is happening. If you don't change this kind of behavior, you'll continue hurting your spouse, and you're going to damage your marriage. So you have to make a decision to change. That may involve outside help, such as counseling. You may need some kind of treatment program if alcohol abuse, drug abuse, or other addictions are part of the picture.

How can you recognize and deal with these types of disrespect? Let's take the two basic situations one at time—first, if you are the spouse who's being disrespected; second, if you are the spouse who is expressing disrespect.

IF YOU'RE ON THE RECEIVING END

Precisely because disrespect is often part of a pattern that develops over time, you may not even be acutely aware of what's happening. The first step to dealing with disrespect, then, is to recognize that it exists. Here are the most common forms of disrespect within a marriage:

- **Chronic irritability**—snappy, grouchy, or dismissive behavior

- **Stereotyping the other person,** especially by means of gender clichés—"You men are all alike!"; "Isn't that just like a woman!"

- **Condescending or demeaning behavior**—treating the other spouse like a child rather than as an adult peer

- **Hostile or domineering speech "strategies"**—manipulative use of words or the "silent treatment"

- **Verbal abuse**—cursing, threats, or accusations

- **Physical abuse of any sort**—hitting, "slapping around," or sexual domination (including marital rape, obviously, but also demanding any sex act from an unwilling or uninterested spouse)

If you experience any of these behaviors from your spouse, it's clear that respect is out of balance within your marriage. You should face the situation as soon as possible and, if necessary, receive outside help. Ignoring these sorts of disrespect won't make them go away; on the contrary, ignoring them will probably aggravate the problem in the long run. It's important, too, to acknowledge the disrespecting spouse's primary responsibility for what's happening. For instance, some women tend to believe that disrespectful treatment they receive within the marriage is partly or entirely their own fault ("If I weren't so demanding, he wouldn't shout at me so much"). But this self-blaming attitude is a mistake. Every spouse has a right to be treated with dignity, respect, and kindness. Although you and your spouse will have to sort out your problems together, nothing justifies any husband or wife demeaning, belittling, threatening, or abusing the other partner. My recommendation: accept the fact that there's a problem, get outside help if possible, and deal with your difficulties as soon and as thoroughly as possible.

WHAT IF YOU'RE ON THE "DELIVERING" END?

It's difficult to admit that your own behavior may be disrespectful toward your spouse. First, because disrespect is often habitual, thus part of your moment-by-moment, day-by-day behavior, which makes it "hard to see the forest for the trees." Second, because it's embarrassing and even psychologically threatening to realize that you're behaving in ways that are harmful toward another person. Third, because admitting to disrespect toward your spouse means that you'll have to change—and change is a challenge. How, then, can you deal with this issue if you're caught up in this problem?

The first step is to recognize what's happening. Read over the disrespectful behaviors I listed. Do you see your own attitudes or actions reflected in this list? If so, there's nothing to be gained—and much to lose—if you ignore the situation. On the contrary, you may do irreparable damage to your marriage and risk losing a precious relationship. It's far better to admit that you've somehow gone astray and resolve to face the problem and change your attitude and behavior.

The second thing to do is to take specific steps to rectify the situation. As soon as possible, speak openly with your spouse about what's happening. Listen with real empathy to what he or she feels about the interactions between you. Although you can't change patterns of behavior overnight, you can resolve to start. If necessary, seek help from a member of the clergy, a marital therapist, or a counselor to gain perspective and specific "tools" that will help you regain respect and learn better ways of communicating.

Task #2
Express Your Appreciation

A lot of spouses don't even notice each other. Oh, I know they see each other in a visual sense. But do they truly *see*? "See" in the appreciative sense? Often they don't.

I suggest that you look around. Open your eyes. Look closely at your reality. Who earns the income that supports you? Who looks after you when you're sick? Who cooks your meals? Who cleans the house? Who does the dishes and takes care of domestic business for you? Given what you see, have you been fully appreciative of your spouse? Or have you been a little bit careless—a little unappreciative? Open your eyes and see the goodness you have and all the love you've received.

Now, I'll admit that appreciating your spouse's worth doesn't lead to instant, automatic, total change. You don't simply wake up one morning and say, "Well, I really appreciate him [or her]." Appreciation is a task that you have to work on. You have to try to understand your spouse's contribution to the marriage and your family. But doing so is a choice you make. I urge you to make that choice!

How? In part by *expressing* your appreciation. Spouses in happy marriages often try to express appreciation in ways that will help the other person feel good. Sometimes these expressions involve very simple gestures. Sometimes it's simply a matter of offering a compliment. Sometimes it means giving an extra hug or kiss. Sometimes it means saying thank you for the other person's ordinary tasks—such as cooking a meal, running an errand, making a phone call, or doing a favor. It means not taking the other person for granted.

A major task is to focus on what the other person needs in order to feel appreciated. Maybe you appreciate your spouse in your own mind, but you don't express your appreciation outright. You're just not "getting the words out." What should you do then? In some way or other you need to learn ways of saying supportive, encouraging words. I see a lot of couples who, by struggling with this issue, have learned the basic skills of tuning in to the other person's emotional needs.

Task #3
Counteract Emotional and Spiritual "Dryness"

Sometimes people become unappreciative when they "dry out" emotionally and spiritually. They go through a period of drought, of emptiness, and they forget to smell the roses and see the good things in their life. The resulting state of emotional or spiritual dryness can create feelings of depression, despair, or lack of vitality, which in turn can prompt some people to withdraw from activities and other people. If this emotional dryness is affecting you, how can you counteract it? How can you counteract how this state of mind affects your relationship?

Most of the time, what has happened is that you feel bad internally because what you feel should have occurred externally has *not* occurred. Perhaps your work has been frustrating. Perhaps you have conflicts within your family of origin. Perhaps you have health problems. Perhaps your marriage itself doesn't feel sustaining. You may feel that you haven't been complimented for a long time. You may be wondering if you're a good person, or you may feel that your spouse doesn't appreciate you. It may be just a basic communication problem. The problem may even be more serious than what I'm listing here.

Here's what I suggest about emotional and spiritual dryness: you have to find sustenance. Just as physical thirst means that you need water, thirst of these other sorts mean that you need something to replenish you. Perhaps that means finding sustenance from your relationship through more time together or less stressful time together (such as by setting aside time for relaxation, recreation, or other restful exercises together). Perhaps it means seeking counsel from a

trusted, wise person of the sort I mentioned in Chapter 2—a counselor, therapist, priest, minister, rabbi, friend, relative, or coworker. In
any case, I urge you to find insightful help and not try to proceed
through life in a depleted state. Doing so will harm you—and it'll
harm your relationship, as well.

You can counteract the problem of emotional and spiritual dryness in
other ways. Feeling depleted is a risk that everyone runs sooner or later.
Don't just ignore the problem—find some sort of remedy for what ails
you. How? Here's just a short list of responses to this issue that may help
you find solace and replenish yourself:

- **Keep a journal to explore your thoughts and feelings.** A journal
  or diary can provide a good way to release emotions and vent tensions. It's cheap, safe, and harmless to yourself and other people.
  Don't censor anything, especially events and feelings that make
  you feel uncomfortable. Just "pour out your soul" on paper.

- **Listen to music, sing, or play your favorite instrument.** For thousands of years, human beings have vented their emotions—
  delight, fear, longing, and grief—through music. No matter what
  sort of music you enjoy, it can be a source of great comfort and
  release.

- **Practice some other art.** Art can be a wonderful way of expressing
  your emotions. You don't have to emulate Rembrandt or Picasso
  to experience something worthwhile. Let out what you're feeling.

- **Read.** Poetry, novels, biographies, and devotional literature can
  offer insight, inspiration, amusement, and delight, all of which
  can nurture the mind and soul.

- **Seek comfort in spirituality.** Prayer, meditation, or the liturgical
  rituals of your religion can become a wellspring that eases your
  thirst.

∾ **Give yourself some TLC.** Emotional or sensory treats can recharge your battery. Go see a movie. Take a long bath instead of a quick shower. Find other ways to indulge yourself in easy, safe, affordable ways.

∾ **Get some exercise.** If you feel depleted, physical exercise often energizes you rather than drain you further. Play a sport you enjoy. Go for a run or a swim. Take a walk. Almost any kind of enjoyable exercise can help to recharge your battery.

∾ **Find solace in nature.** Go outside! Many people find consolation in the natural world—in the presence of wildlife, the wind in the trees, the play of light and shadow, the clouds overhead, the shift of the seasons.

Task #4
Deal with Conflicts in Your Relationship

I wish I could tell you that spouses always try hard to respect each other. I wish I could say that couples keep the necessary boundaries in place, and that these boundaries make their relationships successful and meaningful. Unfortunately, that's not always the case. A lot of husbands and wives *don't* try hard enough, and a lot of problems arise because couples ignore the necessary boundaries or fail to maintain them. The result? Well, when your priorities are fuzzy and you neglect the most important aspects of your life, you'll eventually find yourselves in conflict.

There are different kinds of conflict, of course. There are external pressures that can intrude on your relationship, and there are also internal pressures, attitudes, and behaviors that, if left unchecked, can damage your marriage.

Let's begin with external pressures: problems with in-laws; with inappropriate friendships; with finances; with temporary changes such as a new job or a move to a new city. These events are relatively temporary—events that will diminish or end (even if you sometimes feel like they never will). We can learn how to work with problems like that. These are the minor battles, not the major wars. Usually we have to focus on short-term solutions, such as adjusting to a job or coping with an in-law. Doing so eases the pressure and diminishes the marital conflict. In addition, it helps if you and your spouse can remember that you're not fighting each other; you're both trying to solve the same problem. If you can work together as a united front (for instance, by helping each other adjust to the move to a new city or the start of a new job), you'll accelerate the process of overcoming the issue you face.

By comparison, internal pressures can become major wars. Examples include changes of attitude that prompt a spouse to say, "I don't love you anymore," "I don't feel the same way toward you," "I'm not sure we should be together anymore," or "I've fallen in love with someone else." In many instances, statements like these—which reflect major changes of a spouse's affection—are the result of the spouses growing apart over time (such as when they gradually lose a sense of common ground) or when there's a more sudden split between them (such as when one of them is caught having an adulterous affair). The most severe internal pressures, in my observation, result from infidelity. However, even problems that seem less significant than adultery can lead to harmful internal pressures over a period of time. An example of this situation is the husband who leaves dirty clothes scattered all over the house, or who refuses to do his share of the housework. Is this sort of thoughtlessness as bad as sexual infidelity? Of course not. Under some circumstances, though, it can do severe damage to a marriage. It's not these behaviors themselves that are the core issue. Rather, it's the wife's interpretation of these behaviors that creates damaging internal pressures. Dirty clothes on the floor may represent to her her husband's disrespect for her daily efforts to keep the house clean. Refusing to do a share of the housework may symbolize selfishness and lack of consideration. The result: powerful negative forces that can lead to marital "war." And a couple can't move on until they address the issues that are leading the partners toward conflict. You have to take care of them; you have to work through a complex process to understand what's happening in your life—what feelings are real and which are illusory.

To cope with conflicts in a relationship, the first thing you need to do is accept two realities: first, the reality that conflicts *will* arise, and second, the reality that there *are* ways to solve them. Some of these ways to solve conflicts involve working on basic skills—communication, patience, and compassion. But in any case, working through these conflicts means going through a process.

For relatively small problems, you and your spouse can go through the process of conflict resolution on your own. You can discuss your differences, find areas of agreement and disagreement, and figure out how to compromise. Later discussions in this chapter will offer some tools for negotiation within your relationship.

However, you can't really solve big marital conflicts without the help of counseling. Why? Because couples don't have an unbiased perspective about the situation while right in the middle of it. Also, few couples today have the skills to really resolve a big crisis without assistance from a trained third party who can help you work through the issues and resolve your conflicts. Marital counseling is effective partly because it provides well-tested strategies and "tools" to help a couple heal their wounds.

I realize that many couples resist the notion of counseling. Men, especially, are often reluctant to accept the need for professional help. About ninety-five percent of women are more open to counseling than men are. A lot of men say, "I don't want a priest, psychologist, or therapist telling me what to do," or "What does a therapist know about my problems?" Well, I can understand where this attitude comes from: male pride. It's an unwillingness to accept a course of action that many men interpret as weakness. Most men feel they've already got a handle on the situation:

"People say they're going to help me, but they don't have anything to tell me that I don't already know."

This is an unfortunate attitude. It's the psychological and marital equivalent of refusing to ask for directions! Unfortunately, it's really widespread. The truth is, all of us can benefit from others' insight, inspiration, and objective perceptions. We all need support at some moment of our lives. Let me offer this comparison: If you had cardiac disease, would you say, "Okay, I've got a bad heart, but I'm not going to see a cardiologist—I'm going to deal with this problem myself!"? Of course not. You'd go to an expert. You'd find out what type of heart problem you've got. You'd accept the need for an expert diagnosis and proper medical treatment. You can't tackle a heart problem on your own. The truth is that marriages can develop heart trouble, too—disorders that can be harmful, even deadly, if allowed to persist unchecked. You may feel tempted to ignore the symptoms, but pretending there's no problem will let something eat away at your relationship—and even kill your marriage.

Task #5
Learn to Negotiate

Another skill I consider crucial in dealing with conflict resolution is negotiation.

When we think of negotiations, we often think of what takes place in the business sector. But negotiation is really an essential part of all human relationships. We're all different, right? We all have different perceptions of reality. We have available a huge variety of approaches to solve the dilemmas that come our way on a day-by-day basis. As a result, negotiation is one of the most important skills that you can learn and practice in your relationships, including—and especially—in your relationship as a couple.

Learning to negotiate is also a good way to practice the give-and-take of communication: I listen to you and try to figure out your needs, and you listen to me and try to understand my needs. This is very important in all relationships, but especially if you feel you're in a conflict. There's no reason why one person has to lose and the other has to win. Relationships aren't a competitive sport! If you can learn the value of negotiation, it's much easier for you to create a win-win situation.

My pastoral role, as well as my work on my television and radio shows, often includes helping couples with issues of negotiation. Here's a scenario I often see: A couple comes to me for help. They've been married for two, five, ten years—whatever. They're good people, very caring, but they find that a lot of little differences are cropping up. So one of the questions these couples often ask me is whether their problems are individual conflicts that they can solve one by one; or do their problems reflect a bigger, more serious drift away from each other—a more global change in their attitudes? The husband brings out his list of issues, and the wife brings out hers. The spouses obviously have different perspectives. He thinks some of her complaints aren't such a big deal, and she thinks that his complaints aren't so serious. But in any case, something is causing conflicts between them.

In a situation like this, here's what I ask the couple:

- Are you willing to change?

- Or are you completely set in your ways?

- Are you willing to change the behaviors that really frustrate your spouse?

- Are you willing to make things work?

- Are you willing to do everything you can that's humanly possible to make your marriage what it should be—a life-giving, loving relationship where happiness is not unattainable, but is a state you can actually live in?

Sometimes the spouses answer in a way that suggests a complete impasse between them, but often the questions help them find common ground and solve their differences. If you're facing similar conflicts, I urge you to ask yourselves these same questions and use the answers to rebuild your bridges.

When a couple comes to me for help, I say, "Okay, how do you deal with this problem and how it affects your relationship? You tell me you love each other, right? You want to be together. Well, if you love each other and want to be together, you have to reach an agreement to put aside a lot of what's bothering you. You have to negotiate. You have to agree that you're going to let some things into your life, but you're going to exclude other things. You have to learn to agree on that and support each other on this issue."

Tricky? Of course. A strenuous process? Almost always. To reach a win-win outcome, both spouses have to give up something. Or else they both have to commit themselves to develop new skills (such as open communication) and perfect these skills together. Whatever else, both have to agree that if they want their marriage to survive and flourish, they have to work on the issues together. If they love each other, they can't allow anyone or anything else to destroy what they have together. And that's where negotiation comes in.

I need to repeat what I said before: negotiation is not about one side winning! Negotiation is about understanding that you both win when you work together. Unfortunately, our culture tends to see many compromises and negotiations as win-lose situations. Now, it's true that there's never any negotiation without sacrifice. Someone always has to give up something in a negotiation. But in the long run, you're investing in a happier future. You're putting aside something that you may think is very important in order to build up this fundamental relationship in your life. The ability to negotiate is what helps you build a stronger marriage in the long term.

Task #6
Grasp the Consequences of Not Negotiating

One of the struggles I see is that many couples become accustomed to unhappy marriages. They just accept their unhappiness as a given—an inevitable state of being. And people tend to say, "Well, my marriage isn't what it should be, but that's how it goes." But that complacency opens the door to all kinds of damaging situations. If you're unhappy in your marriage, you open the door to seeking happiness elsewhere, to looking for closeness in relationships that aren't as promising as marriage, such as interacting with people on the Internet, and even infidelity. You try to fill the void that's inside.

Are you ready and willing to do what's necessary to change the marriage? Is your spouse ready and willing? If the answer is no for either or both of you, it almost doesn't matter how big or small your problems are. If you're not willing to change and accept your differences, if you're not willing to compromise and negotiate, it's unlikely that you'll reach any consensus as a couple.

To be honest, I'd say that many couples will seek excuses in order to get out of their marriages. They're more interested in ducking their problems than in solving them. If you put more energy into the crisis that you do into the solution, you're always going to have a problem. And lots of couples put more energy into screaming and fighting about the crisis than into trying to resolve it together. Many couples also put too much energy into finger-pointing: "He's the problem—it's not me!" Or, "She's got the problem—it's not me!" But here's the truth: when you're married, everything that happens between you becomes a problem for *both* of you. It's joint property. You can't just dump the blame on your spouse and wash your hands of the whole situation.

My strong recommendation: grasp the abundant, negative consequences of not negotiating. Yes, negotiation is hard. But so is suffering through an unhappy marriage—or watching your marriage collapse.

Task #7
Prevent or Deal with Abuse

If a marriage includes physical abuse, then respect has dropped so far that it hasn't just diminished—it has completely disappeared. This is a dire situation. First of all, no spouse should be subject to violence. Second, physical abuse is symptomatic of deep emotional troubles within the marriage. In a situation like this, what should be done? Is the marriage beyond remedy?

Christina and Rob, for example, have struggled hard with these questions. On one level, you could say that they love each other. They enjoy doing many activities together; they have a passionate love life; and they're both devoted parents. But for reasons that neither of them can understand, Rob's frustrations with certain aspects of life sometimes erupt into wild, chaotic anger. He throws what Christina calls "tantrums," and at times he even lashes out at her—screaming at her, calling her names, threatening to strike her, and even hitting her. Christina feels terrified of her husband when he gets into these disturbed states. Rob seems transformed into a totally different person, a man who's capable of anything. Then Rob's "tantrum" ends and he seems to snap out of an altered state of mind. He realizes what he's done and he breaks down, begging her forgiveness. He promises never to hurt her again. Yet sooner or later, another tantrum hits and the scenario repeats itself. Both spouses are confused and frightened about this situation.

As this couple's dilemma suggests, the effort to deal with marital abuse is very difficult and intense. It's not a quest you want to undertake alone. If you're in this situation—and if both spouses are willing to work through their problems—you need to seek help from a good marital therapist. You need to work through the process that will identify what has gone wrong in your marriage and how to address the issues. How did you reach this impasse? What happened to create an atmosphere in which one or both spouses express themselves through physical violence? What can you do to return to a more respectful way of interacting? Answering these and other questions may involve a series of counseling sessions before you can figure out what your next steps should be.

Some couples are resistant to this process. When I raise the possibility of counseling, most people see a flag go up, a red flag that says *Divorce*. Spouses begin to imagine what life would be like if they took this step, and what they imagine causes a lot of anxiety. That's understandable but unfortunate. Wouldn't it make more sense to imagine what life would be like if they began to *fix* some of these problems? That's easier and less traumatic than divorce. In fact, many marital problems can be repaired. It's true that some kinds of damage to a marriage can be permanent. In most situations, though, there's enough goodwill and love to carry you through to a more positive solution. There are enough good feelings in both partners' hearts that they want to stay together. These positive emotions and intentions will allow a counseling or therapeutic process that will enable the partners to acquire the tools and skills they need to fix the problems in the relationship.

Sometimes drastic situations require drastic solutions. Sometimes the abusive partner needs a kind of marital "shock treatment." I don't mean real electrical jolts, of course. Rather, I mean a temporary separation, a threat of divorce, an ultimatum to change behavior, or just a simple statement, such as one partner saying, "We can't live together until you change what you're doing." Then the choice is up to the other spouse.

If you face this sort of extreme situation, don't expect an immediate fix; however, these measures can serve as a wake-up call, leading the abusive partner to realize the need for change and to take action. Unfortunately, there are times when these methods won't work at all. You may need to not only *threaten* a separation but go ahead and actually separate. Don't remain in a relationship where your health, safety, and life itself may be at risk! It's hard to predict what will happen in a marriage where physical abuse is present. Sometimes the abusive partner will face his or her other problem, get help, and change. But if disrespect and abuse con-tinue—and if the abusive partner shows no desire to fix the problems—it's time for the couple to question the viability of their marriage. If the abusive partner claims a desire to change but doesn't follow through, I suggest that the other spouse disengage until there's a clear indication of improvement. Don't wait around in hopes of change if waiting endangers you and your children.

Task #8
Practice Forgiveness

Without forgiveness, it's impossible to have a good relationship. And I believe that we learn to forgive simply by *practicing* forgiveness. And you'll have to learn how to do it eventually. If you're going to live in a successful relationship, there's no other way.

Unfortunately, a lot of people resist forgiving others. This resistance isn't necessarily a result of being harsh or cold; rather, I sense that peo-ple can't forgive others because they haven't really experienced forgive-ness themselves. Perhaps their parents criticized them whenever they made mistakes—or, worse yet, punished them, mocked them, or sub-jected them to the silent treatment. Sadly, what I'm describing is a common scenario in many families. Other families foster an atmosphere in which kids grow up believing that conflict isn't a setting for finding solutions or forgiving others, but rather an arena in which winning is everything—and where there's always a clear winner and a clear loser. Under these circumstances, concepts like forgiveness, common ground, and negotiation are totally alien. Rather, the ruling attitude is one in which power determines all outcomes and forgiveness is tantamount to weakness. And it's impossible to understand forgiveness as a virtue if you can't disassociate forgiveness from winning or losing a battle or a competition.

If you weren't given a good amount of forgiveness as a child or as an adolescent, you'll have to work harder in practicing forgiveness as an adult. Here's the truth: forgiveness isn't about competition. Forgiveness isn't even about being right or wrong. Forgiveness is about being able to say, "I forgive you because the love I feel for you is greater than anything else." This is why I really find that forgiveness is much more than a merely human quality. As the poet Alexander Pope said, "To err is human; to forgive, Divine." If you can understand from a spiritual perspective that God is all-merciful and all-forgiving, and if you're able to experience God's redemption and forgiveness in your life, you'll probably be able to see how this applies to your life in marriage, and you'll be willing to forgive as a way of moving on with life. Forgiving your spouse is a way of learning to live together effectively.

So if you're struggling with issues of forgiveness, what can you do? Should you just force the words and say, "I forgive you" in hopes of setting up a new pattern? How can you get started on this process? Here are some steps I recommend:

❖ *Step 1:* FACE THE SITUATION

In the kinds of situations I'm describing, you and your spouse are in pain because of what has happened. But if you can't offer forgiveness, you'll stay in pain—and the pain may even intensify. So the first step of solving the problem is to recognize that you're in a bind and to admit that doing nothing will only make it worse.

❖ *Step 2:* ACCEPT THE NEED TO LET GO

It's hard to forget about traumatic events within a marriage and pretend that nothing has happened. But forgetting isn't what I'm advocating. Rather, I'm recommending that you *let go and move forward* rather than constantly *hanging on and looking backward*. Move on.

✤ *Step 3:* TAKE A LEAP OF FAITH

At least one partner must gamble and decide to forgive. Will this leap of faith solve all your problems? Of course not, but it may open a door that has been closed up until now. I've seen many relationships where one partner's ability to forgive allowed the relationship to flourish and continue to grow. To take an extreme example: I've counseled couples in which infidelity has occurred, and the husband—the spouse who was unfaithful—is amazed by his wife's ability to forgive him, move on, and start rebuilding the marriage. The wife, reassured by her husband's efforts to start over in response to her forgiveness, in turn gets to work on the marriage. Each of them inspires the other to try harder. For this reason, I believe that forgiveness can have a great impact on both parties.

Of course it's best if both partners have acquired this ability to forgive and move on. Otherwise, when a transgression occurs, the relationship can't continue to grow. But if you can each accept your spouse's fallibility, your forgiveness will help to heal the woundedness you feel.

✤ *Step 4:* MAKE AN EFFORT TO EXPRESS FORGIVENESS

It's not enough to feel forgiveness in your heart. It's not even enough to say, "I forgive you." You have to be able to project that you really mean your forgiveness and that you're going to move on emotionally. If you keep bringing up the transgression, you haven't really forgiven. You haven't really let go of it. Any act of forgiveness, mercy, or kindness that you give authentically teaches a great lesson, and it affects the other person greatly.

✤ *Step 5:* PUT YOUR NEW KNOWLEDGE OF FORGIVENESS TO WORK

Some hurtful events will take place in any marriage. Sooner or later, every spouse will speak some hurtful words. But does the inevitability of some hurtful actions and words mean that you should hold them all against your spouse? Should you give them all the same "weight"? Does a spouse's irritable comment following a hard workday matter as much as his or her committing infidelity? Of course not. We'd all agree that there are different transgressions, some more serious than others. It's appropriate to gauge them according to their real impact on the marriage. It's also appropriate to forgive these transgressions—to practice forgiveness and see its day-to-day benefits.

Task #9
Learn to Say the Magic Words: "I'm Sorry"

There's a specific issue located inside the bigger issue of forgiveness that I want to raise in its own right. This is the crucial act of learning to say "I'm sorry."

Why do we find it so difficult to apologize? Saying *I'm sorry* is something we cannot take for granted. We have to learn to say it often, especially when those words truly come from the heart. If you've violated your partner's respect, a sincere apology can be the best, most healing remedy. And if you can grasp the wisdom in this act, you'll begin to observe the great power of forgiveness.

Unfortunately, a lot of people *don't* grasp the impact of a heartfelt apology—or at least they tend to struggle accepting it. "Talk is cheap," some people say. But that's not always true. Sometimes an open-hearted apology is the most valuable gift you can bestow, especially if it's a gift for someone you've hurt.

Admitting that you've done wrong is a necessary condition for asking forgiveness and choosing to improve your life. But it's just the beginning. It's not enough to say "I'm sorry" to the police officer who stops you for running a red light. The fact is you broke the law, and now there are consequences. When you break the law within your relationship, there are consequences there, as well, and you have to face up to them before you can receive forgiveness and move on.

Whenever there's love in a relationship and a desire to make things better, many spouses will accept a request for forgiveness and look to the future rather than the past. For this reason, saying *I'm sorry* and truly living with those words in our hearts and minds can help us be more conscious of how our actions can foster healing in the painful situations we experience. But here's the catch: real apologies must always be accompanied by a desire to change bad habits and replenish the respect both of you need. You must renew yourself—and your relationship must renew itself—in order to survive, grow, and thrive.

Solving respect problems is easier if you and your spouse can master the tasks I've outlined in this chapter. You'll acquire a better "tool kit" of perceptions, insights, and skills to help you deal with many issues that arise during married life.

However, I need to double back on what we discussed at the start of Path Two. Respect may be partly a matter of skills, but it's first and foremost a matter of compassion. Even if you acquire all the skills we've been discussing—appreciation, negotiation, conflict resolution, forgiveness, whatever—you can't really respect your spouse without compassion (the ability to "feel with") in your heart. Who is the person you share your life with? Who is the person who's across from you at the dinner table? Who's the person on the other side of your marriage bed? You may say, "That's my husband," or "That's my wife"—but can you *really feel* what that person feels as he or she lives and breathes and goes about the hundreds of activities that make up your life? Sadly, many husbands have no idea what their wives are thinking and feeling, and many wives have no idea what their husbands are thinking and feeling. And, saddest of all, many spouses really don't even try.

This is why Path Two is so important. If you can simply respect each other—and if you simply can strive for the compassion that energizes respect—then you're already on your way to real life and real love.

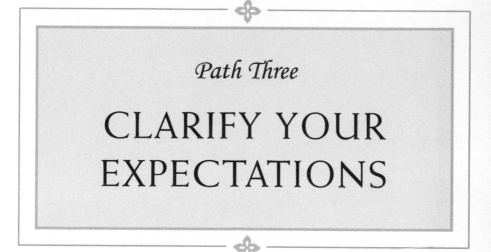

Path Three

CLARIFY YOUR EXPECTATIONS

A dear friend of mine didn't like roller coasters. One day, his fiancée and I decided to take him on one anyway. I told him that as part of his marriage preparation, he should ride the roller coaster several times, since there are many similarities between this experience and our daily lives. He didn't understand what I was getting at until after the ride. Then he got the picture. The roller coaster went up and down, took twists and turns, slowed down and sped up, went into a dark tunnel and then came back out into the light.

Sound familiar? Relationships, too, go up and down, take twists and turns, slow down and sped up, and include times of darkness and times of light. No matter how stable or happy, relationships will include all sorts of roller coaster–like motions. At some points we'll be sad, at other times joyful and uplifted. Troubles will come, and they'll twist and turn our lives and even take us to places where we never expected to end up. We may be busy, with our life going full speed ahead—and then suddenly our relationships will hit a bumpy patch, such as an illness or loss of a job. There will be times of gloom, but we'll emerge again into the light. If you make a commitment to friendship, marriage, or any other strong relationship, you're certain to get a roller coaster ride. Life is just like that.

What does this have to do with expectations? Simply this: if you expect married life to be easy and smooth, you'll be disappointed, frustrated, or both. If you can accept that marriage will be a roller coaster ride, however, you'll deal more easily with all the changes that your commitment will bring. Your expectations should be realistic enough to take into account the unpredictability of married life.

For all these reasons, Path Three to good relationships is, first, to learn to deal with expectations; and second, to undertake a sequence of tasks to clarify them.

Chapter 6

Learning to Deal with Expectations

The path of clarifying expectations sounds simple, even simplistic, but it's surprisingly difficult, and it's a process that many couples neglect or purposely ignore. I frequently see evidence of this situation in my pastoral work. Many (perhaps most) marriages begin without the spouses having a clear idea—either separately or together—of what they expect from each other or from married life. Even long-married spouses may not have discussed their expectations. Although I can't provide any hard data, I'm convinced that most couples base their relationships on vague, often starry-eyed notions of marriage rather than on a clear sense of what their shared life will be like.

What's the result of this romantic, keep-your-fingers-crossed approach? Well, it's no secret that over 50 percent of marriages in this country end in divorce. There are many reasons for this sad outcome, but one reason is a "disconnect" between what people expect from marriage and what the reality of married life presents. Spouses often expect married life to be easy, smooth, and consistently (or constantly) fun; they can't accept a roller coaster ride that's far more unpredictable.

Let's look at the nature of expectations, then consider how a couple can clarify them as they work to strengthen their relationship.

WHAT INFLUENCES OUR EXPECTATIONS?

Each person brings a great variety of expectations to his or her marriage. These expectations concern issues such as husband/wife roles, work roles, marital communication, family finances, sex, and parenting tasks, among others. Where do these expectations come from? To some extent they have familial and cultural origins. Each of us has grown up in a family that influences what we expect to happen in a marriage—who will earn the income, how to raise children, how the spouses should behave toward each other, and so forth. In addition, the local community (neighborhood, town, or city) and the wider community (society as a whole) also influence what we expect in marriage. The media, too—movies, TV programs, books, magazines, popular music—powerfully affect what we believe will happen throughout the course of a marriage.

In general, these expectations tend to be highly idealistic. Think of all the magical imagery people use, for instance, when describing weddings and newlyweds: "They're the perfect couple," "He's her knight in shining armor," "She looks like a fairy-tale princess," "They're a match made in Heaven." Idealism is wonderful in some respects, but marriage requires a healthy dose of realism, too. We touched on this issue in Path One—how the images of perfection influence (and probably distort) our ability to deal with the complexities of day-to-day life. If you enter into marriage seeking and expecting perfection, you can't help but end up disappointed. We're all imperfect human beings. You're imperfect; so is your spouse. Once your courtship, engagement, and wedding are over, you'll have to accept the often wonderful but always complex tasks of living with another imperfect person.

REALISTIC VS. UNREALISTIC EXPECTATIONS

Whatever else you do, you need to distinguish between realistic and unrealistic expectations. Doing so involves making two distinct efforts.

One is to learn what marriage really involves. Given the amount of wishful thinking and misinformation that TV shows, movies, and other media disperse about married life in our culture, gaining a more accurate impression about marriage can be difficult. If you're not married yet, I strongly recommend that you and your partner attend some sort of premarital counseling through your church or temple or other facility. Counseling or workshops of this sort can help you better understand the nature of the commitment you're about to make and what day-to-day married life will be like. In addition, premarital counseling can provide you with a "tool kit" (such as communication skills, conflict resolution skills, and so forth) that you can apply to real-life situations after your wedding. What if you're already married? Well, even couples who have been married for many years can benefit from "marriage encounters," which are workshops in which trained facilitators help couples to learn new communication skills and to deepen their understanding of the marriage commitment.

The other effort is our main agenda in Path Three: to clarify expectations. Individual men and women are so different that there's an enormous range in what people need and want from married life. If you don't know what you expect from marriage, and if you don't know what your spouse wants, how can you possibly find the common ground between you? You won't even know where you're coming from, much less where you're going! So by some means or other, you have to define the issues that are important to you, understand what's important to the other person, and then find out where there's room to compromise. Much of Path Three concerns this process. All of the issues we'll discuss can apply both to couples who are just embarking on marriage as well as to those who have been married for a long time.

UNDERSTAND YOUR EXPECTATIONS

The more realistic you are in facing the issues in your marriage—including the issue of expectations—the better off you'll be. To undertake this process, you need to identify your expectations and compare them with your spouse's. You need to do a "reality check" to see if these expectations are in sync with the real world.

One of your most critical tasks as you start a relationship is to make sure that you both understand your own expectations. This is certainly true for couples heading toward marriage, since the partners will presumably base their shared life on an agreement of what they feel is most important. It's also true for spouses who want to nurture their marriage as it changes and develops over the years. In both situations, the partners need to know *what they expect from each other and from the relationship.* What do you expect from your partner? What are your emotional needs? What are your physical, financial, and domestic needs? As you answer these questions, you should do more than just make a list; you should also consider *why* you find certain needs important. Do you need a good-looking spouse on your arm in order to feel good about yourself? Well, maybe so. But don't just stop there. Why is this need important to you? Is it possible that you're focusing on a value that really isn't so significant after all? My hope is that exploring these issues will lead to some introspection about yourself as well as about the other person.

Part of what I'm saying is that it's all right to be open about your expectations in a relationship. Does this mean that you can have *anything* you want in your marriage? No—life doesn't work that way. But you need to identify your needs and expectations from the very start of your relationship and "compare notes" with each other as time passes and your expectations and needs evolve and change. If you don't openly express what you need from your partner, it's going to be more difficult for both of you to perceive each other clearly. You can only fulfill real expectations when you're open and honest about your needs.

UNDERSTAND YOUR EXPECTATIONS FOR A MATE

Clear-eyed acceptance of your spouse isn't possible unless you begin to understand what qualities you saw in this person when you first fell in love or considered this person as the right mate. If you're like most people, you have a tendency to accept others at face value. Then, as you begin to dig deeper, you start to find imperfections or incompatibilities that may prompt you to say, "Oh, this could be a real problem. Maybe this person isn't right for me." But in fact there are many issues for which you'll never be 100 percent in agreement with any other person. If so, what do you do? We just have to learn to live with differences of character, differences of taste, preferences, ways of doing things, and personal idiosyncrasies. After all, we come from different places, different backgrounds. For this reason, acceptance is about understanding between two very different people who have come together—two people who don't necessarily see eye to eye.

The task is to understand that two different people *have* come together, but you don't lose your individuality when you go into a relationship. You continue being your own person. You have your own good features and flaws, your own virtues and vices, your own strengths and weaknesses. The other person has his or her own strengths and weaknesses, too. Some people find this situation relatively easy to accept—they have no problem with it. Others will always have more difficulty.

If you enter a relationship with a narrow understanding of what the other person can provide for you in the long term, you'll be frustrated. Why? Because you'll discover over time that you require a lot more than you thought you did. And that's why some people's marriages become frustrating or dry. You never took the time before the wedding to communicate openly your needs, your desires, your dreams, your ambitions. Couples grow apart because their needs aren't met. What they end up doing is finding either someone else or something else to fill the void, and this usually leads to the partners growing apart. One partner heads off in one direction with one dream about life, while the other heads off in a different direction with a different dream about life. They forget to dream together! Why? Because they never communicated their needs properly.

I can't tell you how many times I've heard someone say, "You know, things are so-so, but I know that with time it's all going to get better." Well, I don't know that with time it *will* get better. The situation certainly won't get better if you don't do anything to make it better. How can you fix a problem if you don't know what it is? The core task you face here is to define your expectations, share your insights with each other, and clarify what you want from your spouse. Discuss the situation. Share your hopes, fears, concerns, preferences, and aspirations. If you have doubts, express them, deal with them, and work through them. Otherwise you'll be prone to what may be merely wishful thinking.

THE IMPORTANCE OF AUTONOMY

I need to emphasize another important aspect of this situation. When I say that you need to clarify your needs, I don't mean that every need you identify is valid. For example, let's say that you need your spouse to ease your loneliness. Well, the easing of loneliness is certainly a potential benefit of marriage. But if you expect your spouse to ease *all* of your loneliness *whenever* you're lonely, your expectation isn't realistic. Loneliness is part of the human condition. Easing all of your loneliness isn't a burden that your spouse can carry single-handedly. You need to find multiple ways to address this issue: certainly by nurturing a good marriage, but also by establishing strong friendships, maintaining cordial relations with your family, and finding solace in God.

Similarly, it's not reasonable to expect that your spouse will fulfill certain other needs that are your own responsibility. Your spouse can't take responsibility for your self-esteem, your self-acceptance, your overall sense of purpose in life. Your spouse can help you deal with these issues, but he or she can't undertake the whole task on your account; rather, they are needs that depend on your own autonomy, strength of character, and psychological or spiritual development.

SHARE YOUR EXPECTATIONS AND GROW TOGETHER

Many people have a tendency to suffer silently in their relationships because they can't adequately communicate what they feel, need, and desire. My suggestion: communicate openly and with total honesty to get your message across. Express your expectations—but be realistic about them.

As a rule, most good relationships take time to develop and grow before they can begin to flourish. There is a necessary period of discovery—of getting to know each other, of finding common ground—a stage that cannot be ignored. This early phase is where you begin to understand the type of nurturing you need throughout your married life. Clarifying this issue of expectations is the type of task that you and your partner should clearly undertake before you tie the knot. Get to know each other fully.

The situation is a little different for couples before marriage compared to the situation for couples who are already married.

FOR COUPLES BEFORE MARRIAGE

Don't marry someone who doesn't possess the sorts of qualities you want in a lifetime companion. It may sound simple, but choosing the right mate is more than half the battle. If you need someone to affirm you and constantly express affection, don't marry the distant, introverted, unexpressive type. If your boyfriend doesn't send you flowers before the wedding, it's unlikely that he'll do so after you get married. If he doesn't pay much attention to details during your courtship, he'll be much less attentive to these things after the wedding. I guarantee it! Don't delude yourself. Give yourself enough time to let your expectations clarify. Rushing into marriage won't solve your disagreements.

Are you realistic about the people you admire and love? Maybe so—but most people aren't. In fact, we often admire or even idolize certain people in ways that can set us up for disappointment. It's easy to expect more from others than they can truly give. Being too idealistic or starry-eyed can be risky. Part of having realistic expectations about relationships is being able to accept this truth. The more you can connect with this reality; the better off you'll be in the long run. Part of living in relationships is accepting differences and challenges as they come, day to day.

FOR COUPLES WHO ARE ALREADY MARRIED

Sharing and clarifying your expectations isn't just a premarital task; it's a task that you should undertake on an ongoing basis. Why? First of all, because you'll understand your own and your spouse's needs better and better as your relationship deepens. Second, because your needs actually change over time. You'll need to discuss a whole range of issues as you face different stages of marriage over the years.

Marilu and Ted, for instance, had achieved a pretty good sense of each other's needs during their first five years of married life. Then Marilu became pregnant. Both spouses were delighted by this development, but they were confronted by a whole new phase in their relationship: parenthood. They hadn't talked much about the enormous changes they'd face on becoming parents or how they'd cope with them. Would Marilu quit her job or just take some time off after she gave birth? Would Ted try to arrange for paternity leave so he could help out? How much involvement would Ted have in day-to-day childcare tasks over the long term? Would the couple hire a childcare provider at some point, or would they look after their child throughout his development? These and many other questions came up and prompted discussions of the spouses' expectations as Marilu's due date loomed.

Parenthood is only the most dramatic of many developments that should prompt a couple to discuss their needs and expectations over the years. Issues concerning work, leisure, sex, communication, health, and retirement are just a few of the others that most couples will need to explore and talk about as their marriage develops and changes. You can't just have a few conversations, then figure that your needs and expectations will stay stable for the rest of your years together. Just as marriage itself involves constant change, so, too, do your needs and expectations.

The foundation of this process is always good communication. You can't expect your spouse to be a mindreader. You need to discuss these topics openly and frequently.

LEARN TO EXPECT THE UNEXPECTED

Even if your expectations are reasonable, you may find that they're unmet simply because of life's unpredictable events. (The old saying puts it this way: "Life is what's happening while you're busy making other plans.") Some of what happens will almost certainly be negative. You or your spouse may lose a job. You may face other financial hardships. You may suffer a serious illness or an accident. Members of your families may experience personal difficulties that require your help. You may be confronted with loss and grief. Even positive events, however, can cause stress. For instance, a great job opportunity may present you with major challenges. The birth of a child will bring joy to your life but also new responsibilities. Buying a house will give you more space for raising your family but will result in expenses and domestic tasks, too. Both negative and positive changes in your life will require flexibility, imagination, and hard work.

To be realistic, you must learn to expect the unexpected. A lot of couples think they can plan everything in advance—or else draw a clear map of where their relationship is heading—but this kind of expectation will set you up for a big surprise. Sure, you can predict to some degree, and you can plan certain aspects of your relationship. It certainly helps if you and your partner relate well to each other and work hard to understand each other. But the truth is that if you're really going to have realistic expectations, you need to be prepared for anything. Is this a pessimistic attitude? Not at all. People with realistic expectations can prepare themselves for the challenges that are inevitable in life—and I can assure you that challenges will come. The key to success in dealing with these situations: learn to weather the storm when life doesn't fit your "plan."

UNDERSTANDING THE PLACE OF CHANGE

This brings us to a crucial topic: where change fits into married life.

What if you have needs and expectations that your spouse can't meet? Does this situation mean that you have the right to make your spouse change his or her behavior or attitudes? Is change of this sort even possible? And when change isn't feasible or desirable, how do you deal with the situation you face?

The issue I'm raising shows up in a lot of marriages. Even partners who are generally responsive to each other's needs and expectations may fall short in some respects, or there may be "blind spots" in their mutual attention. When this situation occurs, it's tempting for one spouse to feel a need to change the other. It's an understandable but potentially problematic response. Let's examine each of the several aspects of this subject.

THE RISKS OF TRYING TO CHANGE YOUR SPOUSE

Martina is a gregarious, vivacious young woman. Twenty-seven and employed in the fashion industry, she enjoys socializing at work, hanging out with friends, and spending time with her husband, Hal, whom Martina married a year ago. The couple is close and deeply in love. But even during their first year of marriage, they have already encountered a tricky problem. Martina enjoys a much wider range of social activities than Hal does. Parties, work-related gatherings, restaurant meals with friends, lunch out with girlfriends—all sorts of interactions appeal to her. By contrast, Hal would rather have dinner at home with Martina or visit with a few of their mutual friends. Tension has started to build in this couple because of the difference in their attitudes toward socializing.

Martina's solution: "Hal needs to loosen up. He's a great guy. People really like him. But he needs to come out of his shell. I think it's a shame for him to hide like he does." So Martina has decided to coax her husband "out of his shell" by prodding him to get together with people who don't really interest him, such as her pals from work, and by taking him to social occasions that bore him, such as fashion industry events. She's convinced that her "campaign," as she calls it, will transform her husband into someone who's as gregarious as she is.

I feel that Martina's efforts, though well-intentioned, are a mistake. Martina is a social butterfly. Hal is like a friendly dog who just likes to hang out at the farm. I honestly don't think that this shy man is likely to change—and if he does, it won't be because his wife *forces* him to change. Can this couple compromise and find common ground on social issues? I believe they can. Hal isn't antisocial; he's just not the good-time Charlie that Martina wants him to be. Just as Hal accepts Martina's gregarious nature, Martina should accept Hal's nature as a homebody. Otherwise he'll probably start to resent her zeal to "convert" him, and he'll withdraw from her instead of opening up. Her plan will have the opposite effect from what she intends.

Unfortunately, the situation I'm describing is lamentably common. When one spouse feels that his or her needs aren't being met, there's often a temptation to try to change the other person. Some women I know seem to have a program for "reforming" the men in their lives. Sometimes this means relatively superficial changes, such as convincing the guy to get a more appealing haircut, to buy classier outfits, or to improve his manners. Sometimes it means a broader, more ambitious set of goals, such as encouraging him to get a different job. I've known men who take a similar approach to the women in their lives—attempting to change their partner into someone that more closely meets a set of predetermined expectations. This may mean pressuring their girlfriends or wives to take an interest in sports, cars, or politics, or it may mean attempting to change their personalities or physical appearance. The core issue is similar even if the "programs" differ.

Why is this situation a problem? First off, the person being "reformed" may have no interest in the program. Second, the program may fail to work or even backfire. Third, most people resent being "overhauled." Fourth, these efforts generate little more than resentment in the person who is intent on creating change. I'm not saying that all efforts to change the other person are wrong—there are some exceptions. Generally speaking, though, neither member of a couple has the right, the wisdom, or the clarity of mind to take on the task of transforming the other. Changing your partner is a risky business!

WHEN CHANGE IS APPROPRIATE . . .

So is there ever a time when it's appropriate and even necessary to try encouraging or forcing your spouse to change? Yes—when the behavior or attitude or personality trait you're seeking to change is harmful to you, your spouse, or your relationship. (An example: when a spouse's behavior is part of an addiction. I'll address that issue in a moment.) But what about seemingly minor things that just drive you crazy? Here are some examples to contrast and compare as you consider issues of changing the other person.

First, let's say that your husband sings a lot but not very well. In fact, he's . . . *vocally challenged.* It's annoying that he sings so much and so often out of tune—and in public, no less! However, what he's doing isn't really a major transgression. He's not hurting you; he's just indulging himself in a harmless way. There's no point in changing your husband's pesky habit.

Now consider a second example, one that isn't a major transgression, either, but which could lead to a marital conflict. Let's say that your husband strews his dirty clothes all over the house. You try repeatedly to convince him that he should put his laundry in the hamper. No such luck. You think it's only fair that your husband should pitch in more, and he shouldn't make your life difficult by leaving clothes all over. You're tired of feeling like the maid service. Your husband's messiness isn't a mortal sin, but it's not as harmless as singing off-key, either. Is it all right for you to say, "Look, I'm not trying to change your whole character, but I want you to clean up after yourself. I want you to be fair to me. Is that unreasonable?"?

What you're asking for is a realistic expectation. There's good reason for your husband to clean up his act. How do you communicate to your spouse that his behavior really gets to you? How do you explain that some things really bother you, that seemingly little things hurt you and could eventually hurt your relationship? Well, it's not easy, but it's important to try. Your spouse needs to know how his actions make you feel. Maybe his intent isn't to be so inconsiderate, but lack of consideration is the ultimate effect. His sloppiness demoralizes and burdens you, and you need to make him aware of that.

The issue I'm describing comes down to a balance between acceptance and consideration. Yes, you need to accept that your spouse is different from you. While you may value a tidy home, your spouse may value comfort and lack of hassle. After a long day at work, he just wants to come home and relax. He changes into something comfortable and tosses his dirty clothes on the floor. Of course he intended to pick everything up, but he just forgot. The upshot of this situation is that you and your spouse have different ways of thinking, different ways of doing things, and different preferences. You end up having to balance the situation. Which is more important: your need for neatness or his need for comfort? Should you accept his personal style and live with a temporary mess if he eventually cleans up after himself? Or should he be more considerate of your needs and delay his relaxation a few minutes to clean up after himself first?

There's no pat answer. It's crucial, however, that you and your partner clarify where you stand in situations like this. Different couples will reach different conclusions as they sort through this kind of dilemma. For you to reach your own conclusion, you need to discuss your individual needs and feelings and learn how to be considerate of each other.

WHAT ABOUT SITUATIONS WHERE CHANGE SEEMS NECESSARY?

Sometimes spouses face situations that go beyond issues of whim, preference, and personal style—situations that present far greater challenges and hazards to a marriage. Some of these situations may prompt you to expect or even demand that your spouse change his or her behavior.

Let's say that your husband is a compulsive gambler. His obsession with games of chance frustrates you, but it's also an issue that goes far beyond just frustration, since he's risking your well-being by wasting money on cards and dice. He's an addict. He's not addicted to drugs, but he's addicted to gambling, which can have severe consequences both for an individual person and for a family. How do you face this issue? Is your husband's obsession with gambling one of those cases where it's fair enough—even necessary—to demand that he change? Can you just tell him, "Either you stop gambling or you're out of this marriage"?

Compulsive gambling isn't just a personality quirk or an eccentric habit, as was the husband's singing off-key. It's also not simply unfair, as was the husband who scattered his dirty clothes around. We're talking about a much more serious problem—a problem that can have devastating consequences for the husband, his wife, their children, and even their extended family. So, yes, it's reasonable to confront this issue. It's sensible—I'd say it's *crucial*—to demand that the husband change his ways.

One of the most difficult but necessary situations facing any relationship is an addiction. It's bad enough if an unmarried man or woman is trapped in a cycle of addictive behavior, but the problem is even worse when a husband or wife has become addicted. The potential stress on family life and the risks to the other spouse and the children raise the stakes for everyone involved. The specific addiction could be alcohol, drugs, gambling, sex—you name it. The issues are pretty much the same regardless. In any of these cases, addictive behavior rarely stays under control. Addictions have a way of causing progressive damage. Unless you face the problem head-on, deal with it, and go through a process of rehabilitation, the addiction will only get worse.

If you were to say, "I'm going to accept this behavior," you wouldn't be doing your husband a favor. On the contrary, your acceptance would be negligent. It would be codependence, which is a type of collaboration with a troubled person that feeds into the problematic behavior. Unfortunately, many spouses do accept behaviors that shouldn't be easily accepted—behaviors that need to be addressed professionally and need to be transformed.

Many couples have to deal with an addiction issue, but very few couples do so until there's a crisis—a DUI arrest, a drug bust, or an empty bank account. Only then do they face the problem. Sometimes people say, "We didn't want to confront the situation because we didn't want to create a crisis." Well, sorry—the crisis was already there. They were simply trying to ignore it, or else to shove it underneath the carpet.

I'll say it again: you have to face problems of this sort and deal with them directly. In the second chapter of Path Three, I'll explain the steps you need to take.

THE RISK OF WISHFUL THINKING

One thing is for sure, though: change and compromise in marriage aren't the result of wishful thinking. Unfortunately, though, a lot of people resort to wishful thinking rather than learning to compromise through mutual consideration, listening, and hard work.

For instance, I can't begin to tell you how often I speak with women who are concerned about their fiancés' behavior or attitudes but are convinced that "he'll change once we make it official." Sorry, but it doesn't often work that way. In fact, usually nothing can be further from the truth. The situation often changes for the worse. The problems, flaws, and defects that are evident before the wedding don't wither away; they suddenly multiply and expand. Slipping a wedding ring on your finger—and on your spouse's finger—won't magically resolve whatever conflicts are present in your relationship.

My recommendation: don't resort to wishful thinking. Clarify your needs and expectations. Understand your partner's needs and expectations. Then openly, thoughtfully, and earnestly work together toward accommodation and compromise.

THE GREAT LESSONS OF SUFFERING

Our discussions of change, unpredictability, and problems within relationships bring us to a difficult subject: suffering.

The longer you live, the more likely it is that you'll face challenges, hardships, and pain. None of us wants to think about this aspect of life, but it's inevitable. Each of us will encounter suffering—either physical suffering, such as an illness or an accident; or emotional suffering, such as grief or unrequited love; or spiritual suffering, such as struggles with faith, guilt, or despair.

It's also certain that our relationships will include the experience of suffering. No relationship occurs without an element of conflict, and conflict will invariably cause anguish or pain. Difficult or unhappy marriages contain abundant pain. Even happy marriages include events that cause unhappiness, grief, and sadness: difficulties with children, misunderstandings between the spouses, financial strains, accidents, and illnesses. It's also true that even the happiest, longest-lasting marriage will come to an end someday. No one, and no relationship, is exempt from suffering.

Why is there suffering? Each of the world's great religions has struggled to answer that question. From the Book of Job onward, our Judeo-Christian heritage has offered counsel and consolation to anyone who struggles to make sense of human pain. My purpose in writing this book isn't to address this huge, complex issue in general terms. But precisely because suffering does affect our day-to-day relationships, I feel it's crucial that we explore how this issue may affect you as you build your relationship as a couple. Facing the reality of suffering is the first step to take if you and your spouse want to learn how to draw closer together rather than to pull away from each other in times of suffering.

SUFFERING—WHAT'S IT ALL ABOUT?

I don't believe we were created to suffer, but I certainly acknowledge that life can be difficult and even painful. Do we have to like this fact of our existence? Of course not. But resenting the situation won't make it go away. If we don't acknowledge the reality of suffering, we'll live in a state of constant denial. Refusing to acknowledge suffering leaves us more vulnerable, not less so, to its consequences on our lives.

In one of my favorite books, M. Scott Peck's *The Road Less Traveled,* the author writes, "Most do not fully see this truth that life is difficult. Instead they moan more or less incessantly, noisily or subtly, about the enormity of their problems, their burdens and their difficulties in life as if life were generally easy, as if life should be easy." But life *isn't* easy. And our relationships aren't easy. If we expect a smooth ride—and with it an absence of suffering in our significant relationships—then we're bound to feel disappointed or hurt by our disconnectedness from reality. We can't run from this truth: life includes ups and downs, unpredictability, and even outright pain, especially when we give ourselves in love to another.

HOW, THEN, SHOULD WE RESPOND?

In our contemporary culture, we tend to run away from anything that hurts. Just look at your local drugstore—you'll find hundreds of over-the-counter remedies for almost any ailment. We flee from pain and see it as something to be avoided at all costs. This is true not only for physical pain but even for emotional pain. It's true that many people suffer from clinical depression, and it's appropriate for them to seek treatment, including medication, for this malady; but there's a growing trend for people to pop antidepressant pills to counteract even the most routine forms of sadness. Well, I believe that emotional pain—including pain caused by dysfunctions in relationships—won't go away just by popping a pill. There's no quick fix for a whole range of human experiences that include a measure of suffering. Those experiences may include separation and divorce, illness, loss of a job, economic instability, family problems, addictions, aging, loss of a loved one, and many other difficulties.

So how, then, should we respond to the suffering we encounter—including the suffering that's part of our relationships?

I feel that the answer isn't in *how to avoid suffering*, or even in *how to get rid of suffering*, but rather in *how we should respond to suffering in our lives*. How do we interpret the many situations in life that bring us struggles, difficulties, and pain? How do we react so that these sufferings don't remain solely a burden, but instead become useful lessons that deepen us and help us change and mature? How do we adapt to suffering so that the experience helps us in all our relationships? These are difficult questions! They don't have easy, clear-cut answers. But how well we approach them will make a huge difference in how we cope with the suffering that ultimately comes our way.

The truth is that if we pay close attention, we can find great lessons in suffering. Benjamin Franklin wrote that "the things that hurt, instruct." The great Saint Augustine also maintained that a human being who hasn't suffered is like a cathedral that hasn't been blessed. Suffering isn't just part of the human condition; it's also a great teacher. Among other things, people who haven't experienced suffering often have a difficult time being realistic about life and compassionate in dealing with their own and others' pain. Ironically, the struggles and difficulties that our most significant human relationships cause may possess a unique power to make us all more human and more compassionate.

When I think of life's trials and tribulations, I often think about a book that I consider one of the finest testimonies on the subject of suffering: Rabbi Harold Kushner's *When Bad Things Happen to Good People*. This book isn't a direct commentary on couples' relationships, but many of his statements are relevant anyway, so I want to raise some of them as part of our discussion.

Rabbi Kushner tells the story of how he and his wife learned that their young child suffered from an incurable disease called *progeria* (also known as "rapid aging disease"). His testimony is especially moving because, through his own suffering and inner questioning, Rabbi Kushner has helped millions of people understand that bad things do happen even to the best people. Here he was a rabbi, doing what was right before God, yet he felt that God had wronged him. Why had this happened? Through his own personal struggle with these issues, the good rabbi has taught us that we must be realistic in our expectations. We must accept the limitations of the human condition if we truly intend to understand this life we live.

I relate deeply to Rabbi Kushner's thoughts, especially as they pertain to dealing with suffering, and I often recommend his book to people who write me or come to see me. I also feel a connection with the rabbi because his own experience has helped me cope with events in my own life. When my father was diagnosed with terminal cancer, I, too, felt confused. I felt that I was a pretty good person and that my dad and my family didn't deserve to go through such pain. Here I'd given my life to God as a priest, so surely He was on my side! I'd never expected to lose my father at such an early age. This event was certainly a big twist in my life—something I'd never expected. So how could I deal with this situation and make sense of it?

Well, I struggled with these issues for a long time. I can't say that I've found the perfect answer—far from it. But I feel that I've reached some insights about what my father went through in his illness and death, and I also feel that I have a better grasp of what I went through, too, in experiencing the loss of my beloved father. Here's how I see it.

All of us have a tendency to blame *someone else* for our sufferings. For believers, the ideal person we usually blame is God! Where is God in all this suffering? If my father got sick, wasn't it because God wasn't on his side? If I suffered the loss of my father, wasn't it because God wasn't on my side? If your marriage or relationship isn't going well, isn't it because God is not on your side?

Well, the truth is that God doesn't cause all this suffering and pain. Suffering and pain are simply part of life. We have to learn to live with suffering and pain, and we need to learn to get through the hard times they cause. We have to trust that every moment of darkness in our lives can be transformed into light. Perseverance will always pay off as we try to make sense of this dilemma. Unfortunately, many couples lose the battle because they lack perseverance—they can't deal with the pain and suffering that life's problems can bring. The "pain-free" society we live in has gotten us accustomed to eliminating any type of pain—even before it starts. Unfortunately, that mentality can only destroy relationships.

WHAT DOES SUFFERING MEAN FOR COUPLES?

In relationships, as in life more generally, there are sunny days, rainy days, and even stormy days. You may live a happy existence overall, but your relationships will be subjected to some degree of suffering. Suffering is just part of the human condition. Just the fact that you're alive creates the potential for all kinds of suffering. So we're here, which is wonderful, but that doesn't mean that everything will be a fairy tale, happily ever after. At some point you're going to face suffering.

In addition, it doesn't help that the images of suffering we see in movies and TV shows are often simplistic. Pain on the tube and on the silver screen is often stylized and easily resolved. Storylines exploit accidents and illnesses for dramatic content but leave out the agonized waiting, the physical struggles, and the patience that recuperation usually requires. Even deathbed scenes tend to be tidy, not too messy, and neatly resolved for maximum poignancy and benefit to the plot. As viewers, we want the characters' suffering to ennoble them and not frighten us too much. All problems should be tied up nicely and, ideally, allow room for a happy ending before the final credits roll. Even talk shows that deal with real-life problems tend to shy away from the ambiguity and severity of true human suffering. We witness dysfunction and pain and family conflicts, but the host often resolves the guests' problems, provides handy tips to fix years of distrust, infidelity, and so forth, and ends the show with a smile and a jaunty theme song.

As a result of these sanitized media images, we get used to the idea that suffering will go away quickly, so we don't have to worry about it. The truth is, much of the suffering in our lives will endure, and many of our struggles will be with us for the long term. Fallout from situations from our past will travel with us into future relationships. Even struggles that you have overcome early in your relationship linger on. The conflicts, emotional pain, and confusion that people experience in a relationship won't conveniently disappear overnight following a single heart-to-heart talk. Yes, talking and listening are essential steps toward mending your relationship, but couples often need to work hard to solve their problems, and the process of growing and reaching mutual understanding often takes a long, long time.

In a marriage, couples must be ready to face all kinds of suffering—suffering that may be the result of work situations, of children growing up to become far different from what you hoped they'd be, of family conflicts, of disagreements, of disappointments, and of marital conflicts. Will these various kinds of suffering inevitably diminish your relationship? Not necessarily. It's true some marriages do fall apart as a result of suffering; some crises put so much strain on a couple that there's danger of separation or divorce. But suffering can actually strengthen a relationship. For example, I've seen couples who've had to cope with the hardship of a child's illness—a great struggle for any family. It's difficult in its own right, and it also puts a strain on the marriage. Many marriages have broken up because the parents have trouble dealing with such a severe crisis. The suffering is too great, the pain destroys one or both parents, and a huge rift develops between them. But some marriages become stronger, not weaker, as a result of suffering. The spouses support each other; they see each other through the hard times. And their mutual support makes them stronger. It deepens their love.

I know a remarkable couple who faced much hardship in their relationship and grew stronger not just in spite of the suffering, but because of it. Adrian was a medical doctor, and he himself had experienced many other families' medical difficulties and struggles. Then his only child was diagnosed with cancer—a terminal illness in a young teenager. I saw Adrian and his wife, Lisa, fight all the medical battles together. In the past, there had been a lot of tensions in that family over in-laws, money issues, and attitudes toward parenting. But I remember one Thanksgiving when I visited with them in the hospital. They were cutting the turkey right there on their son's hospital bed and talking with each other. I looked at them and thought, What a close family! What a strong bond of love they have there even in the midst of their crisis.

Eventually the son died. I attended the funeral Mass. Just looking at that couple, I thought about how these people had struggled with so much. The father, Adrian, had been a political prisoner in Cuba for years, and you could certainly imagine that something that hard would have hurt his marriage. But he had survived, even prevailed, and his whole family had made it through that crisis with him. And now they struggled together through their son's long and painful illness and even made it through the son's death. The pain they suffered could have devastated them, but their love and mutual support held each other up and made their marriage bond even stronger.

You can't help wondering, of course, why people have to go through so much suffering. But those are questions we can never understand. The question we should ask isn't why, but how. How do we deal with this? How do we get on with life? How do we find what makes us strong? That's why I believe firmly that if we are to have a realistic understanding of suffering, we need to see it not as a curse, but as an opportunity to grow and to develop and to try to be more fully present to each other. If we can do that, then suffering has meaning. But if suffering is seen as a punishment—if you regard it as nothing but hardship—you limit your ability to cope with it.

As I stated earlier, we'll all suffer to some degree in this life. The question isn't *if* we'll suffer. We will. The question is how we deal with the suffering that comes our way. And I believe that if a couple is willing to expect the inevitability of suffering, the more prepared they will be to face the struggles of life.

"IN GOOD TIMES AND IN BAD"

The current generation has generally escaped the effects of war, famine, and political suffering of the sorts that our parents and our grandparents have often experienced. Many of us have been spared the direct consequences of most recent world tragedies. Yes, we now have the threat of terrorism, and that's a genuine risk to our well-being. But, in general, we have a pretty safe life. I don't know how many of our young people today are aware of the fact that suffering is real and that they will suffer at some point in their relationships as a couple and in their families. To some degree this situation has left us somewhat starry-eyed about some hard truths.

When you marry your spouse, you say to that person, "in good times and in bad." What does that mean? Does it mean just the good times? No, it means what the words say: in good times and in bad. And, frankly, bad can be very bad. Bad can mean illness. Bad can mean problems with children. Bad can mean death. Even the best relationship in the world will end in death, and you'll lose the person that you love so much. So the question is: Are you ready for the suffering that, inevitably, we all have to face? And will the suffering you experience ruin your relationship—or will it strengthen it? I believe that when a couple has a strong bond of love, suffering can make the relationship stronger.

Chapter 7

How to Clarify Your Expectations

A young bride named Meg called her mother immediately after getting back from her honeymoon. Crying into the phone, Meg said, "Mom, ever since we arrived home, Jack has been using terrible four-letter words when he speaks to me."

The mother replied, "How can that be? What did he tell you?"

The bride responded, "He said: cook, iron, wash, and dust."

"Don't worry, sweetheart," the mom told her daughter, "I'll be there to pick you up in fifteen minutes!"

Well, okay, so it's just a joke. But like many jokes, this one makes a point about a genuine issue that many people face. Here's what I regard as the point: too many couples haven't clarified their expectations, and the reality of marriage comes as a terrible shock. They somehow imagine that putting gold rings on their fingers will magically settle any unresolved issues facing them. Maybe it's a legacy of the fairy tales they heard as children. Maybe it's a result of watching too many romantic movies. In any case, husbands and wives often have a lot of illusions about married life.

I see the fallout from these attitudes all the time. Many of the cou ples I counsel seem disappointed, frustrated, even bitter about how they interact as husband and wife. They often resent each other for being different from what they expected. They are anxious or scared about what the future will bring, given the dramatic differences between what they anticipated from marriage and what the reality is like. What I'm describing is a sad and unfortunate situation. These are good-hearted men and women; they entered marriage with good intentions. But for many of them, something has gone seriously wrong.

I urge you to avoid falling into this same trap. There's so much at stake that I strongly recommend that you take the time to clarify your expectations *now* rather than wait for misunderstandings to occur in the future. If you and your partner haven't yet married, this is the perfect time to undertake this task. If you're already married, it's not too late. You can benefit from clarifying your expectations at any point in your relationship. It's true that doing so requires some effort, patience, and shared commitment. But it's worth it—there's much to gain if you proceed, and significant risks if you don't.

TASKS TO HELP YOU CLARIFY YOUR EXPECTATIONS

Building on our discussions in Chapter 6, here are seven tasks that can help you and your partner understand your needs as a first step toward mutual fulfillment.

Task #1
Identify Your Needs

How should you figure out what your expectations are, where you and your partner agree and disagree, and whether your expectations are realistic or unrealistic? For all couples, clarifying expectations is based on good communication. (I'll have more to say about this crucial issue in Path Five of this book.) Some couples can undertake a useful, creative discussion entirely on their own and achieve the necessary goals. Many, however, need outside help as they talk over the issues. I often provide this sort of assistance to couples. Task #1 is an exercise similar to what members of the clergy use for this purpose.

I've found that one of the best ways to make progress in this complex process is by using a *marital inventory*. The marital inventory is a list of statements that each partner reviews and responds to, indicating that they agree or disagree with each point. Their responses then provide a means for assessing what their needs are—and more important still—whether each partner's needs are in harmony with the other's.

Here's how to use this exercise. Read the inventory's comments and respond with how they apply to you. Your partner should also read and respond to the comments to determine how they apply to him or her. Both of you should respond openly and honestly. There's no right or wrong answer—only the answer that's *true for you*. Your partner needs to respond in the same spirit of openness. At this stage, you should note your responses separately, as it's important for you not to second-guess each other. Be as specific as possible. Once you've worked through these questions separately, then compare your answers to see where your re-sponses are similar and where they differ. Use this comparison as a "springboard" for further discussions.

Can a couple make full use of this exercise on their own? Some cou-ples can; others find it a little difficult. I believe that, ideally, you should have a guide of some sort—a pastoral counselor, a priest, a minister, a rabbi, or a marital therapist—who can help facilitate your discussions and help you clarify the issues as you go, offering suggestions and mediating if you and your partner reach misunderstandings.

What if your partner isn't willing to do this exercise? Well, that would be unfortunate, but his or her reluctance shouldn't prevent *you* from proceeding. Using the inventory can still help you clarify your own needs, understand how they affect you, and reach insights about your relationship.

Here's the inventory:

- For me, the commitment we're making to marriage means a sacramental commitment to love each other under all circumstances.

- On a scale of 1 to 10 (with 10 being the highest and 1 the lowest), rate the following for how much they matter to you:

Security	Possessions
Status	Travel
Leisure time	Charity
Education	Sense of community
Money	Contact with relatives

- Having children is a strong need for me.

- When something concerns me, I need to handle it by discussing it directly with my spouse.

- On a scale of 1 to 10 (with 10 being the highest and 1 the lowest), rate the importance of your sexual relationship.

- I need our sexual relationship to adapt to my moods.

- When my spouse and I disagree about something, I feel a need to reach a compromise as soon as possible.

- I have a strong need to practice my religion and express my religious values.

- I need to have my own personal, individual bank account.

- I need to look my best.

- I need to express my personal feelings to the persons I'm close to, including my spouse.

- I need my spouse to share all of his/her personal feelings with me.

- I find it difficult to say "I'm sorry" when I'm wrong.

- I need as little conflict as possible in my marriage.

- To be fulfilled in my marriage, I need to avoid getting married too soon.

- It's important to me that our expenses never exceed our income.

Please note: some of the questions may not apply to your situation. However, the more issues you can address, the better chance you have to clarify your expectations, both individually and as a couple. Again, I urge you to consider finding a marital therapist or a pastoral counselor to assist you with this important process!

Task #2
Clarify Your Expectations

While Task #1 focused in general on what you need for yourself, Task #2 now focuses on what you need in another person. As with the earlier exercise, it's ideal for you and your partner to answer the questions separately, then compare notes on your answers. I want to repeat that there are no right or wrong answers—only honest, open answers. Consider this task, like the previous one, a springboard for discussion.

Here's the inventory:

- I think my spouse spends too much time with his or her friends.

- In our marriage, I expect domestic tasks to be divided as follows:

  □ All my responsibility/Not at all his or her responsibility
  □ Mostly my responsibility/Minimally his or her responsibility
  □ Equally shared responsibility
  □ Minimally my responsibility/Mostly his or her responsibility
  □ Not at all my responsibility/All his or her responsibility

- In my marriage, I expect the money-earning responsibilities to be divided as follows:

  □ All my responsibility/Not at all his or her responsibility
  □ Mostly my responsibility/Minimally his or her responsibility
  □ Equally shared responsibility
  □ Minimally my responsibility/Mostly his or her responsibility
  □ Not at all my responsibility/All his or her responsibility

- Although I enjoy being with my partner, I expect each of us to have some time alone. I need _____ hours alone each week.

- I hope that after the wedding, my future spouse will change some of his or her behaviors, such as _____.

- When I'm upset (anxious, scared) I need my spouse to _____.

- I expect my spouse to spend money wisely and save for the future.

- I expect parenting our children not to become more important than our couple relationship.

- When my spouse is angry, I expect him or her to _____.

- When change affects us, I expect my spouse to _____.

- I expect my spouse to be flexible in dealing with challenges.

- I expect my spouse to be very involved in his or her work.

- I expect my spouse to have a good sense of humor.

- I expect my spouse to participate in practicing our faith as a family.

- Regarding the responsibilities of parenthood, I believe that they should be:

  ☐ All my responsibility/Not at all his or her responsibility
  ☐ Mostly my responsibility/Minimally his or her responsibility
  ☐ Equally shared responsibility
  ☐ Minimally my responsibility/Mostly his or her responsibility
  ☐ Not at all my responsibility/All his or her responsibility

Task #3
Check in with Your Partner Regularly

Let's say that you and your spouse have each clarified your personal needs and your expectations. You've also discussed how you feel about these issues and, ideally, you've made compromises that will help to accommodate each other. So far so good. If you've undertaken these first two tasks, you're ahead of the game compared to many other couples. Congratulations!

But those first two tasks are just the start. Clarifying your needs and expectations isn't a static, one-shot effort. Instead, it's important to reassess your needs and expectations periodically and to make adjustments on an ongoing basis. How do you carry on with this process? What I'd recommend is what I call "checking in." Here's how I see the situation.

Needs and expectations change over time. You and your spouse are constantly learning, growing, and developing in many ways. This is all to the good—a sign that you're vibrant, creative human beings. But if you don't have an ongoing dialogue with each other on the issue of expectations, you risk losing track of what you need from and what you can offer each other. You may grow apart and feel progressively more conflicted rather than more harmonious over the years. Checking in, however, allows you opportunities to stay in touch and aware of what each of you is thinking, feeling, hoping, fearing, and needing.

To undertake this check-in process, I urge you to talk periodically and, in the course of your conversations, to ask each other a brief series of questions and then discuss your answers. Here are some suggestions for the target questions:

- "What do you need from me that you're not getting?"

- "Is there anything I'm doing that troubles or frustrates you?"

- "What can we do that would help us work better together as spouses or as parents?"

- "Would you be willing to do _____, which would help me a lot?"

- "Would you be willing to *not* do _____, which I find frustrating?"

The key to checking in with your spouse in this way is to ask the questions with an open mind and an open heart. If your goal is to pressure, manipulate, humiliate, or "manage" your spouse, the exercise will backfire. It only works if both of you can ask the questions and listen to the answers in a spirit of generosity and common endeavor. Doing so, however—especially if you can repeat the process on a regular basis—will go a long way toward keeping you both clear about your needs and expectations.

Task #4
Recognize When Asking Your Partner to Change Is (or Isn't) Appropriate

What I'm about to advocate now is one of the most difficult tasks that married couples must undertake on a routine basis.

Change is inevitable. Change is also crucial. If you have no capacity or willingness to change, you're likely to end up stagnant. The same holds true for marriages. The capacity for change is part of what keeps a marriage lively, flexible, and enjoyable. However, different people have different capacities for change. In addition, some issues are more important than others. And so, taking these several factors into account, you and your spouse each need to recognize which issues warrant change and the degree to which each of you can accommodate change. Let me put the matter this way: there are basically three kinds of issues that prompt the possibility of change in a marriage.

- **Issues that you can live with no matter what.** These issues are quirks or personality traits that don't necessarily require any change. Examples:

  - A spouse who shouts too much while watching televised sports

  - A spouse whose preferences in attire annoy the other spouse

- **Issues that might reasonably prompt a request for change but are negotiable.** These issues aren't really harmful as such, but they may be frustrating in ways that suggest the advantages of change. Examples:

  - A spouse whose cooking style doesn't suit the family's tastes

  - A spouse whose business socializing takes him or her away from the home too much

❧ **Issues that require change for the survival of your relationship.** These issues do real, potentially severe damage to the marriage, the spouses, or their children. Examples:

- A spouse who is addicted to alcohol, drugs, sex, or gambling

- A spouse who is psychologically or physically abusive toward the other spouse or their children

So how should you assess what's going on in your marriage, whether one or more aspects may require change, and whether change is appropriate? There's no sure way to answer to this question. As I've noted elsewhere in this book, I believe that most couples can benefit from having a mentor help them with many issues, this one included. If that option isn't either feasible or desirable, however, I suggest that you ask yourself some questions that will help you clarify the situation on your own. Here are some suggested questions:

❧ Does the behavior in question seem harmless or potentially harmful?

❧ If it's harmless, is it something you can tolerate or ignore?

❧ If it's harmful, what is the potential for harm?

❧ Could it injure you or your spouse?

❧ Does it affect your relationship?

❧ If so, how does it affect your relationship, and to what degree?

❧ How does that behavior make you feel?

❧ Do you believe that your spouse is behaving in this manner to bother, annoy, frustrate, demoralize, or hurt you on purpose?

❧ Does your spouse know that the behavior bothers, annoys, frustrates, demoralizes, or hurts you?

∾ Have you discussed this behavior with your spouse in the past?

∾ If so, what was his or her response (both verbally and in his or her behavior)?

∾ What do you feel is the likelihood of your spouse responding to a request to change this behavior?

By answering the questions on this list, you have a better chance of identifying behaviors that may warrant changing—or, for that matter, that may warrant ignoring. With most behaviors there's no simple "litmus test" that will determine if they are subject to change. Each couple will have to create their own system for perceiving what the spouses do within the marriage and which behaviors suggest a need for change. Whatever else, though, I guarantee you that the couples who are most likely to change successfully are those that somehow maintain respect, patience, and good communication as the "ground rules" for the process.

Task #5
How to Prompt Change in Your Spouse or Marriage

So let's say that you identify some frustrating but basically harmless aspect in your spouse's behavior that you feel is burdening you or your marriage. How can you cope with the situation? Specifically, how can you prompt your spouse to change? (This task will focus only on relatively benign issues. For discussions of major crises and unacceptable behaviors, see Tasks 6 and 7.)

Here's an example. Marge and Russ have an ongoing conflict over Russ's bathing habits—or, more accurately, Russ's habits concerning what *doesn't* happen after he bathes. Russ is very hairy. When he showers, the bathtub ends up strewn with a great number of black hairs. Russ never cleans the tub after his showers; he leaves that task to Marge, who feels more and more frustrated by having to clean up after her husband before *she* takes a bath. This situation is hardly a major calamity in their life together, but it's a source of ongoing and increasing friction.

Here are some ways in which Marge can prompt Russ to change. You can adapt these approaches to your own purposes.

- **Be direct but not accusatory.** Marge tells Russ, "This messy bathtub situation really bothers me," rather than "You're such a slob, always leaving the bathtub such a mess."

- **Focus on "I-messages"—how the situation makes *you feel*.** Marge says, "I feel really frustrated by having to clean up after you."

- **Point out issues of fairness, not the other person's character.** Marge goes on to say, "I just don't think it's fair that I should have to do this cleanup every time you take a shower."

- **Be specific, not general, about your request.** Marge then asks, "I'd like you to wipe out the tub after you shower. I'm not saying you have to scrub the whole thing—just take a tissue and mop up all those little hairs."

- **Be open to the reciprocity.** When Russ notes, "Well, hey—*your* long hair is a problem, too, 'cause it's clogging the drain and the trap," Marge admits, "Okay, then *I* need to clean up, too. I'll use that hair strainer and also wipe out the tub."

Is this approach foolproof? Of course not. Different situations will require different approaches, some more time-consuming and complex than others. But adapting the method that I've suggested here is flexible and fair to both parties. If you and your spouse use it with good intentions, you can resolve a wide range of problems and create the potential for comfortable change.

Task #6
How to Handle Times of Suffering

Because every marriage will encounter crises, it's crucial for you to under-stand how to handle the burdens of stress, uncertainty, suffering, and pain. No brief summary can cover this complex subject in all its subtlety; how-ever, here are some important steps that will help you weather the storm:

✤ Step 1: TALK ABOUT WHAT'S HAPPENING

When facing hard times, many husbands and wives tend to withdraw from each other rather than seeking support and solace from each other. Husbands, especially, may fall silent and "hunker down" alone. This re-action is understandable in some respects: you may feel so overwhelmed during a crisis that you try to conserve your emotional energy as you deal with the situation. Also, many emotions are difficult to express at such times, such as when coping with job loss or the illness of a family mem-ber. But self-isolation is a mistake. You need the consolation and mutual assistance you can offer each other.

A better approach: keep talking about the situation you face. Share your frustrations, anguish, and worries. Strategize and plan together on how to solve your problems. An ongoing conversation about your crisis won't be easy or fun—in fact, you may find it emotionally wrenching—but taking this route is far better for both of you.

✤ Step 2: STAY ON THE SAME TEAM

This step builds on Step 1. If you can keep your communication channels open, you have a better chance of staying together as you face the crisis. By doing so, you gain two great advantages.

First, you give yourself a better chance to strategize about the situation and plan your responses. You're far stronger as a team than each of you would be on your own. You'll come up with more (and better) ideas about how to proceed. You'll also present a united, more persuasive "front" when dealing with the world (such as in coping with doctors, lawyers, institutions, or whomever else you have to face).

Second, you'll have a better chance of staying close as a couple. Crises of every sort are stressful, and stress often serves as a wedge between the spouses. The divorce rate for couples following the death of a child, for instance, is high. Working hard to stay in touch with each other—through verbal communication and through emotional support—is crucial and will pay off in the long run. I urge you to do whatever you can to maintain a sense of mutual emotional support.

❖ *Step 3:* AVOID VENTING PAIN AND ANGER AGAINST EACH OTHER

It's common that when facing a crisis, husbands and wives will vent their frustrations against each other as a "safety valve." If you have a sick child, for example, you're more likely to express your anguish against your spouse rather than against the doctors and nurses at the hospital. This is understandable but still problematic. Still, I strongly urge you both *not* to use each other as scapegoats during a stressful time. Talking over the situation honestly and openly will help you avoid resorting to demoralizing marital warfare.

What should you do if your spouse vents his or her anger against you anyway? That depends on the specifics of what's happening. Physical abuse is unacceptable under all circumstances. If you feel you're in danger of spousal abuse, seek help immediately. Don't put yourself in danger. If, on the other hand, the abuse is verbal, you face a more complex situation. Verbal abuse, too, is unacceptable, but it may be more understandable during an acute crisis. My recommendation is, again, to find external support—a pastoral counselor or a psychotherapist—who can help you and your spouse deal with this stressful situation. And what if the outbursts are emotional but not abusive? In such instances I recommend that you shouldn't back off when your spouse expresses anguish, frustration, or anxiety related to your crisis. Part of your role as a spouse is to help your husband or wife deal with these emotional stresses. The same role is true for him or her. However, I believe once again that trying to deal with these situations alone is less helpful than if you have resources available, such as a pastor or a counselor.

✧ *Step 4:* GIVE EACH OTHER TIME ALONE

Just as you should try to provide support to your spouse, you need to know when to back off. Crises are often so depleting that each member of a couple will need a chance to recuperate from the physical and emotional demands of coping. Yes, communicating and standing together is important. But so is having time alone. Almost everyone needs a measure of solitude to rest, reflect on the situation, and generally "recharge." This is especially true if you're facing a protracted crisis, such as a family member's illness, recovery from an accident, or rehabilitation from an addiction.

My recommendation: don't be offended if your spouse needs to pull back now and then and seek solitude. It's part of the normal human coping mechanism. Grant yourself this same opportunity. Each of you—and your marriage as a whole—will benefit.

✧ *Step 5:* KNOW WHEN YOU CAN FIX THINGS . . .

. . . and when you can't. I'm all for pushing hard when doing so will make a difference. There will be times, however, when you can't solve the problem facing you. There are times when you can't make everything better. If your spouse's mother dies, for instance, you can't undo the death. You can't even take away the burden of grief that your spouse is feeling. You just can't fix the situation.

What should you do at such times? First and foremost, you need to accept that there are some events in life that are beyond our control. Some problems are too big for us to fix. We're only human. If you can accept the limits that are part of being human, you'll take off some of the pressure you'll feel otherwise. The result is—perhaps oddly—liberating. Once you accept your inability to solve the problem, you're free to do more fully what is within your power as a husband or as a wife: to offer your spouse love and support.

✤ *Step 6:* GET HELP

One of the most common mistakes that couples make during a crisis is to try to deal with the situation on their own. I regard this approach as unfortunate for several reasons. First of all, many issues are too complex to resolve alone. Second, flying solo risks increasing the stress you feel, which can lead to psychological problems such as depression and anxiety, or even to physical health problems. Third, it's just not necessary to carry these burdens on your own shoulders. A wealth of resources is available for almost any health- or mental health–related challenge you may be facing. For instance, almost every major illness in existence— from Alzheimer's disease to Zollinger-Ellison syndrome—has prompted someone to set up a foundation, research center, or support group to help people deal with it. You can find information, coping strategies, referral services, and sometimes direct personal assistance that can make your situation easier and a lot less stressful. For information about available resources, see this book's Appendix.

✤ *Step 7:* BE STRONG FOR EACH OTHER

Finally, I urge you to stay loyal to each other and see each other through the crises. This is easier said than done, I know. But in addition to offering so many other benefits, one of the extraordinary gifts that marriage provides is the possibility of offering a safe haven in the middle of the storm. If you and your spouse can stay steady with each other, you will be granting each other support and solace of a sort that almost nothing else in life can provide. This isn't something that just *happens*. Loyalty and supportiveness require active choice. I urge you to make that choice.

Task #7
Deal with Addictions

One of the crises you face may start with discovering that your spouse is subject to an addiction. The most common sorts of addictions in our culture involve alcohol, illicit drugs, gambling, and sexual obsessions. Each of these addictions presents its own special challenges, but your response will generally require taking the following steps:

✤ *Step 1:* ADMIT THAT THERE'S A PROBLEM

You can't even begin to solve a problem if you pretend that it doesn't exist. This statement is never truer than when applied to an addiction. Unfortunately, most addicts live in denial about their addiction, and their spouses often share that state of denial. ("Oh, he's not really an alcoholic—he just drinks a bit too much now and then.") Recognition of the problem is essential.

Facing the fact that your partner has an addiction is a difficult step to take. Dealing with and overcoming an addiction can be emotionally draining, painful, and challenging to your relationship. But you have to accept the reality of what's happening. Until you do, you're stuck. Once you do, you can move forward.

✤ *Step 2:* GET HELP

Very few people can overcome an addiction alone. Succeeding takes more than just willpower or positive thinking. You need help from people who are experienced in tackling this sort of problem. Success will require some sort of treatment program—Alcoholics Anonymous, Al-Anon, Gambler's Anonymous, or whatever applies to your situation. Your spouse needs rehabilitation, a program that helps him or her get a handle on the problem and takes your spouse through the steps necessary to rebuild his or her life.

Are you reluctant to ask for help? Many people are at first. They feel ashamed that they're coping with an addiction or that someone they love is addicted. They may be tempted to blame themselves or accuse themselves of failure or sin. Well, self-blame won't help the situation. Addictions are diseases, and you need to see them as such. If you or your spouse developed cancer or heart disease, you wouldn't respond by accusing yourself your husband or wife of failure on moral grounds, would you? You'd go find a good doctor and a good treatment program for the specific disease. When someone you love is an addict, you need to respond in a similar way and seek the help he or she requires to overcome the addiction.

See the Appendix for information on resources to treat many kinds of addictions.

✤ *Step 3:* BRACE YOURSELF FOR A BACKLASH

A word of warning: as part of their physiological and psychological problems, many addicts lash out at the people closest to them. Your spouse may accuse you of indifference, cruelty, lack of love, and all sorts of other failings. Your husband or wife may claim, "Now you're hitting me when I'm down"—or even trying to destroy him or her. Alcoholism and drug abuse, especially, often distort the thought processes to the point of paranoia. As a result, you can expect a backlash against your efforts to help your spouse. Your earnest efforts to help may earn you little more than accusations, temper tantrums, and threats.

Many spouses struggle with this situation. They often feel guilty confronting their addicted partner, as if they *are* hitting their spouse when he or she is down. The truth is, both spouses have already been dragged down, because addictive behavior burdens the marriage and the whole family. So, in response, you might rightly say, "I'm not hitting you when you're down. We're seeking help because you have a serious problem. And we can't move on until you face it. You have to accept that you have an illness."

✤ *Step 4:* GET RESOURCES FOR YOURSELF

As a result of some of the situations I've described, it's crucial for you to find resources that will support you emotionally during the process of your spouse's rehabilitation. Alcoholics Anonymous, Narcotics Anonymous, and other organizations devoted to treating addictions include programs for the addicted person's spouse and family. Specific resources may include information about addictions, counseling, and support groups. I strongly urge you to take advantage of these resources.

In addition, I recommend that you locate and rely on whatever emotional and spiritual resources you have available: support from family and friends; from your priest, minister, or rabbi; from a counselor or therapist; and from your church or temple community. Don't hesitate to find sustenance from the people who care for you. You'll need their help to maintain your energy and stamina over the long haul.

✤ *Step 5:* GO THE DISTANCE

Treating an addiction is a long-term commitment. Many experts in the field would describe it as a *permanent* commitment. (For instance, proponents of Alcoholics Anonymous say that no one is ever a "recovered alcoholic," but, instead, a "recover*ing* alcoholic.") So I'd never state that the process of overcoming this problem is smooth or tidy. But what choice is there, really?

WHAT WE EXPECT

"Life is under no obligation to give us what we expect," wrote Margaret Mitchell in *Gone with the Wind*.

How true—and it's true as well that much frustration and misery results from our all-too-human tendency to believe that if we expect something, we have a right to have that expectation fulfilled. I know many single people who fall prey to this belief; I know many married people who do as well. What complicates the situation in marriage, however, is that each spouse must cope with both his or her own expectations and with the other person's as well. Perhaps it's the potential for a double dose of dashed hopes that makes the issue of expectations so difficult for couples.

It seems to me that, ultimately, the way to address this dilemma is through a combination of clarity and flexibility. Clarifying your needs and expectations will help you know what you want. Flexibility will help you adjust, adapt, and compromise if you don't or can't get what you want. Ideally, marriage partners help each other through a process of growth that increases both spouses' clarity and their flexibility. One of my wishes for all couples is that they strive for this combination of goals.

I want to close with a quote from the novelist Pearl S. Buck: "A good marriage is one which allows for change and growth in the individuals and in the way they express their love." [*To My Daughters, With Love* (1967)]

Path Four

BE HONEST

Here are four people speaking about the role of honesty in their respective marriages:

"Jason and I disagree about a lot of things, but we have an agreement that no matter what else happens, we'll always level with each other. Sometimes we argue because we see things so differently. We're both very opinionated! But we always know we're hearing exactly what's on the other person's mind. We always know exactly where we stand."

—Melinda, thirty-eight

"My wife watches me like a hawk. She knows I'd never cheat on her, but it drives her crazy that I work around so many women, and her imagination kind of gets the best of her. I end up feeling kind of paranoid. I can't even kid around with these female coworkers without feeling guilty. And to be frank, I resent that."

—Adam, twenty-seven

"Janice has taught me so much about being open to each other. She'll say, 'What's bothering you?' And like any red-blooded American male, I'll say, 'Nothing. I'm fine.' And she'll say, 'Oh, come on, I know something's bugging you.' Nine times out of ten, she's right. Maybe even I don't know it, but she's right. So we'll talk. And what's so great is that I know she'll always listen to me, and she'll accept whatever is on my mind without judging me. And then we deal with it together."

—Alvaro, forty

"What hurt me the most about his affair wasn't the affair. That was bad enough! But the whole time it went on, which was over a year, he acted like everything was normal. He treated me like I was the center of his life. But I wasn't *the center of his life. Someone else was the center of his life. So everything he did to me and everything he said to me that whole time was a lie."*

—Nanci, twenty-five

These four spouses—two wives and two husbands—are all dealing with where the truth fits into their lives. To their credit, the first and third have somehow created a strong foundation of honesty in their marriages. For the second and fourth, however, honesty has a weaker, even unstable place in the relationship they share. These couples, like all couples, will have to cope with issues of honesty throughout their married lives. There's really no way around it—honesty is, in fact, one of the central issues in any relationship.

HONESTY: A COMMANDMENT— OR JUST A HELPFUL HINT?

Many people nowadays regard the Ten Commandments as little more than God's suggestions, but I assure you that they are much more than helpful hints. In addition to providing explicit instructions, the Commandments also contain the wisdom and guidance we all need in order to live happy lives. And telling the truth is so important that God even made it one of his Commandments: *You shall not lie.*

A few theological comments will be useful here. The Commandments that God gave to Moses on Mount Sinai (Exodus 20:2–17 and Deuteronomy 5:6–21) can be divided into two basic categories: the first three and the last seven. The first three have to do directly with our relationship with God. You could say they are the "vertical" Commandments—they deal with the "God-and-you" relationship. The remaining seven are the "horizontal" Commandments that deal with our relationships with each other—all of our human relationships and interactions. They present a formula for living our relationships with honesty and transparency. In fact, the last seven Commandments provide almost everything we need to know about this topic, for each of these commandments touches on various problems that so frequently come up in our lives when we stray from being truthful and sincere.

(These Commandments are: 4—You shall honor your mother and your father; 5—You shall not kill; 6—You shall not commit adultery; 7—You shall not steal; 8—You shall not lie; 9—You shall not desire your neighbor's wife; and 10—You shall not covet your neighbor's goods.)

In terms of our discussions of relationships, the Eighth Commandment—"You shall not lie"—is a fundamental concept. First of all, honesty is the foundation of any open, giving relationship, including marriage. In addition, honesty is the central concept around which the other six "horizontal" Commandments cluster. Why? Because all the other Commandments also deal with basic issues of truth and falsehood. Issues of killing (the Fifth Commandment), adultery (the Sixth and the Ninth), stealing (the Seventh), and covetousness (the Tenth) all have to do with the fundamental concepts of honesty. For this reason, all of these commandments apply to issues of relationships. And if we take them to heart, God's Commandments can keep us honest and out of trouble in all of our relationships, including marriage. The Eighth Commandment confirms the saying that "Honesty is the best policy." The world of our human relationships is complicated enough already without all the deception and lies that lack of honesty adds to the mix!

Here's the heart of the matter: you and your spouse can't develop trust, respect, and loyalty without building them on a foundation of honesty. The absence of honesty damages all relationships, but the lack of it is especially harmful to husbands' and wives' efforts to create strong, loving marital bonds.

For these reasons, Path Four—Be Honest—explores the nature of honesty and how it influences couples' relationships.

Chapter 8

Honesty—The Core of Openness

When we speak of honesty in the context of relationships, what are we really talking about? Do we mean simply speaking words that are factually accurate? Or is there a deeper set of issues at the core of what we're discussing?

I personally believe that there is a deeper set of issues. Honesty isn't just stating words that aren't false. Honesty is also a matter of being able to be fully yourself and to speak your heart and mind to the person you love most—the person you're sharing your life with. Honesty is about expressing what's true to you and consistent with your love of your partner or spouse. Honesty is the core of openness.

Good marriages—solid marriages, happy marriages—all contain this element of honesty. The spouses don't try to hide things from each other to satisfy some selfish aspect of their own personalities. On the contrary, they share what is most important in their minds, hearts, and souls. The kind of honesty I'm referring to means fully sharing yourself with your spouse.

In Christianity, we speak about how the two spouses become one. This concept comes from the book of Genesis—the idea that the man shall leave his father and his mother and shall be joined to his wife, and the two shall become one. What does that mean—"the two become one"? Can you have your own set of truths, your own separate life, without your spouse really knowing who you are and what's going on inside you? I don't believe that's possible. For a relationship to be true and good, there has to be honesty. There has to be a uniting bond between you. Maybe the right word is *transparency*—a lack of guardedness, a lack of emotional stinginess. There should be nothing in your life that you have to hide from your spouse. When two lives come together in this profoundly intimate way, there should be a radical openness to each other. There should be sincerity in everything you do. In a sense, you and your spouse really *do* become one. This concept isn't just an ideal. I believe that it happens in practice. There are couples that simply look at each other and know what the other person is thinking. They totally "get" each other.

Trouble occurs when there's an absence of transparency. The spouses aren't open to each other. They aren't true to the vision of their marriage. This is sad—even tragic. If you can't be true to the person you love most—the person you've given your life to, who can you be true to? What binds you together to this person if it's not the ultimate truth of striving to be one?

I'll admit that it's easy to misinterpret what I'm saying. Am I saying that you always "lay it on the line" and state the first, most impulsive, and most simplistic comment you're thinking? No, not at all. Honesty in marriage can involve subtlety and complexity. Honesty can—and should—include the larger vision that I mentioned a moment ago.

Here's an example. A man named Sam once heard this question from a friend: "At what age do you think women are at their most beautiful?"

Sam thought a while and said, "When they're my wife's age."

Sam was almost sixty. His wife was that age, too. Sam could have said, "When they're twenty"—or twenty-five, or seventeen, or thirty. He could, in short, have given any of the standard answers based on our culture's predominant attitudes about feminine beauty. But he didn't. Was

Sam's answer the most objective one possible? No. But I think he was speaking honestly by stating what he believed: that his wife was the most beautiful in his eyes. A person who is deeply in love with his or her mate would probably think that the most beautiful person is that spouse. So in an important way, Sam *was* being honest. This was his perception of beauty. And his answer suggests that honesty is more than just a question of "facts." Honesty in marriage takes into account the importance of the marriage commitment and the spouses' shared life.

In this chapter, let's first consider the general issues of honesty and how they affect couples' relationships. Then let's examine three specific threats to honesty: jealousy, greed, and infidelity.

THE POWER OF OUR WORDS

When we consider how honest we are, we have to assess how much value we place on the power of our words. Do we really say what we mean and mean what we say? Do we consider the vows we take to be sacred? When we make lifetime promises, do we keep our word? I believe that taking our words seriously is essential if we are to live as human beings and not just as instinct-driven animals.

In the past, "giving your word" was as valuable as a written agreement. Before checkbooks and credit cards were common, many people simply used the honor system. Giving your word on other commitments, too, was legally and morally binding. Does this system still exist? To some extent. Even today, for instance, the marriage vows remain a solemn expression of a verbal commitment intended to be honored forever. When a man and woman face each other at the altar and promise to love each other "all the days of our lives," they are making a radical statement. I often ask the bride and groom a few days before the marriage ceremony if they are prepared to say these words with full intent to honor them. They often look at me with a sense of awe and respect in their eyes. This response shows me that they're preparing to make a serious commitment. Yet with the current divorce rate so high—and with the indissolubility of marriage constantly in question—I have to wonder if the value of these solemn, sacred words will continue to have the same impact on future generations of married couples. Have we altogether lost our respect for words and the binding commitment we've always attributed to them? I hope not.

Here's the bottom line. We must be honest. To be honest, we must be motivated to be honest. Maintaining this motivation may take some focused attention—an awareness that honesty doesn't just *happen*, it requires us to think about what we're doing. We need to work to keep our promises. We need to stay aware that a sloppy attitude toward truth—a tendency not to take our words seriously—can damage our ability to love openly and build lasting relationships. Simply wanting to love and to build good relationships isn't enough; we have to act on this desire through thoughtful attention and hard work. We must keep our vows and renew what we promise each day—even if doing so isn't so easy.

There's another important issue here: the relationship between trust and truth. We can't talk about honesty without also talking about trust. I know everyone would agree that trust is one of the fundamental elements of an intimate relationship. How can you be completely open with someone—how can you allow him or her into your sacred center—if you don't trust this other person? How can you risk the vulnerability that this openness involves? How can you be confident that the other person won't betray your openness and hurt you? How can you give your heart to someone without trusting him or her not to break it? If you don't feel trust, you risk living in ways that focus on protecting yourself—building a barricade around your heart, not letting anyone come close to you—which can lead to a lonely, solitary existence.

But trust doesn't exist in a vacuum. Trust in a relationship is paramount, but you can't feel complete trust unless you sense that your willingness to trust is justified. And what would prompt this sense of confidence?

Well, both you and your partner must be committed to the truth. You have to establish a pattern in which each of you assumes that the other person's words are fundamentally truthful. How can a couple build confidence and trust without a fundamental, consistent pattern of both partners telling the truth? If your commitment to the truth is inconsistent—not necessarily because you lie all the time, but because you lie often enough that your partner can't feel confident in what he or she is hearing—then you can't build trust. It's for this reason that violating the Eighth Commandment—"You shall not lie"—is a big part of many relationship problems.

Even seemingly minor lies can do major damage to a marriage. It's a problem that requires a lot of attention, for we are accustomed to fibbing without thinking much about it. We have even created the concept of "the little white lie" to make ourselves feel all right when we lie.

Lying isn't just a bad habit; it's a long-term burden. Many people carry a lifetime of lies into their relationships—a legacy that can harm or even destroy a marriage. I'm not referring only to major lies and betrayals—the shocking issues that prompt endless discussions on daytime talk shows: infidelity, personal secrets, and all the rest. Even those "little white lies" that we tend to make habitual can cause severe damage to our relationships. With time, these little white lies often grow bigger and darker. In a marriage, especially, a pattern of habitual lying can destroy the couple's trust and confidence in each other. I've seen this phenomenon far too many times to consider it routine and harmless.

HONESTY IN CRISIS

There's no question that the core issue of honesty in a couple's relationship is the partners' "radical openness" to each other. It's not just a question of saying words that are factually true; it's also a matter of each person being openhearted and attentive to what the other thinks and feels. A tall order? No doubt about it. But this is the reality of what's involved in a healthy relationship.

It's inevitable that each of us falls short in our various relationships. It's inevitable, too, that spouses fall short in their interactions within a marriage. That's just part of being human. We are fallible creatures. One of the reasons that a man and a woman unite in marriage is to support each other, to help each other develop, and to encourage each other throughout their earthly life. Don't beat yourself up because of day-to-day shortcomings; these are all part of how you'll learn and grow. But what about really serious shortcomings in a couple's honesty? What about problems that cause not just frustrations or irritations, but major relationship trouble? Sometimes couples fall short in ways that do grievous harm to each other—or to the relationship itself. Sometimes a crisis develops in a couple's ability to be honest.

I talk with a lot of unmarried couples about the vows they're going to take, about the commitment they're making when they get married, and all of them accept the fact that marriage is a big deal. Unfortunately, my experience shows me another side of the picture as well. I receive about five thousand letters a week through my newspaper column, and I'd say that 70 percent of them have to do some sort of marital dysfunction. A large percentage of those—80 or 90 percent—involve a wife stating, "My husband has cheated on me."

What does this situation tell us? There's a sad contradiction here. Although a great majority of people say they grasp the words "all the days of our lives," a lot of people aren't keeping their half of the bargain. I speak with these couples about what these words really mean. Now, the secular perception of marriage is that it's an agreement between two people who come together and say, "We agree to live together in this way. If things don't work out and we need to break this paper agreement, we'll get divorced." But in the Catholic perception of the sacrament, you get married in the Church because you understand that as a human being, you lack the strength to keep your commitment all the days of your lives, so you're requesting God's help. The sacrament exists to give you the grace to help you fulfill the radical commitment you're making. Two people become one forever. They don't enter into an ordinary agreement—they enter into a *covenant*. A covenant means it's not just two people involved; there's a third party in on the deal, too: God. The covenant is an agreement you make in the presence of God; there *is* a legal part, but there's a stronger part—the sacramental part—and that's why a Church marriage is such a big deal to Christians of all denominations.

So when someone feels that his or her relationship was betrayed, that phrase "all the days of my life" becomes a big problem. Why? Because you feel, *Wait a minute, I went into this relationship thinking that he understood that we're both going to do everything possible to be together, and now he's doing something else.* So betrayal creates a huge violation. Someone hasn't kept his or her part of the deal. This is what I mean about honesty not just as *speaking words* but as *living a commitment*.

The aspects of honesty that I believe cause the most severe relationship troubles are *jealousy, greed*, and *infidelity*. It's true that smaller-scale forms of dishonesty can cause damage, too. As I mentioned earlier, even a pattern of "little white lies" can undercut a lot of the trust and confidence within a marriage. But jealousy, greed, and infidelity do the most severe damage, so I'd now like to consider those problems and how you can avoid them. Following this discussion, Chapter 9 will explain how you can cope with these issues in practical ways.

JEALOUSY

I recently spoke with Sander and Alicia, who are engaged and soon to be married. Sander works in one city; Alicia works in another. They've had a long-distance relationship for many years. In several important ways they're a happy couple. But Alicia claims that she can't trust Sander because several of his ex-girlfriends live in his city, and his work involves interacting with other women as well.

Sander responds to these concerns by saying, "True, they're in the area, and now and then I interact with women at work, but I don't mess around with anyone. Alicia is my girlfriend. She's the only one I care about."

Alicia's response: "I don't care. I can't deal with it."

This is a troubling situation—one that won't improve until Alicia can put her concerns aside and trust her fiancé. If she doesn't, I predict that her jealousy will corrode this couple's relationship.

Jealousy is a manifestation of one person's insecurity and lack of trust in the other. It can become an obsessive, even sick part of a relationship. Few behaviors can be as damaging as jealousy, especially in the long run. A common issue is jealousy over previous relationships—even relationships that are now long past. Jealousy is also common in relationships between couples who are trying hard to rebuild their marriage following one spouse's extramarital affair.

Why is jealousy such a problem? Generally, it's because one or both partners insist on living in the past, and this fixation limits their ability to grow together and move forward. This situation is unfortunate. Without trust, a lasting, mature, and happy relationship can't survive. Jealousy can suffocate good feelings that are trying to grow and thrive in a relationship.

Sometimes the situation isn't even the "other woman" or "other man" scenarios that come to mind when we think of marital jealousy. I know a couple in which the wife is incredibly jealous of her husband's interactions with *anybody*—even his childhood male friends. Susana is also jealous of her husband Pete's interactions with his coworkers and clients at the veterinary practice where he works. She is fundamentally insecure about his interactions with *everybody*. I often wonder if Pete feels suffocated by his wife's suspicions of his every move. Yet far from protesting, Pete has actually made further concessions to his wife's jealousy. Is this response a sign of healthy flexibility? Maybe—but I doubt it. This is not a healthy situation! I worry that Pete will gradually feel so constricted by his wife's jealousy that his resentment will build and build until it explodes. Or else the couple's world will shrink until this marriage becomes nothing more than two unhappy people trapped together.

I've also heard about cases where the man is jealous of his wife's girlfriends from college—how they go out to lunch, how they talk so intimately, how they have such a great time together. It's not that he suspects his wife of any homosexual involvement—far from it. But he feels envious of the good time that these women have when they're together. Perhaps he fears that his wife prefers their company to his own. I don't know. I do believe, however, that such expressions of jealousy are a troubling symptom of mistrust in the marriage, and jealousy hints at further problems down the line.

Here's how I see it. There's a healthy type of jealousy in a relationship—the jealousy in which you insist on an exclusive relationship with the person you love. That's understandable. That's not a sick type of jealousy; it's a normal type of jealousy. That's a sense of mutual possession: "You belong to me and I belong to you." There has to be a certain amount of mutual belonging in a marriage, because it is, after all, an exclusive relationship.

But the other type of jealousy—the troubling kind—is an insecure lack of trust, a lack of confidence in the other person. This kind is always destructive. Why? Because the jealous partner puts the other person in a place where he or she never feels free. The situation can end up feeling claustrophobic. This leaves the other person feeling not at liberty to be him- or herself or to relate to other people. It also implies a kind of weakness in the marital bond, and that's not a good feeling. When jealousy enters a relationship, the jealous partner will inspire a sense of fear in the other person, who will wonder, *Is she watching me? Does she think I'm doing something inappropriate?* When fear is part of the equation, there's a big problem. In marriage as in many other situations, fear isn't a good motivating factor—or, if it motivates at all, it's a *negative* factor. When you're motivated by fear, you're headed for trouble.

If you love someone and you give yourself to that person out of love, you should feel trust in the love you share. No one wants to be tied down by a compulsively jealous person who says you can't do anything with anyone else. There are all kinds of extremes—from the man who won't allow his wife to leave the home because some other man might look at her, to the woman who goes through her husband's cell phone record to make sure he hasn't received any phone calls from any other women. E-mail is a big thing now, and sometimes people suspiciously review each other's messages. When I hear about that sort of obsession, I have to wonder where the trust is. Where is the privacy? Spouses should be able to treat each other as adults, not as potential criminals who need to be monitored. If you have reason to believe that your partner is behaving in ways that violate the spirit of your marriage, you should openly discuss your concerns. If you have no reason to feel that something is amiss, you should honor the trust that's the foundation of your relationship.

How should you deal with jealousy if "the green-eyed monster" shows up in your marriage? Chapter 9 will offer a variety of suggestions to help you tame this beast.

First, though, let's have a look at another issue that complicates honesty for many couples.

GREED
"HE WHO DIES WITH THE MOST TOYS, WINS"

This famous bumper sticker has always troubled me deeply. First of all, didn't anyone tell "the guy with the most toys" that he couldn't take all those toys with him? But in addition, the bumper sticker's attitude bothers me because it makes a joke of a worrisome aspect of our culture: our obsessions with acquiring things, power, wealth, and status. In short, it offers a kind of humorous approval of greed—the desire to acquire more stuff than we really need. It may seem funny, but greed can be a destructive force in our lives.

I believe that we live in an age of addiction. All kinds of addictions abound—most obviously addictions to alcohol, drugs, and other substances. But there are other addictions, too, including addiction to possessions, money, power, sex, and status. All of these addictions are essentially forms of greed. Why? Because we desire both material and nonmaterial "stuff." We want more money, more power, more sex, more status. We become focused on the acquisition of these things. Why, you ask, are these goals a problem? Shouldn't we aspire to success? Shouldn't we strive for comfort? Sure, success and comfort are worthy aspirations. However, I believe we run into trouble when success and comfort become our primary goals—when we make more stuff a higher priority than family, friends, health, compassion, love, and wisdom. When greed takes over our lives, we're not free. In fact, greed can burden us, distract us, and separate us from the people we love.

The sad result of greed is self-deception. The greedy person believes the solution to life's problems lies in having more stuff—and nothing could be further from the truth. We human beings were not created to be greedy. As a matter of fact, our true nature is really to be generous and giving, not selfish and hoarding. If we don't accept our inherent generosity, it's difficult for us to live well or find happiness. But when we learn to give generously, we let go of greed and learn to live beyond ourselves. By contrast, greed traps us inside ourselves, and we have little time to value others—including, sadly, the people we love the most.

HOW DOES GREED AFFECT RELATIONSHIPS?

You may be wondering what greed has to do with honesty and with a couple's relationship. The short answer: a lot. The reason is that many couples focus on acquiring stuff rather than attending to each other. It's not hard to imagine why. We all face a constant onslaught of advertising, media propaganda, and social pressure to acquire more and more things. It's central to our consumer culture. Greed ends up being a distraction from the interpersonal issues that should concern us most, such as spending time with the people we love and responding to their needs for attention and affection. It tends to constrict our openness to others; it shuts the door to the sacred center and keeps out even the people we care about. Here are two brief examples.

Sheldon, who is an accountant, likes to buy and sell stocks online. It's an easy way to pick up some extra cash, and he can do it in his spare time after work. Sheldon sees his part-time trading as a hobby that's not only harmless but positive, since his net gains will benefit his family's bottom line. But what started as an intermittent pastime has become more and more engrossing. An occasional hour spent at the computer after dinner quickly expanded into a whole evening's commitment. Sheldon's wife, Mindy, soon grew frustrated with the situation. Her husband wasn't available to help out in childcare activities, and he ignored her even after the couple's kids went to bed. Was there something intrinsically wrong with this man's eagerness to play the market? No. But his growing desire to "hit it big" quickly grew disruptive. Sheldon's obsession with online trading displaced his interest in his kids, his commitment to family activities, his domestic duties, and his wife's desire for intimacy. This otherwise good-hearted husband's eagerness for material well-being had become distorted and potentially destructive.

What I see happening to a woman I'll call "Norma" is a little different but risks similar emotional and marital damages. Norma, a twenty-six-year-old homemaker, loves to shop. This avocation is common these days—many people adopt the motto, "When the going gets tough, the tough go shopping." But Norma's shopping sprees are a problem. Her husband, Jesse, works as a lineman for the local electric company. He earns a decent salary, and the couple has a pleasant suburban house and a comfortable life, but Jesse's paychecks don't leave them with a huge amount of discretionary income. Unfortunately, Norma's frequent trips to the mall to purchase clothes, furniture, high-tech appliances, jewelry, and all kinds of other consumer goods have "maxed out" the couple's credit cards, made it difficult to pay their monthly bills, and created a lot of stress between them.

What complicates matters is that many couples aren't on the same page about the place of possessions and wealth in their married life: How should they share what they have? How should they distinguish between what is necessary and what is a luxury? It's not necessarily that one person is more materialistic than the other. Rather, the issue is that because we live in such a consumerist culture, there's often a disparity between the spouses regarding what they really need and what they want.

This issue can become a problem because, as our society places more and more importance on the size and price of our toys, the pressure rises in the relationship. If, for example, a man gives his fiancée many gifts—starting with a huge engagement ring—there's going to be a material value placed on the love that one partner feels for the other. It's almost as if *more stuff* equals *more love*. Her fiancé provides her with many things, so that means he loves her a lot, right? By this logic, providing her with fewer things—even if he's actually more affectionate, more loyal, more trusting, more emotionally giving—means that he must love her less. Can you see what I'm suggesting? Our relationships become warped, not based on *how much we love* but on *how much things cost*.

In my experience, the couples with the best marriages are the ones who don't place material wealth high on their priority list. Instead, they value the nontangible aspects of their relationship. Unfortunately, I've found that many young people in today's society feel they have to have a lot more stuff to be happy. This concept is so foreign to me! Even before I became a priest, I didn't need or want a lot of things. Maybe this attitude was simply a result of my upbringing. My parents had a very happy, complete marriage with very few *things*. For instance, my father had a 1969 VW Bug that he bought a few months after I was born. It's the same car I drove when I was a teenager. All of my father's coworkers had nice, brand-new sports cars. He was their boss, and they'd ask him, "Why do you drive such a beat-up old car?" And he'd answer, "Because it's good enough. It drives perfectly fine." He was comfortable with it. He didn't need a fancy car to be happy. That's the message I received as a child. So when I look at the situation now, I wonder to myself, Why is it that that so many of my peers seem to equate their happiness with the number and expense of possessions?

Frankly, I find material stuff a big distraction for relationships today. Many couples struggle with this issue. Sometimes both partners want more and more and more stuff, and their cravings burden the marriage because they're up to their eyebrows in debt. Or else there may be a big disparity within the couple, with one spouse wanting more stuff than the other, or else one of them wondering if the gifts they give each other signify enough affection: "I sure wish she'd given me a better birthday present. . . . I wonder if she really loves me."

Just as I'll offer some suggestions for dealing with jealousy, I'll suggest ways for addressing greed when it's complicating your marriage. But we have a final aspect of honesty to explore before we proceed to the nuts-and-bolts issues in Chapter 9.

INFIDELITY

I was sitting on a plane right before takeoff. As usual, I'd booked a window seat—a great place to read and have some rare moments of time to myself. Then a middle-aged man sat down near me in the aisle seat. No problem. I figured we'd exchange a few pleasantries, then settle in for the flight and read, doze, or watch the movie. But this time, to my great surprise, the man turned to me and said, "Father, I'm not Catholic, but I need to talk with you. I know you'll understand."

"Sure," I replied, "what's on your mind?"

Then, before he could say another word, the man began to sob. He cried like a child and couldn't get another word out. Well-dressed in a business suit, he looked like a professional—a lawyer, a businessman, maybe a doctor—certainly the type of person who seemed to have his life totally together. But there he was, breaking down next to me while I waited for him to be able to speak.

At last he said, "Father, I just found out that my wife of thirty years has been unfaithful to me." He was emotionally destroyed, to say the least. "I need to tell you about it."

We spoke for the remainder of the flight, and I promised to pray so that his marriage could be restored to full health.

Unfortunately, I hear this kind of story all too often. Infidelity in marriage has certainly reached epidemic proportions. In the letters I receive daily through my columns and on my radio and television shows, the issue of infidelity comes up time after time. Helping couples cope with the aftermath of infidelity is, in fact, one of the hardest and most wrenching things that I deal with as a pastor. I repeatedly end up confronting two very wounded people. One spouse feels betrayed, while the other feels that he or she has let down the couple. There's a great sense of insecurity. The unfaithful spouse wonders, "Will she forgive me?" or "Will he be able to get over it?" The other spouse wonders, "Can I trust him?" Both wonder, "Will our marriage ever be the same?" It's a huge burden for both of them. And it's a terrible problem, since infidelity betrays the honesty and respect that a couple has promised to create between them from the moment they take their marriage vows.

I believe that few human disloyalties affect people so intensely as infidelity in marriage. It's truly at the top of the list of betrayals. And if my experience as a confessor is any indication, I'd say that committing infidelity is a sin that prompts many people to feel deeply ashamed. Many can't even admit to it except by stating what they've done in a roundabout way: "I have violated the Sixth Commandment." They can't force themselves to say the words: "I have committed adultery." In the meantime, the victim of infidelity—the loyal wife or husband—also suffers greatly, for his or her mate's dishonesty makes it difficult to regain a sense of trust. The wronged partner may also suffer from low self-esteem, and often blames him- or herself for the other partner's behavior. In short, the pain caused by infidelity leads to real and severe wounds for both spouses.

INFIDELITY—AN "EQUAL-OPPORTUNITY" BETRAYAL?

There was a time when men had a monopoly on infidelity; very few women had the time to involve themselves in this activity. With the changing roles in our society, however, and with more and more women working outside the home, we now have achieved "equal rights" in this sinful arena as in many others. Cause for celebration? I don't think so! It's interesting, though, that men and women seem to commit adultery for somewhat different reasons.

For many men, infidelity is a result of sexual desire or a craving for adventure. It begins in the mind with a fantasy. Unfaithful men often justify their infidelity by stating that they'd never actually *leave* their wife and children—they love their spouse too much, and they want to be a good husband and father. So why were they unfaithful in the first place? That's a tough question to answer. Some men don't regard infidelity as a problem if no one discovers it. This situation reflects an immature attitude that "you're not guilty unless you get caught." The guy just doesn't consider it a huge issue. When the problem gets discovered, though, and when his wife feels hurt and angry—well, that certainly catches the man's attention. Getting caught usually makes the male see that he's wounding the relationship. There's often a huge burden of guilt on the unfaithful party's shoulders. The unfaithful party may say, "I don't want to lose my wife. I don't want to wreck my marriage. What can I do? How can I convince her that I love her?"

Women, on the other hand, seem to have a somewhat different experience of infidelity. When a woman commits adultery, she has often sought the understanding, compassion, and even physical affection that she lacks at home. An indifferent, dismissive, or abusive husband can prompt his wife to look for affection outside the marriage. Some wives even feel that they had no recourse, as they felt they were starving to death emotionally and needed to find sustenance. When caught having an affair, they may respond defensively about the situation and claim that their actions were a result of desperation. I don't believe that what they do is justified, but it's probably true that some reach out to other men as a kind of rebellion against an indifferent husband.

A wife's infidelity usually shatters the male ego. In my opinion, the female ego is much more capable of handling infidelity. The male ego is damaged because the husband usually wonders if someone else can satisfy his wife better in the bedroom than he can. Perhaps for men it's primarily a sexual issue; maybe it's a self-identity issue; maybe it's a protectiveness issue. But there's definitely something in the male ego that says, *Maybe I'm not man enough for her.* Their wives' infidelity becomes a personal commentary on them. Men feel very deeply wounded by infidelity, and they have a much harder time moving on than many wives do when they've been the victim.

Women who are the victims of infidelity don't usually perceive the situation as men do. They don't take their husband's infidelity as much as a commentary on their own sexuality. They're probably furious, but they're more likely to ask, "Why did he betray me?" or "What does he see in that woman?" or "What did she do to get him going?" Also, women more often than men have had ongoing suspicions about infidelity. I believe that women are much more likely to discover a husband's infidelity than a man is likely to discover his wife's infidelity. Many wives have an intuitive sense that something is amiss; they often have a much greater sense of what is going on in interactions between people, and they often pick up cues that men don't even notice.

Both partners often want to speak to a confidant, whether it be a family member, a minister of the Church, a counselor, a priest, or a therapist. Most often what they're seeking is a way to ease this pain they're feeling. Usually, the other partner has found out, the infidelity has been discovered, and now both are in pain and both of them are looking for help together. And when they're both there, the effort to deal with the issue can begin.

Infidelity is one of the most difficult problems that any couple can face. It's the result of drastic deficiencies of honesty between the partners, and it almost always creates a legacy of further distrust, pain, resentment, and suspicion that is hard to heal. But it's a big mistake to assume that *not* addressing the problem will somehow be better than tackling these tough issues. You really have no good alternative but to face reality, wrestle with your problems, and heal your wounds as well as possible.

OTHER KINDS OF INFIDELITY

Before we address how to solve these problems, I'd like to touch on issues different from what we might call "traditional" infidelity—that is, one spouse having an affair with a lover.

Unfortunately, modern culture presents a growing number and variety of sexual temptations that some people find appealing, among them various sorts of pornography. Strip clubs and other kinds of sex clubs are one example of this phenomenon. Another involves sex-oriented media, such as pornographic videos and DVDs. The most recent phenomenon is Internet porn—X-rated Web sites oriented toward photos, video clips, or real-time interactions with other people online. All of these kinds of porn have a primarily male audience. The sad thing about all of them is that they can damage a couple's intimacy, since the husband may end up leading a fantasy life that's separate from the reality of his marriage. He may feel that it's easier for him to deal with the illusions on the computer screen or the TV screen than to interact with the real human being who's waiting for him in the next room. He may find it more exciting to watch a woman dance nude at a club than to make love with his own wife. All of these activities can both reflect and contribute to marital dissatisfaction and sexual dysfunction. I've seen some men reach such a state of obsession that they just can't disengage from the computer and relate to their wives.

Is what I've described something we could call infidelity? Well, maybe not in the most traditional sense. It's obviously not adultery with another woman. I believe, however, that sex clubs, DVDs, and Internet porn are a *kind* of infidelity. When a man takes a vow "to forsake all others," the word *others* refers primarily to living, breathing human beings. But if he ignores his wife in favor of fantasy women—whether in the form of strippers, pornographic movies, downloaded photo files, video clips, or online chat with anonymous strangers—I think it's clear that he's shifting his loyalty from his wife to something else. In this sense he is violating the letter of his vow to be faithful. He's certainly violating the spirit of his vow "to have and to hold" and, above all, to cherish, value, and love the woman he married because she is the center of his life.

What happens when a couple faces this kind of situation? Usually it's the wife who forces the issue. Men rarely come for help for a sexual addiction. The wife usually asks for help when she has discovered what's going on. One woman told me, "My husband spends three hours a night looking at those Web sites, but he won't even come and kiss me good night." Other wives discover that their husbands are going out to sex clubs. These are the sorts of events that can trigger the crisis.

What should the couple do if the husband is damaging the marriage through a sexual addiction—either to a "traditional" pastime such as going to strip clubs or to a newer activity, such as Internet pornography? How should the wife respond? What if the husband seems incapable of responding to his wife's entreaties for change?

The first step is to determine what type of behavior has occurred. All of the behaviors I've described are troubling and damaging to a marriage, but some of these behaviors are even worse than others. A husband who visits prostitutes is engaged in a far more hazardous behavior than one who visits online porn sites, given the risk of bringing home HIV or some other sexually transmitted disease.

Next, you need to clarify whether the situation occurred once, a number of times, or on an ongoing basis. The frequency and recurrence of such behavior makes a difference, since it may suggest how much the husband has distanced himself from his marriage. The more often he has engaged in this behavior, the bigger the problem the couple faces.

Also, it's important to find out whether the husband can accept that his behavior is a problem. Can he admit that he's done something that will damage his relationship? Or does he insist on denying the whole situation? His acceptance of his problem is crucial.

Alexa, for instance, had been married to Robert for thirty-five years, and they had several children together. It turns out that Robert had been unfaithful to her by going to prostitutes over a period of many years. Alexa found out about her husband's betrayals through friends and family members. But Robert never, ever admitted it. He denied everything. So what can she do? Confronting him over and over never made a difference. And if he can't even admit to what he has done, there's very little that his wife can do to make him change. The same holds true for other sorts of sexual behavior—whether it's a matter of hiding in a room and watching pornographic videos, staying up late each night visiting Web sites, or going out alone to sex clubs.

What if a husband can admit that he's got a problem? What if he can say, "Okay, I know I've done something that hurts you. I know that's not good, and I'm deeply sorry. I'm willing to stop. I'm willing to seek counseling and get control of myself." That's an entirely different situation. With the husband's acceptance that he's got a problem, he's opening up to the possibility of communication and the possibility of change.

*   *   *

All of these situations—jealousy, greed, and infidelity—reveal something out of balance in a couple's honesty. All of them can produce crises that may threaten the integrity and viability of a marriage.

So how should you respond if you face one or more of these crises?

That's the question we'll explore next.

Chapter 9

How to Solve Honesty Problems

I believe that honesty isn't just a fundamental respect for truth. It's also a day-to-day expression of that respect. Your honesty—or lack of honesty—creates the context for how you respond to the world and interact with the people in it. If you believe that honesty is a noble ideal to strive for but you ignore, bend, or violate the truth, you'll damage your relationships with others. In particular, you'll damage the relationship that's most central to your life—the relationship with your spouse.

I encounter many couples with honesty problems. Sometimes the problems are relatively minor, such as a tendency to fib over small matters (forgetting to pick up the dry cleaning, claiming to be stuck in traffic). Sometimes the problems are severe, such as committing adultery. In these, and many instances that fall between the two extremes, husbands and wives wrestle with how to be honest and stay honest with each other. Dealing with honesty is, in fact, one of the ongoing issues that all couples face.

I see couples facing two basic kinds of honesty problems. One is keeping honesty strong within a marriage. The other is dealing with specific honesty problems that develop because of jealousy, greed, and infidelity. Here are some ways to solve each of these kinds of problems.

HOW TO STRENGTHEN HONESTY

Although we'll discuss these specific topics in this chapter, I want to comment first on how you can strengthen your overall honesty as a couple.

Task #1
Practice Openness

Even if you're honest on a day-to-day basis, I believe that it's important to *practice* maintaining a fundamental openness to your spouse. What I'm calling "openness" goes beyond the specific facts of what you say. Openness is the quality of having an open mind and an open heart. If you're open in this sense, you are available to your spouse—ready to hear about his or her worries, troubles, and hurts, as well as his or her interests, enthusiasms, and delights. You're willing to make your spouse's concerns your own. You're ready to cherish your husband or wife despite his or her imperfections and limitations. Openness of these sorts is a type of honesty because it honors what matters most: the love and warmth you share with this other person.

Part of what matters about openness-as-honesty is that it goes beyond—but also energizes—factual honesty. Openness transcends a focus on facts alone. Let's say that a wife asks her husband, "Honey, does this dress make me look fat?" His thoughtful answers—"I think the other outfit is a lot sexier," or "You look absolutely wonderful"—may be more "honest" than saying, "Yeah, a little," because it answers the hidden question she's really asking: *Do you still find me attractive?* It honors the love and warmth of the couple's relationship. Similarly, if a husband asks his wife, "Don't I look a lot more buff now that I'm working out twice a week?" she could answer, "Not really." But even if he's still more of a chunk than a hunk, her positive response is more openhearted and thus more able to honor the relationship.

And our first task is to practice openness. How? Here are some suggestions:

Stay mindful of each other. It's easy for spouses to lose track of each other as the center of each other's lives. All the daily tasks and obligations tend to blur the vividness of this other person you love—to diminish the intensity of what you feel. If you can stay aware of each other, though, you've already done half the task of practicing openness.

Set aside time together. Creating a brief "haven" for just the two of you will help you honor and focus on each other. What I'm suggesting can be simply a quiet time together—a walk in the park, a brief interval in the backyard, or twenty minutes of sharing coffee at the kitchen table. No matter what the setting, time together gives each partner a chance to hear what's on the other's mind. Share your feelings, dreams, concerns, or needs. Raise issues you've had no time to discuss. Tell each other thank you for all you're doing for each other and your family.

Express disagreements openly rather than in veiled ways. All couples experience conflicts. All couples have differences of opinion. All couples must cope with frustrations, miscues, and misunderstandings. Something that makes a major difference in couples' success or failure is whether they can address the issues honestly rather than through roundabout, veiled, or sneaky ways. I'm not talking now about "telling the truth" versus "telling a lie." What I'm referring to is the tendency of some spouses to face issues directly, while others can't even look each other in the eye about even the most minor matters. Resorting to sarcasm, hidden threats, or "subliminal advertising" aren't good ways to solve problems together. It's more productive to put your cards on the table, sort out whatever concerns you, and stay open to possible solutions.

Learn new forms of openness. Perhaps you like the *idea* of openness, but you're not sure exactly how to achieve it. Fair enough. Marriage involves lifelong learning, so there's no reason for you to know everything from the start. But you can acquire skills in a marriage just as in any other realm of life. Part of that openness is precisely this willingness to learn. Learn from whom? Well, any number of therapists, pastoral counselors, and marriage workshop leaders can help guide you toward new insights and skills. I'll have more to say about this topic in Path Five—Communicate.

Task #2
Eradicate Little White Lies

You're late getting home because you stopped at a store to buy some clothes on sale—but you call your husband and say you're stuck in traffic. Or you forget to buy some ingredients for dinner, but you tell your wife the store was out of stock. It's so easy to tell little white lies! No harm done, right? Well, I'm not so sure. Maybe these lies aren't so terrible one by one, but they're harmful anyway—a slippery slope that can do other kinds of damage in the long run. Even small lies chip away at the fundamental honesty that should be central within a relationship.

If you decide you'll eradicate little white lies, what's the best way to do so? My recommendations:

Be consistent. If you can avoid lying *at all*, you avoid the slippery slope altogether. Consistency will help you avoid the temptation to lie a little here, a little there, until the situation gets out of control. You may not make your marriage a "lie-free zone" overnight, but striving for consistent honesty is a crucial goal.

Work together. Sometimes a couple makes a silent pact to play loose with the truth. "If he [or she] can fib," one spouse may decide, "then I have a right to lie, too." Fair enough? Not really—because making lying an equal-opportunity habit just makes things worse. A better idea: work together to be honest. Make a commitment that you'll *both* tell the truth.

Be supportive as you strive for honesty. Oddly, it's tempting to punish your spouse for telling the truth. Let's say that a husband admits that the store wasn't really out of those ingredients—he just forgot to go shopping. If his wife berates him ("I knew it! You *never* remember to buy what I ask you to!"), he's less likely to be honest in the future. Fibbing will save him the trouble of getting scolded. If you're supportive of each other, though, you're more likely to encourage future honesty. However, note that both partners have to commit themselves to accepting these admissions. You can't use them to start a battle ("You're always late," "You're so irresponsible," and so forth).

Now let's look at ways of addressing the specific honesty problems—the "Big Three" we discussed in Chapter 8.

HOW TO DEAL WITH JEALOUSY

Are you dealing with jealousy in your relationship? If so, I recommend that you face the issue and deal with it as soon as possible by undertaking these tasks:

Task #1
Identify the Sources of Jealousy

When I counsel couples who are struggling with jealousy, I try to help them identify any possible behaviors that might justify this attitude. I ask,

"Do you have a *reason* to be jealous? And if you do, what are those reasons?" Many times what I hear is that in the past, one partner has violated the other's trust. And if violations of trust have occurred, the jealous person has a tendency to wonder, "Is he being truthful? Is he being straightforward with me?" Once burned, twice careful. This situation means that the couple does, in fact, have issues to work through. A deeper dialogue may be important—perhaps with a therapist or a pastoral counselor present as a guide.

Once you identify the sources of jealousy, you have to move into new territory: the territory of trust.

For the person who is the object of jealousy, this means making sure that you never give your partner a new reason to be jealous. You have to "walk the straight and narrow path" to reestablish trust.

For the jealous person, the goal is to realize how much harm he or she is doing to the relationship by being so jealous. Even though you've entered a relationship that is exclusive, you both still need a certain amount of freedom—a certain amount of room to grow and to develop and to be yourself.

Task #2
Grasp the Damage That Jealousy Can Do

If you're coping with jealousy, you need to grasp as soon as possible that this emotion will damage your relationship in the long term. Jealousy can't do anything good for their relationship. You're dealing with a demon—what Shakespeare called "the green-eyed monster." This monster can attack and even devour your whole relationship if you allow it to. So if you don't deal with it head-on, jealousy can ultimately ruin what you and your partner are trying to build together. Do you realize that this attitude demonstrates that you don't have a very mature relationship? Because when you have a mature relationship, there's a sense of freedom, of trust, of willingness to let the other person *be*. Let your spouse develop. Otherwise you're clinging to a rather adolescent attitude.

Here's another important question that you should ask yourself: Does the person you've married belong to you as a *thing you own*? Or is he or she a *gift you've received*? Your husband or wife is autonomous—a separate person. If you perceive the other person as a thing—an object you own—it's not only a false assumption, it also suffocates the other person.

Think back to a time when you felt jealous and expressed how you felt to your spouse. Now answer these questions about what resulted from that situation:

- How did your partner react?

- What was the outcome of the situation?

- Looking back now, did you have cause for jealousy?

- What were the circumstances?

- Can you see now how you might have misinterpreted the situation?

- Did your expression of jealousy strengthen your relationship—or weaken it?

- Did your expression of jealousy deepen communication between you and your partner—or make it more likely that he or she would hold back from you?

As you think over the answers to these questions, I think you'll probably agree that your expression of jealousy probably had the opposite effect from what you may have intended or desired. Instead of fostering closeness, it probably became a wedge that drove you and your spouse apart. Instead of encouraging your partner to confide in you, it probably prompted him or her to hold back from you. Jealousy isn't a force that strengthens a couple's relationship. On the contrary, it's often a "solvent" that loosens the ties between the partners.

Task #3
Learn to Deal with Jealousy

Next, you need to face jealousy head-on and deal with it. This task involves two separate actions—one for the jealous spouse, another for the spouse who is the object of jealousy.

If you are the jealous spouse . . . Next time you feel that green-eyed monster rear its ugly head, stop and ask yourself the following questions:

- ∽ Why am I feeling this way? What am I afraid of?

- ∽ Has my partner given me a reason to fear this?

- ∽ Could there be another explanation for his/her behavior?

- ∽ Are there ways I can cope with my uncertainties that are better than subjecting my partner to jealousy?

Answering these questions will help you widen the scope of your insights so that you don't fall into habitual jealousy.

If you're dealing with a jealous spouse, ask yourself these questions the next time you're confronted by jealousy and accusations:

- ∽ Why would my spouse feel this way? What is he/she afraid of?

- ∽ Did I do anything to contribute to this fear?

∽ What can I do to ease this fear in the future?

∽ Are there ways we can discuss the situation so that we can diminish the risk of my partner's habitual jealousy?

Here again, the goal is to widen your understanding of the situation and avoid reflexive responses that can decrease your compassion.

Task #4
Consider the Possibility that Jealousy Is Part of a Bigger Problem

---

Sometimes jealousy can be part of what's called *obsessive-compulsive disorder* (OCD). This disorder can be a serious mental health problem—a disorder in which obsessive thoughts and/or compulsive behaviors plague you. An example of this would be a husband who can't stop obsessing over his wife's whereabouts and activities, or who compulsively tracks her movements, phone calls, or e-mail. Sometimes OCD is the result of personal trauma in the past. There may also be a biochemical aspect to the disorder.

If you believe that you (or your spouse) may be suffering from OCD, I urge you to seek professional mental health counseling. This disorder isn't a situation that should cause you feelings of shame; it's a genuine health problem, not a moral failing. It isn't your fault. But it is a situation that you can't ignore, and you must address it as soon as possible. Speak with your physician or call a referral service to find a mental health professional, or else raise the issue with your pastor.

HOW TO DEAL WITH GREED

Now let's turn to greed—an issue that many couples face in our materialistic culture. Here are some tasks that may prove challenging in the short run but helpful in the long run.

Task #1
Take Stock of Wants vs. Needs

I often ask couples, "Are you satisfied with who you are and what you have? Or are you looking for satisfaction in *things*?"

Wanting more and more and more is often an attempt to fill a sense of emotional or spiritual emptiness. You have to have so much stuff to feel fulfilled! If that's the case, I believe you're trying to fill a void that really can't be filled with things. Some people feel empty because of psychological wounds—a craving for love or a lack of self-esteem. But even people whose emotional needs have been met may feel empty anyway. Deep within each of us is a God-shaped void that only God can fill. But out of confusion or stubbornness, many people look in the wrong places for relief from emptiness. Instead of filling the void with relationships—relationships with a loving spouse, with family, with God—they try to fill it with things. Will that effort be successful? No way. You'll waste your time. You'll just crave more and more and more.

What would be a better approach? I recommend that you take stock of *needs* vs. *wants*. Do you need a house or an apartment? That's fair enough—you need a good, safe place to grow as a couple and raise your children. Do you need a ten-thousand-square-foot mansion with a pool, a three-car garage, and a private tennis court? I don't think so. That's a want, not a need. The same probably holds true for the car you need vs.

the one you want, the clothes you need vs. the ones you want, the vacation you need vs. the one you want—and so on. You get the picture. If you can clarify these issues, you'll ease a lot of stress not only on your family budget but also on your marriage itself.

Task #2
Communicate About These Issues

Are you and your spouse on the same page about material things? Some couples are; some aren't. Compare what your expectations are. Clarify your goals. Here are some of the questions you should ask yourselves and discuss:

- What material goods do you really need?

- What material goods do you *want* but don't necessarily *need* (that is, things that may be luxuries)?

- What makes you happy?

- What type of life do you want together?

- What are your expectations about material wealth?

- What do you consider to be an adequate income to meet your personal and family needs?

- What are your assumptions about which one of you—or whether both of you—will support your family?

- What are your assumptions about whether you should have individual or joint checking accounts (or both)?

- What are your assumptions about the assets and/or debts that each of you brings (or has brought) to your marriage?

- What are your goals in terms of possessions?

- What are your plans or methods for making financial decisions together?

- What are your goals regarding saving money vs. having money available to spend?

These and other questions are critical as starting points for discussions about financial issues and preferences about material possessions.

Task #3
Shift to Nonmaterial Ways of Expressing Yourself

The next time you feel that you should go out and buy your spouse an expensive gift to prove your love, do something nonmaterial—or at least nonconsumerist—instead. Write a letter expressing your love and leave it on his pillow. Draw her a goofy little cartoon. Give a gift of some flowers from your own garden. Tell her something about her that delights you, amuses you, or makes you happy. These are simple but priceless gifts. You can discover or create many nonmaterial gifts you can share with your spouse. These will have a much greater long-term impact on your marriage than if you buy a thousand-dollar purse or watch. If you have to give something that's a material object, make it yourself instead of buying it. A gift from your heart matters far more than something that comes from a shop. You can learn how to do that for each other.

HOW TO DEAL WITH INFIDELITY

Finally, let's consider ways to deal with infidelity—a form of dishonesty that causes severe damage in every couple that it affects.

Task #1
Don't Give in to Infidelity!

Before we discuss how to cope with the aftermath of infidelity, I need to suggest this "preemptive" task. Perhaps certain situations in your life tempt you toward infidelity. Perhaps a certain person offers what seems a kind of relief from the challenges of married life. Perhaps a certain set of circumstances—excitement, mystery, physical pleasure, you name it—promises to add a "spark" to what you consider your humdrum existence. Well, I strongly urge you not to take this path! We could discuss the moral issues forever, but that's another discussion for another book. From the standpoint of your relationship, though, I believe that infidelity simply can't add anything positive to whatever you have. If your relationship is good, it will damage and perhaps destroy what you've built so far. If your relationship is troubled, it will intensify your troubles a hundred- or a thousandfold.

In short, you need to figure out a different approach to whatever ails you and your relationship. I recommend that you seek guidance from your pastor, from a marital counselor, or from some other source of thoughtful, objective help.

Task #2
Determine What Happened

If you've already committed adultery, the fundamental questions you must ask are: What happened? Were you looking for something that wasn't present in your marriage? Was it an impulse? Was it a way of "punishing" your spouse for some real or imagined wrong?

The causes of infidelity can range from simple loneliness to physical attraction to a need for adventure. Sometimes it's blind temptation—

getting drawn into casual sex. You must start by exploring what happened, and why.

It's important to note that there are other types of infidelity, too—not bedroom infidelities but subtler, less physical kinds. Some people don't have sex with someone other than their spouse, but they develop a relationship so intense and complex that it takes time and space more properly allotted to the husband or wife. When speaking with some couples, I hear one or the other spouse, in his/her own defense say, "I communicate with this person so well, and we have a great relationship." Or he or she will say, "We chat on the Internet a lot, so we're really close." When the "wronged" spouse discovers this communication, he or she often wonders, "Why is this communication so strong? Why are they calling each other ten times a day?" These nonsexual relationships can be destructive and hurtful even though they don't fit the usual image of infidelity. They can leave the other spouse feeling like an outsider in his or her own marriage. Depending on the circumstances, they can be as damaging as an illicit love affair.

To get control of the situation, you need to honestly and openly assess what has happened, why it happened, and how you plan to move forward. Once again, I suggest that you seek help in undertaking this process. Which brings us to . . .

Task #3
Get Help

Marital counseling isn't a cure-all. A counselor or therapist won't solve your problems for you. A couple's success in marital counseling depends first and foremost on the spouses' making an immediate and ongoing commitment to examine both what's good and what's problematic about the marriage. So why, then, is marital counseling often crucial? Because a good counselor can help you and your spouse start talking again when communications have broken down; can provide a "referee" for difficult discussions; can provide a sense of perspective that you may have lost. These benefits often make the difference between, on the one hand, a total "meltdown" in a marriage and, on the other hand, a reestablishing of trust, confidence, and good faith. In my opinion, the need for help is never more critical than in the aftermath of infidelity.

If you feel that you and your spouse would benefit from marital counseling, I urge you to ask your pastor or physician for a referral. In addition, you can find a toll-free number for a marital counseling referral agency in this book's Resource Guide.

Task #4
Try to Move On

Only couples that can learn to forgive and move on will survive an infidelity. To start the process of moving on, however, two things must happen.

First, the unfaithful spouse needs to swear off any further "adventures." If infidelity remains an option—such as when the unfaithful partner still has a connection with the adulterous partner—then the couple usually can't move on. There must be a willingness and ability to draw a line and say, "Okay, it's over now." You can't heal the wounds in your marriage if you keep picking them open—or even if you leave the impression that you're not serious about healing them in the first place.

Second, the other spouse needs to be capable of forgiveness. Forgiveness won't solve all your problems, but it's a necessary first step as you start to accept the need for solutions. You can dwell on the infidelity forever and punish your spouse emotionally and mentally every day. You can say how awful this situation is, rage against him or her every day, and depress yourself. Or you can say, "This is a terrible chapter in our life together. I'm sorry it ever happened. It's never going to happen again, so let's move on."

Regarding both of these topics, I need to underscore yet again the importance of having a "guide" as you undertake this process. Recovering from infidelity isn't easy, fast, or guaranteed to work. I don't believe that this is a do-it-yourself project. A wiser course is to find someone to help you follow this complicated path. And by that I mean (again) a well-trained, thoughtful marital counselor.

Task #5
In Cases of Repetitive Infidelity, Consider a More Drastic Approach

On my talk shows and in my columns, I've heard from at least five or six women recently who have said, "My husband has always been unfaithful," or "He's been unfaithful to me for twenty years now," or "He's been with five, six, seven, eight different partners." I hear all kinds of appalling things. Now, it's true that in some cultures, infidelity is acceptable behavior. But we're in the twenty-first century now, and spouses should respect each other no matter what the culture. Men and woman are equal; we should be granted an equal dignity and respect. Nobody should get to play around, cheat on his wife, and risk bringing home AIDS or some other disease. Anyone who does that repeatedly has lost his privilege to be in a marriage. Anybody who is that promiscuous and irresponsible has forfeited his rights. To earn back those rights, he needs to show a radical change of behavior, including a willingness to enter therapy and to reshape his behavior. A person who is constantly out there looking for action and who neglects his wife should be out of the marriage. Unfortunately, there will be times when the right thing to do is say, "Sorry, this marriage isn't going to work. Fix your life; then we'll talk. And if you don't fix it, the story is over."

The truth is that for a lot of addicts—drug addicts, alcoholics, but also sex addicts—the behavior won't end until the person faces an ultimatum and has to change. That's exactly what happens to the compulsive adulterer, too. There's a point where you have to say, "Okay, maybe I can change, maybe I can't. But in any case, I can't risk the lives of my family."

HONESTY—A PROCESS, NOT AN EVENT

My hope is that following Path Four will help you make honesty a stronger, more central force within your relationship. In stating what I've written here, however, I don't mean to imply that you need to accomplish perfect honesty all at once. We are all imperfect, fallible human beings. All human relationships are imperfect. We all make mistakes and fall short of our ideals. Honesty is a process we undertake over the course of a lifetime, not an event we accomplish and simply check off our "to-do" list. However, honesty is so crucial within a couple's relationship that I hope you take it seriously, stay mindful of it, and give it your best efforts—both separately and as a couple.

Path Five

COMMUNICATE

A man named Robert was walking along a beach in California while deep in prayer. He said, "Lord, can you hear me?" He repeated this appeal several times.

At last, the Lord responded: "Yes, I hear you. And because you've been so faithful to Me, I'll grant you one wish."

Robert thought long and hard and then said, "Well, Lord, I've always wanted to go to Hawaii, but I'm afraid of flying and I get seasick on boats. Could you build a bridge from California to Hawaii so I can drive over there to visit whenever I want?"

The Lord laughed and said, "A bridge to Hawaii? Think of how difficult that would be to construct! The supports would have to reach down to the bottom of the ocean. The span would extend for thousands of miles! All that concrete—and so much steel! What a daunting task. Listen—how about if you try again and think up another wish?"

So Robert thought awhile longer and tried to imagine a really good wish. Finally, he said, "Well, my wife tells me I'm insensitive. And I think she's way too demanding. She always wants me to express my emotions, but I feel overwhelmed by *hers!* Neither of us can really make sense of the other person. We love each other, but so often we seem worlds apart. So here's my wish: I wish you could show me an easy, reliable way for my wife and I to communicate and truly understand each other."

The Lord was quiet for a while. Then he replied, "On second thought, do you want two lanes or four lanes on that bridge?"

Just a joke? Well, yes—but it touches a nerve in men and women alike. Let's face it: there's no easy, reliable way for husbands and wives to communicate. Despite their love, men and women often *do* seem worlds apart. Many spouses are convinced that truly understanding each other is a more hopeless task than building a bridge from California to Hawaii.

Frankly, though, I'm not convinced. Is marital communication difficult? Absolutely. So difficult that it's hopeless? No way. In fact, I believe that couples can build a "bridge" within their relationships that will lead to compassion, love, and understanding.

You're probably wondering what I'll offer as evidence for this claim. The evidence is communication in the husband-wife relationships around us that truly work. In my own extended family, my grandparents showed me one such relationship. My parents showed me another. I also have friends, relatives, and acquaintances whose fine marriages reveal good communication. I see plenty of couples like this in my own parish. You probably know such people yourself. Perhaps your own marriage is further proof that a husband and a wife can listen to each other thoughtfully, speak honestly and respectfully, and work hard toward shared goals.

Here's what I believe: good marital communication takes hard work but isn't impossible. You don't need divine intervention to keep the channels open in your relationship. You just need good intentions, hard work, and maybe some new ideas to try out. Communication is a set of skills you can learn and practice.

To focus on these issues, Path Five will consider some general issues that affect couples' communication; then we'll explore some tasks that will help you and your spouse strengthen your efforts to communicate.

Chapter 10

The Importance of Communication in Relationships

When couples come to me for counseling, at least 75 percent of the problems they describe concern communication. The figure may be even higher—80 percent, 85 percent, even 90 percent. It's certainly a communication issue when a woman says, "My husband never talks to me," or when a man says, "My wife doesn't understand me." It's also a communication issue when a spouse says, "We've grown apart." But the problems that clearly involve communication are just the start of what I see. If a couple has fights over money, the conflict will concern how they talk as much as what they spend. If a couple is sexually unhappy, the reason will have as much to do with words as with intimate acts. Almost any marital issue you could name will, at its core, have to do with communication. I'd venture to say that communication has at least a partial role in every problem that couples experience.

All bad news? No. The good news is every couple can improve, deepen, and enrich their communication as husband and wife. In fact, learning to communicate well is probably the most adaptable set of skills you can acquire and apply to your relationship.

Before we consider how to improve your communication skills in practical ways, though, let's first explore why this subject is so crucial to a couple's marriage.

HOW COUPLES' COMMUNICATION CHANGES OVER TIME

Just as so many other aspects of a relationship change over time, a couple will experience a lot of changes in how the partners communicate. The nature and degree of these changes will vary a lot, of course. The partners' age, cultural background, education, and personalities will all make a difference in how they communicate. But if a couple is together for a while, the odds are strong that their patterns of communication will change and evolve.

THE "SPARKLE STAGE"

During the early phase of a couple's relationship—that intense, dramatic, almost intoxicating first few months that some people call "the sparkle stage"—communication is, well, intense, dramatic, and almost intoxicating. The partners just can't say enough or hear enough about each other. Many couples spend hours on the phone talking about everything and anything. You can often see such couples in restaurants or other public places, in rapt conversation and often oblivious to everyone else on the planet. It's tempting to mock their spellbound state. But communication of this sort is crucial—a way that the partners get to know each other with great focus and intensity. They just can't get enough of each other. In a way, this sparkle stage can be almost heavenly, for the partners often seem to feel a profound bliss in being so aware of each other, so open to each other's being, so delighted in each other's existence.

SETTLING IN TOGETHER

Then, as the relationship progresses and stabilizes, communication changes. A couple in which the partners have known each other for a few years may be deeply in love, but they probably don't talk as often or for as long on the phone a they did earlier. They know more about each other now. There's less to discover. By the time the partners marry, they share the details of their lives to a great degree, since they're now experiencing the same events. What was previously a state of mutual exploration now gives way (at least ideally) to a state of mutual trust. As a result, communication may focus less on discovery and more on maintenance of the relationship. This stage has pros and cons. On the one hand, the partners know each other better now, so their discussions may be more relaxed and confident. On the other hand, there's a risk that the partners may become blasé about communication, since there's a possibility of taking each other for granted.

THE PARENTING YEARS

When kids enter the picture, the spouses' communication often changes radically, along with everything else in the marriage. The situation is what one friend called the "good-news/bad-news joke" of marital communication with kids in the house. "The good news is," he said, "that you always have something to talk about. The bad news: you never have any time to talk!" Other friends who have kids have described a different but frustrating scenario: when the spouses organize one of those rare occasions when they can leave the kids with a baby-sitter and go out for a date, all they do is talk about the kids!

It's true that many couples find parenthood deeply satisfying. The risk during the parenting years, however, is that the spouses may forget that they're husband and wife, not just Mommy and Daddy. This is especially common if the couple has traditional roles—she's the stay-at-home mom and he's the breadwinner. In marriages of this sort, there's a risk of communication limiting each partner's insights into the other's life. The husband must realize that his wife needs some time off and, also, some time with other adults. She still has interests and dreams besides her kids, even if she feels deeply committed to being a mother. At the same time, the wife needs to realize that her husband is out in the world, which may involve significant stresses and demands. Couples in these and many other situations often struggle to keep communication channels open so that they continue to understand and sympathize with each other.

I've found that before they have a child, most couples believe that parenthood isn't going to change their life that much. But in fact nothing so radically changes your life as much as parenthood. When they realize that this little baby depends on them for all of his or her needs—for everything, all the time—then suddenly they understand. This is how relationships are tested, because now the partners really have to strive to care for each other and to avoid neglecting each other.

MIDLIFE AND THE EMPTY NEST

Typical of many life stages, midlife presents both challenges and opportunities. Some spouses rediscover each other and enter a new, rich phase of married life when their kids grow up and leave home. The end of parental responsibilities allows the couple to turn inward and focus on being together and enjoying each other as husband and wife. For some spouses, however, the "empty nest" precipitates a crisis. The earlier, intense focus on child-centered tasks sometimes prompts a couple to neglect the marriage itself—or even to use the children as an excuse to ignore marital issues on purpose. The result: some empty-nesters feel out of touch or, worse yet, profoundly alienated, once they are alone again.

What makes the difference between these two scenarios? I believe it's the pattern of communication that the couple has established throughout the parenting years. If their husband-wife dialogue has been open, honest, and energetic all along, it will grow and develop further in the postparenting years. If their dialogue has been closed, guarded, and low in energy all along, communications will be strained now that the kids are out of the picture. Many couples do, in fact, overcome a communication gap of the sort I'm describing. I've seen some previously dormant marriages come alive and blossom anew even when the spouses have almost completely lost touch with each other. Nothing about this stage of life is predetermined. The key to a good outcome under all circumstances is hard work as each partner listens carefully and speaks thoughtfully to the other.

THE GOLDEN YEARS

One of the amazing things I see in long marriages—especially those lasting forty or fifty years or even longer—is that the spouses don't even have to say a word to each other to know what each other is thinking. When I speak to these couples at their anniversary celebrations, the wives tell me, "Father, I know what he is thinking just by that look in his eyes." That's incredible communication. But of course not every couple reaches that level. And while experts agree that eye contact is one of the most effective means of communication—especially to be considered a good listener—we need to learn to verbalize properly what's in our minds and hearts.

Communication of this sort is indeed remarkable and beautiful. However, I feel that it's important not to sentimentalize what these golden-years couples have achieved. Communication of this intense, intuitive sort I'm describing doesn't emerge full-blown out of nowhere. It's almost always the result of a long-standing process within the marriage—the fruit of hard work and careful cultivation. For many couples, it has resulted from efforts to overcome many hardships over the years. The spouses have a profound sense of knowing each other because they've dealt with so many crises together; they have faced and solved problems as a team; they have sorted through complex issues word by word, sentence by sentence, over a period of decades.

It's also worth noting that outsiders may sometimes misread those silent, knowing glances between elderly couples and give the spouses too much credit. We may assume that the spouses know exactly what each other is thinking when, in fact, they're just ignoring each other or taking each other for granted. Some couples just stop talking. They've heard the same stories for years. They've heard the same complaints or requests ("What, tuna casserole again!" or "Can't you clean up your mess?") over and over again. Maybe the spouses *assume* they know what the other person is thinking. Unfortunately, they're not always right. They may have actually stopped listening to their partner and forgotten how to interact.

That said, I'll agree that many couples in their golden years attain a deep level of communication. After decades of living together, raising children, coping with jobs, caring for their own elderly parents, helping each other through retirement, struggling with health issues—they truly know each other. All their earlier efforts to communicate have paid off in ways that all of us should respect and cherish.

WHAT AFFECTS A COUPLE'S COMMUNICATION?

All right, so we agree that communication isn't easy, and that couples go through a variety of stages during their married life. What does this mean for *you*? What are the issues that affect *your* relationship, and what can you do about them?

Let's look at the communication issues that couples face and how these issues can weaken or strengthen their relationship.

THE POWER OF WORDS

To prevent and heal relationship troubles, we should constantly remember the power that our words can exert on others. What we say and how we say it strongly influences other people—both in good ways and bad. We may not even intend to do any harm, but our words can do great damage anyway. A slip of the tongue or a disrespectful phrase can damage or even ruin a good relationship. We probably all know couples who verbally "zing" each other. In fact, some couples are routinely dismissive or demeaning—a depressing situation for both spouses and awkward for the people around them.

Does this mean that spouses should sugarcoat everything they say to each other? Should they avoid telling the truth? Of course not. Being sincere and open are important qualities, but they are more complex than they may seem on the surface. Good communication in a marriage means more than just being positive all the time. It's also a matter of speaking in ways that honor a higher level of truth. For instance, Dana feels that her husband, Lee, is working so hard that he'll damage his health—or the couple's marriage. In the past, she has teased him about his workaholic tendencies. Jokes and jibes simply annoyed Lee, however, and prompted him to ignore his wife. A better approach: direct, honest communication about what has become an increasingly serious problem for this couple.

TWO EARS, ONE MOUTH

Communication in relationships can be truly hard work. It's difficult to understand another person's perspective—and it's equally difficult to get your message across and make sure that it's completely understood. What's the solution to this dilemma? I believe that to communicate effectively, we need to develop our ability to listen more and speak with equal attention and intensity. It's not by accident that God gave us two ears but only one mouth. Keeping that reality in mind is a constant challenge for all our relationships!

Communication skills will play a huge role in your day-to-day interactions with your spouse. To complicate matters, though, communication isn't just a set of procedures; it's also an art. And as with any other art, only practice makes perfect. You become a better communicator by communicating properly and observing some basic guidelines. The most important of these guidelines is that you listen more than you speak. Being a good listener will also make you a better speaker, though, and much more attentive to the needs of your audience. Why? Because you'll be tuned in to the reality of what your spouse is saying. Many communication problems in marriages arise when people close themselves off to others and think that they have more to say than to hear. But in fact it's listening that is most critical. The two-way road of communication requires that you have authentic interest in what your spouse has to say.

THE "HIDDEN MESSAGE": SILENCE

It's important to remember that communication isn't just what we say. What we don't say also matters. It's sounds crazy, but silence is often the "hidden message" we deliver.

For example, Jenny got her hair done and came home to surprise her husband and get his reaction. Her husband, Mike, greeted her but said nothing about her new hairstyle. After a few moments, Jenny asked, "Notice anything different about me?"

Mike looked over again and said flatly, "Yeah—you got a haircut."

Jenny waited for a follow-up comment—or maybe even a compliment—but she came away empty-handed.

Most women find this kind of silence hurtful and offensive. They want some feedback about their "new look," and they want to feel cherished. If a husband is part of the intelligent and insightful 1 percent of the male species—the tiny percentage that actually pays attention to such details—he'll say, "Wow, you look fabulous!" Unfortunately, most don't. And this type of silence—what we don't say—is a way of saying something. In this story, Mike's silence led Jenny to conclude that her husband didn't like her new hairstyle. She may even have concluded that Mike felt indifferent to her more generally. His silence *did* communicate something to her, even though it may have been a totally different message from what Mike was thinking at the time.

Similarly, most men appreciate positive feedback for their efforts—whether as breadwinners or as husbands and fathers involved in domestic activities. A thoughtful wife will offer compliments to her husband rather than falling silent because he's just "doing what he's supposed to be doing" as the family wage earner and parenting partner.

How silence gets interpreted is a constant challenge in all relationships. I assure you that more often than not, silence is misinterpreted. Why? Because we all use silence at times to guard our thoughts. Sometimes people are almost paranoid about what they say. As an old Spanish proverb states: "We are owners of what we keep silent and slaves to what we say." Yet it's possible to go too far. I agree with the popular axiom "silence is golden," but not all of the time—especially when words should, and need to, be expressed. When we withhold what we ought to say but speak freely the words that should be left unsaid, we have a serious communication problem. Striking this balance in communication is one of the most common problems that can arise in human relationships.

REMEMBER THAT WORDS CAN BUILD UP OR TEAR DOWN

Nothing has a greater positive impact on human development and self-esteem than the affirmations we receive throughout life. Similarly, nothing has more negative impact than the insults, slights, and "disses" we receive. In short, words can build up or tear down.

Children tend to be brutally honest. I recently heard about a little boy who watched his mom as she applied one of those "miracle face-lift" creams onto her face. He was fascinated by what he saw, so he asked his mom, "Why are putting that green stuff on your face, Mommy?"

To which she replied, "It's so that Mommy can become more beautiful."

The boy kept watching and noticed that after just a few minutes, his mother began removing all the gunk from her face with facial tissues. Then the boy asked, "What's the matter, Mommy, have you given up?"

Children certainly do have a way with words!

Fortunately, adults—including spouses—can choose their words more carefully. You can avoid unnecessary verbal "injuries" more easily than a child can.

Complimentary statements about your spouse's good qualities can stimulate him or her to grow and develop in positive ways. Similarly, bad or negative statements only tear your partner down and hurt his or her already fragile ego. One of the first American psychologists, William James, wrote of the "craving" that people have to be recognized, appreciated, and affirmed. He stated, "The deepest principle in human nature is the craving to be appreciated." And of course this craving is strongest toward the people who matter most to us: our families of origin, our spouse, our children. This is why silence, indifference, and harsh words from these people do so much damage. All of us need positive words to help build our character and confirm that our lives are important and meaningful. Words have an incredible power. With them we can challenge people to do great things, empower goodness, or destroy the other person's spirit—all by how we choose to communicate.

GENDER ISSUES AND COMMUNICATION

Many women express frustration about husband-wife communications. A common lament I hear: "Father, my husband doesn't tell me what he's thinking." One woman said, "He comes home, he puts his feet up, he plays with the remote control, and he watches TV. That's it." Another said, "He doesn't tell me a thing." It's an unfortunate scenario. She wants to talk. He doesn't. Somehow they're just not in touch. Sometimes the problem is timing—picking the appropriate moment to talk. But sometimes it's deeper than that. Sometimes the husband really *doesn't* want to talk at all. This is a real problem. Each couple should have *some* sort of occasion when it's comfortable for both of them to speak.

Just as men and women are different in so many other ways, there are great differences in communication styles, too. Deborah Tannen and other communications specialists believe that men and women have different preferences in both what they want to say and how they say it. Tannen's book *You Just Don't Understand: Men, Women, and Communication*, offers many insights into gender differences on these issues. Among other things, many women have a strong need to air their grievances and frustrations, and the emotional aspects of doing so feel significant to them. By contrast, many men focus on solving problems as such and are less concerned with the emotional "side effects" of communicating. They'll say, "Okay, let's get down to work. Let's roll up our sleeves and tackle the situation." Given these differences, men may feel frustrated by their wives' "emotionality," while women may feel frustrated because their men seem too "clinical" and overly task-oriented. Men and women alike need to accommodate each other's different needs and perspectives. Men need to realize that women sometimes just need to talk. They're not looking for a solution; rather, they just want to vent, discuss, and share. Women in turn need to realize that for men, the preferable approach is to retreat, grow introspective, and work on the issue on their own. Women shouldn't feel locked out. Men shouldn't feel talked to death. These are just different ways of approaching certain tasks.

It's a common male behavior to try to escape the problem. Some guys stalk out of the house, drive around for a while in the car, and then come back. That's not the right solution, either. On the other hand, it works for some people to disconnect from the issue—to let things cool down before continuing the discussion.

Many women I know speak to me just to vent. They may have already figured out what the problem is and what the solution needs to be, but they need to speak to me just to express their emotional response. So I'll sit there and listen. On some level the conversation serves a good purpose. These women recognize what's happening. At the end they'll say, "Well, thank you—I just needed to get that off my chest." It's a different communication style from what men have, but it's legitimate.

The male response is often more outward-focused. One man I know, Jared, says, "I'd rather not have someone just tell me about their problems. I want to *solve* their problems. My wife teases me: 'You're Mr. Fix-It. You always want to get out there and fix whatever is wrong.' And I'll say, 'Well, of *course* I do! I don't want to waste my time talking about the problem if I can solve it.' "

Where does this situation leave us? Each member of a couple needs to acknowledge that some differences may exist in how to deal with problems. A husband should be supportive about his wife needing a non-judgmental sounding board. Yes, you need to cope with specific issues and solve specific problems, but that's not the whole story. Sometimes you just need to listen. Maybe there's nothing more to be done—no action to take—but you still need to listen. Similarly, a thoughtful wife may need to acknowledge that her husband wants to roll up his sleeves and try to tackle the problem. The husband and the wife may not be on the same page when it comes to dealing with each situation. But if they're thoughtful and respectful, each will acknowledge and accept the other for his or her own way of approaching the issues from a different angle. They need to take a team approach or, at the very least, they need to acknowledge that their emotional needs are different, as they cope with the challenges facing them.

HOW TO COMMUNICATE SUCCESSFULLY

Many of the couples I counsel know that communication is part of the problem they're facing. I often hear comments like these:

- ∞ "I want to talk with her, but I don't know how."

- ∞ "I just can't seem to get across to him."

- ∞ "It's as if we're speaking different languages."

- ∞ "I hear what she's saying, but I don't understand what she's getting at."

- ∞ "We talk and talk and talk and never really get anywhere."

These are poignant remarks—statements that reveal how many couples acknowledge a problem with communication in their relationship but don't know how to solve it. If you share this sense of bafflement and frustration, I urge you to consider ways to communicate more successfully with your spouse.

MAKE COMMUNICATION A PRIORITY

Put first things first. Good communication shouldn't be only a matter of crisis management. If you communicate only to put out brushfires, you're in for trouble. You need to talk about the minor, day-to-day issues, too—to keep the lines of communication open on an ongoing basis. It's true that there will be demands and distractions. When you enter the parenting years, for instance, your children will take up enormous time and energy. But you and your spouse still have to focus on each other and listen to each other. Sometimes the issues will focus on the kids. Sometimes you'll be dealing with job issues, domestic tasks, or other demands on your time and attention. From the beginning of your marriage, you need to realize that all of these issues will be important. But none will be more important than having a strong relationship, because that's the foundation of everything you do. If you don't have a solid foundation, then how do you build the rest of your family life? What makes your foundation strong is good, consistent, ongoing communication. My recommendation: do whatever is necessary to set aside the time, energy, and attention that you'll devote to marital communication.

CONSIDER DIFFERENT APPROACHES TO TIMING AND "STRUCTURE"

How and when you communicate can make a big difference to your overall success. There are times when a couple needs to sit down and concentrate on solving specific problems. At other times, a more casual approach works best: chatting over dinner, while walking the dog, while doing the dishes, while lying in bed before you fall asleep. The important thing is to find settings and times when both of you can feel comfortable.

I'm certainly aware that many husbands find too much structure uncomfortable. The wives are often comfortable saying, "Okay, let's plan what has to happen," but men may find that approach too confrontational. Ironically, men often communicate very well during the courting process, because they have a lot of things to talk about. But then, once the couple gets married, a lot of men go back to their bachelor habits. They get "buttoned down" and less communicative. In response to this situation, I try to help them understand some basic issues and acquire some basic skills. It's important to create healthy habits for their marriage. These options can be activity-oriented, rather than spotlighting the conversation. Many men are more comfortable opening up if talking occurs during a more relaxed activity. This takes the spotlight off the verbal communication.

Here are some suggestions:

∾ Go for a walk in the park together.

∾ Go for a swim at the local pool or Y.

∾ Have a snack at the local coffee shop, café, or diner.

∾ Play cards.

∾ Play some other game.

∾ Take part in some sort of hobby.

∾ Set aside time during any other period of the day that allows you a little peace and quiet.

DIFFERENT STROKES . . .

It's important to remember how many different ways there are to foster good communication. Some couples raise issues outright and address them directly, while some circle around a subject and deal with it by indirection. Some dive right in; others wade in slowly. Some couples communicate with a rapid-fire exchange of statements, with each spouse responding quickly to the other's statements. Others present longer, more detailed statements, with one spouse listening, then reacting. There are, in short, different strokes for different folks.

My only strong recommendation is that whichever approach you use, don't start deciding how you'll comment about a situation until your spouse is done speaking. This is simply a basic part of staying open-minded about the subject in question. In fact, trying to be solution-oriented can cause a lot of difficulties in husband-wife communication. In many situations, it's better not to provide your solution or opinion; rather, it's more constructive to offer feedback regarding what your spouse has said to you so that he or she knows you've been listening and thus feels validated. An example: instead of saying, "Well, you should do X or Y," consider saying, "So what you're telling me is _____. Is that what you feel?" A lot of people think that good communication means learning to "make your case" more effectively. Well, what you say certainly matters. But I feel it's a mistake—often a big mistake—to focus on *talking* instead of *listening*. What matters most in good communication is good listening.

THE IMPORTANCE OF DIALOGUE

What we're really talking about here is dialogue: true verbal give-and-take. Dialogue is an art that takes time and effort to master, but it's also a skill that you need to learn. If you didn't learn this skill at home—if you weren't raised in a household where people really listened to each other—this skill may take some work. The sad truth is that most of us were taught very limited communication skills. We heard statements like: "Do it because I'm you're mother," or "Do it because I told you so," or "I'm your father, so that's that." These statements aren't dialogue; they're a monologue. There's a place for monologue in a parent-child relationship. But when you're married, you're in a loving, equal adult relationship that should have two-way communication as its foundation.

How do you accomplish this goal? Here are some "dos and don'ts" for communicating with your spouse:

- Do speak directly and honestly in a calm, cool, collected manner.

- Don't try to communicate when you're tired, anxious, or stressed by outside demands.

- Do find a quiet, peaceful time and place to talk.

- Don't use unfair fighting tactics such as accusing, blaming, name-calling, or yelling.

- Do stick to the core problem rather than necessarily expanding it to other issues.

~ Do stay open-minded to what your spouse is telling you—even (or especially) if his or her assertions don't make sense to you.

~ Don't set up a program beforehand; listen first, staying open to what you hear, since that way you'll discover truths that you and your spouse are both seeking.

~ Do keep your statements brief—since long-winded "manifestos" will probably work against you rather than in your favor.

~ Don't lecture; if you sermonize on any subject, you'll alienate your listener.

~ Don't bring up old incidents that are irrelevant to what's at hand.

~ Do confront the problem in an assertive, honest way.

~ Don't avoid conflict when something is bothering you; likewise, don't sulk quietly or express your frustrations in passive-aggressive ways.

~ Do focus on the issues, not who's at fault.

~ Don't try to accept all the blame; alternatively, don't blame your spouse.

~ Do listen to your spouse's response without interrupting, judging, or thwarting his or her own feelings and experiences.

~ Don't try to repress your feelings of anger and resentment.

~ Do empathize with and validate your partner's feelings whenever possible.

~ Do focus your communication on the process, not on winning the argument. Lead your discussion to a win-win outcome in which you both feel heard and validated, and in which you find options for resolving your difficulties.

∾ Do look at both the sides of the issues you're facing.

Learning to communicate effectively is more than just dos and don'ts of course; I don't mean to imply that following this list of tips will resolve all the issues you face. But focusing on specific communication issues often goes a long way toward solving problems between couples. The next chapter of Path Five will offer even more "tools" that can become part of your communication tool kit.

LEARN HOW TO ARGUE CONSTRUCTIVELY

There will be arguments in any marriage—even a happy one. Precisely because a couple consists of two individuals—two people with different backgrounds, different perspectives, different needs and expectations, different opinions, and different ways of coping with the world—disagreements are inevitable. When I meet husbands and wives who say, "We never argue," I know there's a problem. Either the spouses aren't facing their problems, they're shoving them under the carpet, they're responding to their issues with indifference, or they're letting their resentments build until the couple becomes a powderkeg that's ready to explode.

CONSTRUCTIVE VS. DESTRUCTIVE ARGUING

The question isn't whether you'll argue, it's whether you'll argue *constructively* or *destructively*. There are good ways to argue, and there are bad ways to argue.

By arguing constructively, what I mean is solving problems together as a couple without damaging each other or your relationship. This process may involve strong disagreements, but constructive arguing means that you disagree while maintaining respect and a commitment to seeking compromise.

Destructive arguing, on the other hand, occurs when the couple disagrees in ways that are oppositional, obstructive, disrespectful, demeaning, or abusive. The process of destructive arguing involves strong disagreements, just as constructive arguing does, but the spouses don't (or can't) maintain their respect for each other, and they often put more energy into the argument itself than into the effort to reach a compromise. Many spouses who argue in destructive ways focus on expressing their anger, not on solving problems. They just want to "get it out of their system," score points, or "win." Your goal in these situations may not be to arrive at an agreement; rather, it's to force the other person to admit you're right, concede the point, or give up. This type of arguing tears couples apart rather than bringing them together. It often damages rather than improves the communication process over the long haul.

In addition, destructive arguments tend to deafen spouses to each other rather than refining their skills as attentive listeners. You need to be open to your spouse's message in order to hear it, right? But openness can't take place if your main goal is to rant and rave. In a destructive argument, you're not exchanging ideas, not listening to what the other person is saying, not brainstorming. Destructive arguing is self-centered, not other-centered. Unfortunately, this mode of communicating isn't a rare thing. Maybe it's always been around. I've certainly known many husbands and wives in the older generations who have spent more time screaming at each other than listening carefully and speaking thoughtfully. No doubt we've all heard about couples in which "dialogue" consisted of shouting, cursing, and throwing crockery. But there's a new "style" of destructive arguing nowadays, too, that is all too common. I call it "TV arguing." You know what I mean: melodramatic speeches, screaming rages, or clever one-liners that "zing" the other person. I guess it's not surprising that people ape the couples they see in the media. After all, TV shows and movies are what shape many aspects of our culture. But this situation is unfortunate. Scriptwriters create dialogue for dramatic effect, not to prompt good spousal communication. Is it really a good idea to model your marriage after the dysfunctional couples in the media? I don't think so! My recommendation: leave that to the Hollywood writers. Strive instead to be open-minded, not sharp-tongued; warm, not witty.

HOW CAN YOU ARGUE CONSTRUCTIVELY?

First of all, don't violate your commitment to honor and respect your spouse. Don't violate your vow to value and cherish him or her. If you are arguing from a place of anger—if you scream and rant—you're probably going to lose the battle. Why? Because doing so will mean that you're not communicating in a way that honors your respect and caring. The end result won't be what you're looking for. After all, the whole purpose of arguing constructively is to resolve a conflict or solve a problem. So if you argue in a way that demeans and insults the person you love most, you've already lost track of your fundamental purpose.

Here are some specific ways to make arguing constructive rather than destructive:

Dealing with anger. If one partner is angry, or both are, it's best to let the storm blow over before you tackle major issues. Take a break from the discussion. Give each other some physical or emotional "space" to cool off and calm down. Later, when the tension has eased, you can proceed. It's best if you don't discuss issues while in the midst of the storm. You need to communicate in a rational, civilized, respectful manner. If you can't manage this approach, if your discussions break down into arguments, or if your disagreements become screaming matches, the situation is cause for concern. This type of corrosive interaction eats away at a relationship. At its worst, it can lead to lack of respect, open hostility, and even physical violence. Unfortunately, some couples don't know how to communicate in a positive way; they only know how to scream, shout, and throw plates at each other! If that's the only way you know how to communicate, there's big trouble ahead.

Once a man said to me, "You know, Father, I resolve all arguments with my wife in the bedroom." When he said that, I looked at him and thought, *Oh, my God, how negative can you be? If you can't converse with your wife when you have a problem, and if you're going to turn your communication into physical aggression in the sexual act, that's certainly going to distance you from your spouse.* There's no tenderness, no love, no gentleness in this situation—it's going to convert all your frustrations into sexual aggression. That's really sick. If you act out of anger and respond out of anger, you're bound to hurt the person you love most.

The importance of timing—and "time-outs." I recommend that if you're having an argument or other conflict that is creating a high level of hostility, you should shelve the discussion and consider leaving the tense environment. Consider taking your discussion somewhere else. Take a walk in the park. Shift to another room. Disconnect from the environment where you feel at odds. Deal with it in a different way and talk about it in a different place.

The man I mentioned earlier is (I hope!) an extreme case. Still, hostile communication is always a problem. If hostile communication is the norm for you, I strongly recommend that you seek professional help. Anger and hostility do great damage to a marriage over the long haul. If you face the problem early, you can save yourselves a lot of grief in the long run.

External influences. A lot of couples argue when they're tired, hungry, stressed, or under pressure from work- or parenting-related tasks. These external influences are sometimes unavoidable. If your child is sick, you're up at 3 A.M., and you're struggling to decide how you should medicate her, you can't just ignore the situation. But sometimes couples get in arguments partly—or entirely—because external influences are clouding their perceptions or making them irritable. A better approach: set aside the discussion until you're better rested or under less stress.

According to Mandy, she and her husband, Jack, have a rule never to argue in the middle of the night unless the situation is a true emergency. "We'll say, 'Look, it's one in the morning,' " Mandy explains. " 'We have to be up at six. We're not going to make any headway on this stuff now. There's a problem we need to solve—we agree on that—and we have to sort it out. But let's do it tomorrow. We're not going to get anywhere in the middle of the night.' " In short, they've learned how to postpone discussions when they're exhausted. It's amazing how trivial a lot of "major" conflicts seem after you've gotten some rest. (Breakfast helps, too!)

My suggestion: reschedule your discussions until you're better rested; then get back to it later. The same holds true if you're depleted because of hunger, illness (colds, flu, whatever), or under pressure for other reasons, such as work deadlines.

Choosing your battles. Finally, when you're headed toward an argument, you have to ask yourself if the subject is truly worth fighting over. You can spend a lot of energy arguing about things that you can't really change—or that aren't worth the trouble. If it's a trivial matter, why waste your time and energy hashing it out? If you know that the argument won't change anything, why argue about it? Are there too many negative emotions tied up in this issue? If the form of communication is mostly negative, you're not going to get good results anyway.

So you have to make a decision. Is this issue worth the trouble? What have been the results in the past? Will arguing again help this situation, or will it only make it worse? I recommend that you look at the bigger picture, take a long-term view, and focus only on the topics that warrant your time and attention.

Many couples argue about their pet peeves. You know what I mean: "You always leave the lights on," "Why can't you clean up your messes?" "You let the kids stay up way too late"— stuff like that. It's about the little things. Many couples also argue about domestic tasks. Often the husband isn't doing his fair share, so that's the flashpoint. Or else the husband is making an effort, but the wife feels frustrated because the husband is inefficient. Are these things really worth arguing over? I don't think so. These are things that may annoy you, but they shouldn't be the cause of anger. Does this mean that you should avoid these subjects? Not at all. But again, you should focus on problem-solving, not demeaning the other person, scoring points, or getting even.

SEX AND COMMUNICATION

Many couples—I'd venture to say most—don't understand how much of their sexual relationship is a matter of communication. They may believe that sex is simply an issue of what happens in bed. This attitude is unfortunate. For better or worse, a lot of a couple's sex life is really a consequence of what happens elsewhere. What you say to your spouse while at the breakfast table, on the phone, or running errands has a huge impact on how you feel in the bedroom. If you're rude and impatient toward your spouse all day long and then, once you're in bed together, you expect everything to be sweetness and light—well, you're going to be disappointed. There's a major connection between your moment-by-moment relationship and what happens at times of intimacy.

Delia, who's been married about seven years, came to me for counseling. She and her husband, Nicolas, were in the middle of a crisis. Delia said, "Father, he never calls me during the day. Even when he's home after work, he never says nice things to me. In fact, he ignores me. I practically don't even exist! And then, when it's time to go to bed, he wants to get all lovey-dovey. He just doesn't understand that I can't be affectionate with someone who's been ignoring me all day!"

I tell the couples I counsel, "Look at the big picture. Don't just think about this or that particular moment of lovemaking. You need to look at the bigger picture, your long-term relationship, and your goals as a couple. Your sexual relationship is one of the best aspects of your married life—or it ought to be! But you have to think about the more general issues of your relationship: how you take care of each other, what your goals are, how your relationship changes and develops over time. All of these more general issues are truly important in their own right. They're central to how you and your spouse grow as a couple. But in addition, the general issues—especially how you take care of each other—will have a huge impact on the degree of sexual closeness you attain.

How can you improve communication in ways that will avoid tension and foster harmony in your sexual relationship? This is a complex question, but here are some aspects of the subject that can make the process easier and more constructive:

Talk open-mindedly and openheartedly. One of the most important things you can do to foster good communication—both in the bedroom and elsewhere—is to talk with your partner about sensitive issues with an open mind and an open heart. It's tempting to ignore sensitive topics precisely because they're difficult to discuss, but this approach is almost always a mistake. In fact, a reluctance to communicate causes the majority of intimacy problems in marriage. Why? Because intimacy is fundamentally a question of what you do with your mind and your heart, not just what you do with your sex organs. Intimacy begins with what you're willing to share with your partner. How much of yourself are you willing to leave open to this other person? How fully are you willing to trust your spouse? To what degree are you willing to be vulnerable?

In marriage, you're giving yourself to someone else. You're sharing your life with this other person. If you're unwilling to talk about core issues in your life, then you're depriving your spouse of love, affection, and emotional intimacy. A better approach: be open to the full range of issues that every couple must discuss.

When sexual intimacy is lacking, isn't functioning well, or isn't healthy, it's usually because the couple has already experienced some type of emotional separation. Men and women interpret that situation in different ways. I think women have a tendency to hold back sex in their marriage as a way of saying, "Well, you don't pay attention to me in other areas, so I'm not going to pay attention to you in the bedroom." Men often wonder, "Why is she doing this to me? What's going on? What am I doing wrong?" A couple facing this situation has more than a specifically sexual problem to solve. If they can address the larger communication issues they face, most areas of their relationship will improve; as a result, their sexual intimacy will probably improve, too.

Face problems directly. When a couple experiences a major sexual problem, such as a dysfunction in one partner or a lack of intimacy between the partners, it's important for the couple to seek what I'd call crisis counseling. This can mean a psychologist, a sexologist, or some other expert who's trained to deal with these issues. What if one of the partners is willing to face the issues but the other one isn't? This imbalance in the partners can cause even more problems. The spouse who denies the problem may feel angry, guilty, insecure, etc. He or she won't face the problem and blocks out his/her partner. The spouse who recognizes the problem may start to blame himself or herself. Often it's the woman wondering, *What am I doing wrong? Am I not attractive to him?* Or the husband may blame himself for what he considers a lack of proper lovemaking technique. But if one partner is closed-minded about seeking help, I still advise the other partner—the one who recognizes the problem—to obtain counseling assistance. Under these circumstances, he or she can at least stop the blame game and learn how to deal with the underlying issue.

In my experience, wives are often much more willing to talk about these subjects than husbands are. I think there's no doubt that women are more open-minded in general; especially when it comes to sexual issues, though, many men feel intimidated by the notion of seeking outside help. They may feel threatened, as if getting assistance implies a lack of manhood. They may be unwilling to speak about a sexual problem with a counselor, especially a female counselor, but often even with a male. They don't want to talk to anyone about their problem.

I recently encountered a couple—I'll call them Frank and Mandy—in which the wife had been trying for years to get her husband to speak with a counselor. Well, the only person Frank would come to was me, because I was the priest who married them. Apparently he felt a bond there between us that put him at ease. Mandy felt happy because her husband would finally speak to someone. A few days later I had them sitting in front of me. After speaking with them for a while, I realized that this husband and wife truly loved each other, but they'd been punishing each other sexually for a long time. Mandy said to Frank, "You never say nice things to me—you never comment on my looks or on my appearance, you know—so I don't really feel comfortable with you." If she changes her hair, Frank doesn't say anything. If she does something special for him, he doesn't even say thank you. She feels that he's indifferent to her all the time. It's only when he's looking for affection and attention in the bedroom that he starts paying attention to his wife. This just gets Mandy angry, so she retaliates by saying, "No way."

Frank responds to this by saying, "Well, it's tough for me, too. It's been so long since I felt close to you. I can't remember the last time we made love. You're always too tired or disinterested. How can I want to be nice to you when you keep pushing me away?"

This is an ongoing conflict in the couple's marriage. Unfortunately, Frank and Mandy haven't been dealing with the core issue. So what's the issue? The issue is that someone in this relationship doesn't know how to communicate affection properly. He doesn't know how to verbalize affection or give the proper attention to his spouse. Affection isn't something you just turn on like a switch because you happen to be in bed. There needs to be an ongoing sense of valuing your mate—appreciating and delighting in him or her. You could say that just valuing each other and doing things for each other is really the best form of foreplay. Showing that you care. Showing that you value his or her company. If you shut the other person out emotionally, ignoring your spouse until you happen to be in bed, well, one of the spouses is going to feel used.

Until Frank faces *his* problem directly, this couple can't really deal with the difficulties facing them, make some changes and compromises, and move on.

The most effective way to deal with any crisis in a relationship is to face the problem and begin to talk about it. Not in the presence of your kids. Not while screaming at each other in the kitchen. Not in the presence of other people, whether friends or family. You have to talk about it one-on-one, in a private setting. You need to set aside time when you sit together and say, "Do you understand why this is happening?" or "Do you understand why this turns me off?" or "Do you understand why I don't like this?" or whatever else is on your mind.

Is this easy? Of course not. On the contrary, it's something that almost everyone finds challenging. Communication of this sort takes a certain degree of selflessness. It's not just a question of getting your own needs met. It's also about giving to the other person, about sharing with your spouse. But I'm not sure that many couples understand that. Close communication on these sexual issues isn't just a means to a goal. The journey itself is what matters. It's part of the process of creating a sense of closeness and a bond. With every act of intimacy between you and your partner—whether that intimacy is physical touching or verbal communication—there's a renewal of the bond between you.

Discuss sexual preferences and other issues affecting intimacy. Regarding the issue of sexual preferences, I want to stress outright that every expression of intimacy between spouses needs to occur in ways that shows mutual respect. It's common for couples these days to forget that in marriage, two people become one. What this means, basically, is that two people—each with a different background, different preferences, and a different personality—are coming together in an act that unifies them. The act of sexual intercourse is no different—the two spouses become one. How can this happen if the partners don't deeply respect and honor each other? For this reason, sexual communication isn't just what happens during sexual intimacy. Sexual communication is also what happens before intimacy and after intimacy.

What does this have to do with preferences? Well, when there's disagreement about physical or emotional or moral issues—when one spouse says, "I don't like that," or "That's not something I want to do"—the other partner needs to pay attention. The couple needs to address these issues together. There has to be open communication about specific as well as general issues so that the couple's intimacy constantly deepens and grows stronger. You have to be as open as possible with the other person regarding your thoughts, your feelings, and your emotions.

Another issue comes up when one partner's upbringing has created negative attitudes about sexuality. If those negative attitudes are severe, they can cause personal and marital tension. For instance, Rosa's family's attitudes about sexuality were so repressed that the only sex act she could tolerate involved hasty intercourse in a completely darkened room. Anything else caused her great anxiety. Her husband loved her deeply, and in many ways his view of sexuality was far healthier than his wife's. He wasn't going to force anything on her. At the same time, he felt that her narrow, tense view of sexuality wasn't good either for his wife or for their marriage.

How should a couple deal with a situation like this? How can one spouse encourage the other to see sexuality not as dirty or wrong, but as a means of communicating love and caring? And—here's an even more challenging situation—how should a couple deal with the situation when one of them has suffered past sexual abuse?

When there's a legacy of sexual trauma of any sort—whether it's the result of outright abuse or of negative family attitudes—the most important step you can take is to get good professional help. I realize that many people will resist this suggestion. I've heard both men and women ask, "How can I possibly discuss such personal matters with someone I don't know? Well, you certainly need to choose carefully whom to discuss these matters with. You need to get a referral from someone you trust—a close friend, your physician, or your pastor. You need to make sure that you have a good "match" with the counselor or therapist you select. But I'll say this much: when someone has a history of sexual or psychological trauma, it's crucial to find outside help. You can't overcome these problems just by means of willpower and positive thinking.

I recently spoke to a woman who said to me, "Father, you know what? Just this year I've been able to understand that I was sexually abused as a child." This woman, who was almost fifty, had needed many decades to reach this insight. Imagine how the legacy of childhood abuse had affected her marriage. It's true that for thirty years or more, she had repressed that experience of abuse, but I can't imagine that it hadn't influenced her attitudes toward sexuality, toward herself, and toward her husband. If a person starts a relationship or gets married but hasn't come to terms with past abuse, those experiences will continue to exert great power. He or she may repress what happened for a period of time, but the past will eventually become an issue. To move beyond the legacy of pain, there has to be some sort of inner healing—psychological healing, certainly, but also spiritual healing. And I'd venture to say that healing is a process that you can't really undertake alone. You need a guide. You need an ally who can help you work through the process.

COMMUNICATION—A PROCESS, NOT AN INSTANT SOLUTION

We've covered a lot of issues in this chapter—so many that you may feel daunted by what I'm advocating. Rest easy. Communication within a marriage is a complex, often contentious subject, but you and your spouse have time and love on your side. By being open to each other, you can change patterns of interaction and learn new skills. You can communicate more openly and honestly, and your openness and honesty will make communication itself easier and easier as the months and years pass.

Many couples want to deal with communication issues just as they deal with everything else: as a quick fix. But you can't fix communication in an hour or two, much less in ten minutes. You're not going to change your way of speaking or your way of listening to each other by making a single decision or by having a single discussion of these issues.

Here's what I recommend: take the long view. Try to see that communication is a process, not an instant solution. Improving marital communication takes long-term, patient, hard work. The changes will be incremental, subtle, and sometimes hard to detect. But if you and your spouse put your minds to it, you *will* make progress.

Chapter 11

How to Communicate Better

So when it comes to couples' communication, we're left with a kind of good news/bad news joke.

The bad news: unlike the four-lane causeway from California to Hawaii, there's no "miracle bridge" that will connect you and your spouse throughout the years of your relationship.

The good news: a truly wonderful bridge is possible anyway—a bridge that the two of you can construct yourselves, one word, one sentence, one discussion at a time.

How will you construct that bridge? What tasks or techniques can help you foster good communication in your relationship? I could offer a long list for you to consider, but here are the things that I find most important and most productive:

Task #1
Make Time to Communicate

"We'd be closer if we just had more time to communicate."

I often hear this lament from couples. Life is busy. Schedules are crazy. Everything else comes first, and time together ends up at the bottom of the list. By the time you and your spouse find time to be together, it's often so late in the day that you're out of energy.

How can you deal with this dilemma? I think the only good solution is to *make* time. If you simply wait for the opportunities to arise, you'll probably wait in vain. Something will always come up and take precedence. A better idea: factor in husband-wife time in advance.

Specifically, I urge you to set aside some time weekly. This goal is especially important if you and your spouse are intent on improving your communication. An hour a week is a realistic option. This time should be a quiet, private interlude for just you and your spouse. Is this arrangement difficult to set up? Probably. But that's all the more reason to go ahead and do it. The very fact that it's hard to set aside an hour a week is all the more evidence that *it won't happen if you don't plan in advance.*

You don't have to have a specific agenda for this one-hour time together. You don't have to make it a formal sit-down "session," which could create too much pressure and make this occasion far more intimidating than it needs to be. It's just a time for the two of you that's conducive to talking. Take a walk. Have a picnic. Sit down for a game of cards or checkers. One couple I know has a regular breakfast date immediately following church. They find that they leave Mass feeling good, and this upbeat mode is conducive to a comfortable time together, including a leisurely, indulgent breakfast, where they review the past week and talk about what's coming up. It doesn't matter what you do—it's just a matter of you and your spouse finding uninterrupted alone time when you can talk, listen, and be open to each other.

Here are some suggestions to consider:

∾ **Do everything possible to prevent interruptions.** Among other things, this assumes that you'll turn off telecommunications gadgets and preserve the "bubble" of privacy you're creating. (See Task 2 below for more thoughts on gadgetry.)

∾ **Set up childcare well in advance to guarantee privacy and calm.** Precisely because children demand so much time and attention from parents, you need to make sure they're safely but completely off-site—or at least fully attended—so that you can focus on each other as husband and wife.

∾ **Plan your time together at least a week in advance, then honor your commitment.** Just as you wouldn't schedule a golf game at the same time that you had an important business meeting or a doctor's appointment, you shouldn't schedule anything else that would conflict with your appointment with your spouse.

∾ **Avoid conversation-disrupting activities.** If your time together will include an activity, make sure that you choose something conducive to talking. Movies, video games, sporting events, and concerts may be enjoyable, but you won't get much talking done in those situations.

∾ **Be fully open to each other.** When you talk, don't censor yourselves or each other. Don't cut each other off or shut down if you don't want to hear something. If something is a touchy topic, say as much to your partner in advance. Perhaps you can talk through the issue now; perhaps you'll have to revisit the issue at another time. But accept the fact that you can't avoid issues indefinitely. You need to face things and be open and willing to talk about all of them.

∾ **Make your time together a no-anger zone.** If you disagree about something, if things get heated, or if you feel emotions getting too intense in a negative way, agree to stop the discussion and resume it at another time.

Task #2
Turn Off Your Gadgets

I sometimes wonder what marital communication would be like if our society wasn't so full of high-tech gadgets. Oh, I know that communications technology has real benefits for many people, couples included. But I also feel that the devices we've all come to rely on have their own drawbacks. I know many couples who depend on electronic entertainment so much—DVDs, iPods, digital TV, and so forth—that they forget to pay attention to each other or spend time together in low-tech ways.

For this reason, I feel that one of the best ways to foster husband-wife communication is turn off all your gadgets now and then. I don't mean to suggest that you reject modern technology altogether—far from it. All I mean is that you take a break from high-tech devices now and then. For at least an hour or two each day (or maybe for a longer stretch of time once a week, such as on a Sunday morning) give yourself a "technological holiday." Yes, that means switching off your cell phone. Shut off your PDA and laptop, too. Turn off the ringer on your home phone and lower the volume on your answering machine. Switch off your TV, radio, and desktop computer as well. Give yourself some silence to work with—a refuge from all the high-tech devices that crowd out ordinary face-to-face communication.

Why is this approach useful—and, I believe, beneficial? Although we have 24/7 access to the entire world, we actually seem to communicate less than ever. Cell phones, fax machines, and many other gadgets keep us constantly in touch with other people—but do we talk and listen effectively to each other? I often wonder. I fear that many of us are getting much more comfortable communicating through electronic means than face to face. We may attribute this situation to speed and practicality, but our gadget mania may also be a way to avoid true personal interaction. I worry that people today often seem to have more time for gadgets than for people. We spend so much of our time interacting with computers, PDAs, TVs, Game Boys, and all sorts of other high-tech devices.

But to foster communication in a relationship, you have to spend quality time with your partner. You have to find a "safety zone" in your life—whether it's in the morning, the evening, or at night—when you can talk about each other's needs. You have to be willing to listen and speak. You need to turn off the gadgets and just focus on each other.

Task #3
Express Yourself in Writing

Remember old-fashioned love letters? They're out of style now, but they did great things for relationships in the past, and many people could learn something from this old method of communication. You don't have to use the flowery language of days gone by, but writing your thoughts to the person you love may help you to articulate and organize what you want to communicate. This may give the message a greater impact than if you were to speak the words. The downside: whenever you write something, it's there in black and white. The words can come back to haunt you in the future. So, admittedly, the option of expressing yourself in writing is a mixed blessing. Here are a few aspects of the situation to consider:

Writing is a way of thinking on paper—almost like thinking out loud. Psychotherapists and spiritual directors have used journaling for many years as an effective way of getting people to express what's inside. Writing can also help us communicate certain things that we may not be able to verbalize clearly or eloquently. This can be especially helpful if you're trying to express thoughts that are complex, intense, or emotionally subtle. The form you use can be a journal, a card, or a letter. Whatever you do, however, make sure that you don't underestimate or abuse the power of communicating through the written word.

Here's how I see the pros and cons of several different options:

Journals. A diary or journal is an almost infinitely flexible way to explore what's going on in your mind. Putting your thoughts on paper can clarify what may seem muddled or completely unknown to you until you start writing. As the American writer William Zinsser puts it: "How do I know what I think until I read what I wrote?" The other advantage of a journal is that you're writing for yourself alone. You're not writing the Great American Novel. You're not trying to persuade, reassure, or entertain someone else. You're just pouring out your heart and soul for your own benefit. You can use a stream-of-consciousness approach and just scribble whatever comes to mind. The payoff: understanding your thoughts and emotions, thus reaching better insights about how your inner state is affecting your outward actions.

Letters can serve either of two purposes.

One purpose is to express something to your spouse and actually "deliver" it to him or her. Let's suppose, for instance, that the two of you have argued recently. You have more to say, but you're not sure if you can express yourself articulately at this point. Writing a letter may provide an opportunity to state what's on your mind in a measured way. You can explain your concerns, pose questions, request clarification, or apologize in ways that might be more difficult if you were simply to "wing it" in person. In short, you can resume or advance a dialogue that has been under way already.

The other purpose for a letter is to express emotions that may seem too risky by other means. That is, you can write a letter that expresses frustration, anger, sadness, or whatever else you're feeling that feels "over the top" and thus not acceptable. Letters of this sort are documents that you do not intend to show your spouse; rather, they are a way to work out your feelings. If you use a letter for this purpose, it's okay to let everything come out—troubling thoughts, furious emotions, whatever you happen to be feeling. Why is this approach useful? Like writing in a journal, it can help you understand what's on your mind. In addition, you may find yourself working through your emotions and coming to a completely different place than from where you started. A letter of this sort may clear the air and allow you a calmer state of mind for the one-to-one interactions that occur later.

Keep these recommendations in mind to avoid problems when you write to your spouse:

- Never write a letter *that you intend to give to your spouse* while in a state of anger.

- If you are angry and you want to write something anyway, stall at least twenty-four hours before doing so, as this "cooling-off period" is crucial.

- It's a good idea to let anything you've written sit for a while (at least overnight) before you deliver the message to your spouse.

- If you really need to vent verbally, do so in a private journal or diary rather than in a letter (since it's better to vent before you sit down and write a message to another person).

- Keep in mind that people tend to read negative messages over and over again and to experience the same (or even increasing) pain as they reread them.

- If you write in a journal, make sure that you can maintain your privacy, since words you've written just for yourself could cause great damage to your relationship if read by someone else.

Here's one other issue to consider: one of the best ways you can use the written word within marital communications is by writing a brief note. You don't have to write a whole letter when you have something to share with your partner. A simple note can do wonders. Saying how much you love your spouse or how much you appreciate him or her is some thing that everyone will appreciate. A funny card or even a Post-it saying "I love you" and stuck to the bathroom mirror can do wonders for communication in your marriage.

Task #4
What I Think You Think

No matter how wonderful your spouse may be, I bet he or she isn't a mind reader. And no matter how great you are, too, you probably aren't one, either. Yet many husbands and wives act as if they can read each other's minds. It's all too easy to think you can guess what your spouse is thinking, and holding this belief may create a lot of tension in your marriage.

To help you overcome this assumption about mind reading—and, better yet, to open up the option of honest communication—I recommend that you try a task called "What I *Think* You Think." Here's how this task works. During your weekly time together, you pick a topic and each independently write down your feelings, thoughts, and opinions about it. You also each write down what you think your spouse feels about this topic. Then you compare notes. The goal: to see the disconnect between that you think your spouse believes compared to what he or she really believes.

For example, Letti and Oscar decided to exchanges views about a loaded topic: "Husbands and Housework."

- **Letti's opinion:** "Oscar, thank you for doing quite a bit of housework! You do lot more than a lot of husbands nowadays. But please stop congratulating yourself so much about what you do! This isn't gonna win you the Congressional Medal of Honor."

- **Letti's guess about Oscar's opinion:** "He probably thinks I'm as obsessive about domestic stuff as Martha Stewart."

- **Oscar's opinion:** "I don't mind doing housework, but sometimes I get the feeling I'll never live up to your standards."

- **Oscar's guess about Letti's opinion:** "She wishes I'd do even more than I do already."

As you can see, some of this couple's opinions came closer to the truth than others did. They do, in fact, have some issues to face regarding the amount of housework that Oscar does in the home, as well as regarding the issue of standards. To some degree, each spouse has some good hunches about the other's concerns. They haven't sorted through these issues, however, in ways that resolve the question itself (that is, a husband's contribution to domestic tasks). But the point of the exercise isn't to tie up the subject in a tidy little package. Rather, the goal is to reveal the couple's actual thoughts and feelings and to open up the discussion.

Here are some possible topics to get you started. Ideally, you should then go ahead and compile your own list of topics to discuss over the long term.

- We spend enough quality time together.

- There are issues that prevent us from communicating effectively.

- Our responsibilities in the relationship are evenly divided (or divided in a way that works for us).

- We are appreciative of each other.

- We spend enough/too much/not enough time with our friends.

- We have planned adequately for the future.

- Our parenting duties are divided sensibly.

- We each have a fair amount of leisure time.

A couple of further thoughts about this task:

- ∾ It's important that you work on only one issue at a time. Doing more than that may prove exhausting.

- ∾ Make sure that you factor in enough time for talking over the topic and exploring it fully. This process isn't something you want to rush.

- ∾ If you agree with the other person or guess right about what he or she has been thinking, that is great. But if you don't, you shouldn't consider your response a failure. This task is an exercise in learning about your spouse and exploring the topics, not mastering the mystic art of extrasensory perception.

- ∾ Consider this task an opportunity for you to learn, to clear up misperceptions, and, if there is a conflict, to work toward compromise.

Task #5
Don't Interrupt Each Other

Here's a behavior I see in many couples: instead of listening to each other, one or both spouses focus on formulating responses while the other person talks. They're so fixated on what they're going to say next that they interrupt the other person before he or she has even finished. This behavior is problematic in many ways. First off, it's rude. Second, it makes thoughtful listening almost impossible. Third, it raises tension when the couple tries to communicate. For all these reasons, I feel that one of the most important tasks a couple can undertake is to avoid this process of habitual interruption.

Many couples constantly interrupt each other. Each spouse is eager—

even frantic—to "control the podium." The result: no one can get a word in edgewise. Both partners feel tripped up and prevented from stating what's on their minds. The tension level escalates. The quality of the discussion plummets. Sometimes a shouting match ensues.

A much better approach is to take turns in a fair way. No, you don't need to follow Robert's Rules of Order. But when it's the other person's turn to talk, don't interrupt while he or she is making a statement. Likewise, you shouldn't get interrupted, either. Each of you gets to state your concerns without interruption; then, while the other person responds, you listen attentively. Is this easy? No. It requires patience, respect, and self-control. But taking turns respectfully and patiently will get you a lot farther (and much faster) than a free-for-all. You don't need to resort to the Native American custom of using a "talking stick"—a batonlike object that allowed the person holding it to speak without interruption. (Frankly, though, I feel that some couples could benefit from this custom!) What you need to do, however, is to make sure that whichever spouse "has the floor" can proceed uninterrupted.

Task #6
Learn How to Argue

Learning how to argue? Why would you want to do that! Isn't it better not to argue at all? You might think so. But I have yet to meet the couple that never argues. And as I said in the previous chapter, *not* arguing at all often leads to problems of built-up resentment, blocked communication, and even violent outbursts. Arguing doesn't mean you have a bad relationship. Arguing in the right way can actually be good for your relationship. Why? Because you get issues out into the open; you have an honest discussion of them; you tackle problems together; and you solve those problems as a team.

As I noted in Chapter 10, the key is to make sure that your arguments are constructive. You need to argue in a way that allows both of you to air your grievances, express your emotions, and work together to find a compromise that serves you both. To accomplish these goals, I suggest the following ground rules:

- **Don't yell, shout, or scream at each other.** Raising your voice won't help your spouse hear you better. Worse yet, yelling, shouting, or screaming will usually damage the communication process, since your spouse will quickly start to shut you out. And if you both end up hollering, neither of you will hear the other.

- **Don't argue in front of the kids (or anyone else, for that matter).** Discussions and arguments should be strictly for you as a couple. Arguing in front of friends or relatives will make them uncomfortable, and kids find their parents' arguments frightening. The only exception to this rule: if you seek outside counseling. In that case, having your counselor present for your arguments may be part of the therapeutic process.

- **Express your concerns without risk of interruption from your spouse.** (See Task #4 for a detailed discussion of this subject.)

- **Avoid sweeping generalizations and accusations.** Problematic phrases include "You always," "You never," "Every time you," and similar constructions. State your concerns without attacking the other person's character. Focus on specific issues.

- **Stop your argument if it gets "too hot to handle."** Schedule the discussion for another time. If your emotions get the best of you, you may say things that you'll regret later. Some couples also run a heightened risk of physical violence when an argument heats up. (If you feel that your safety is at risk, disengage from the argument and, if necessary, seek help.)

Task #7
Use "I-Messages"

One technique I recommend to help make arguments more constructive is the use of "I-messages." Rather than making broad generalizations, frame your comments as nonjudgmental statements from your own perspective. Here's an example. Instead of saying, "You're such a pig—you never pick up after yourself," say, "I feel frustrated because you leave so many clothes lying around." Why is this second statement more strategic and more effective? Because by phrasing your complaint in these terms, you're *talking about your frustration* rather than *attacking the other person's character.* Instead of ranting and raving, you're clarifying the issue. In this case, the real issue is that you feel frustrated by having to clean up all the time. You want your spouse to help out with controlling the household clutter. Your phrasing of the problem *opens up the discussion* rather than *closing it down.* You're not saying, "You're a pig"—words that no one is eager to hear. Rather, you're saying, "I'm frustrated. I get home from work and I'm exhausted. I feel frustrated because you haven't cleaned up your mess." This approach is much more likely to produce an alliance and thus lead to solving the problem.

To practice, make a list of your current grievances and then reframe them as "I-messages."

Here are some examples:

- **Broad accusation:** "You're always late."
- **I-message:** "I feel frustrated when you come home so late."

- **Broad accusation:** "You never pick up after yourself."
- **I-message:** "I feel demoralized when I have to clean up after you so much."

- **Broad accusation:** "You men are so insensitive."
- **I-message:** "I've tried to explain how I'm feeling, but you don't seem to be listening to me."

- **Broad accusation:** "It's so dumb that you've left the lawn mower out, as usual."
- **I-message:** "I'm concerned that the lawn mower will be damaged if you leave it out and there's a rainstorm."

Task #8
Go Back to Dating

Remember what your relationship was like when you first met? Maybe you gave each other little gifts. Maybe you called impulsively at work to whisper, "I love you." Maybe you wrote little notes and slipped them under the door. Maybe you sneaked up on each other to give a surprise kiss. It's not called "the sparkle stage" for nothing. Some couples practically glow in the dark, they're so delighted with each other.

It's true that the sparkle stage can't last forever. All those dazzling sparks of infatuation and mutual delight eventually turn into the warm glow of trust and deep, abiding love. So I'm not saying that you should turn back the clock and strive for a *less* deep, *less* mature love. However, I think a lot of couples could benefit from remembering what their first few weeks and months were like. And to do so, I suggest a task I call "Go back to dating."

To undertake this task, you can be in a long-term relationship, married for decades, or anything in between. The goal is simply to regain the mood you had early on. How? Well, make a date. You don't have to spend a lot of money; just do something special. Get a baby-sitter. Dress up for the occasion. Give each other little gifts. Guys, bring your wives some flowers. Pull out her chair in a courtly manner. Hold hands. And when you're together in the restaurant, don't talk money problems, school issues, or getting the car fixed. Leave all that to another day. Talk about your hopes and dreams. Flirt with each other. Shed your cares for an evening.

Task #9
Express Your Appreciation

Many husbands and wives tell me that they know their spouse loves them, but they just don't feel appreciated. It's common that partners take each other for granted. The stress of work and the complex duties of parenthood, especially, leave many couples too exhausted to do more than meet their obligations. It's hard to find time or energy to offer each other the little pleasures of life together. And one of the things that often falls by the wayside is appreciation.

For this reason, it's crucial to counteracting the drift toward indifference or *seeming* indifference. Here's what I suggest instead: say something nice to your partner each day. Offer a compliment. Express thanks for something. Speak of your admiration. What you say can be short and sweet—you don't have to give a speech. (In fact, it's better if you don't.) The only "rule" is that you need to be sincere.

Here are just a few examples of what I have in mind:

- "You're a great cook anyway, but tonight's dinner was especially wonderful."

- "I like how that shirt makes your eyes look even bluer."

- "You put in so much time with the kids, helping them with their homework—you're such a good dad."

- "I can't thank you enough for all you're doing for our family."

- "You look so pretty with the light in your hair like that."

- "You are so thoughtful."

Performing this task has many benefits. Expressing your appreciation boosts your spouse's ego, helps him or her to feel good, and strengthens your marital bond. In addition, it can serve as an exercise that helps you pay attention to someone in your life who, over the years, may have become indistinct or "out of focus." The positive things you say will actually help you see your spouse in a more positive light.

Task #10
Whisper in the Dark

How often do you and your spouse just fall into bed and call it a day? This scenario is amazingly common. Many couples are too exhausted for lovemaking. Fair enough. But it's a pity when spouses can't have a little "downtime" together to unwind and settle in before sleep. Something to consider: go to bed together fifteen minutes earlier than normal, shut off the lights, and talk in the dark.

There's something about talking in the dark that makes a conversation more intimate. Remember when you were a kid . . . did you share a room with a sibling, or did you have sleepovers with friends? If so, you probably stayed awake after the lights went off and talked about special things. Why shouldn't you capture that secret, private mood with your spouse? It's a special kind of communication that's easy and doesn't take long. It's a time to talk about what you've been thinking about, dreaming about, wondering about. Or you can offer a compliment or expression of thanks. Or you can whisper sweet nothings.

Why not? What better way to end a day than with such a quiet, private, low-key gift to each other?

FOR BETTER OR FOR WORSE . . .

I believe that most couples want good communication, and most work hard to achieve it. The tasks I've suggested in this chapter are just a few of the ways in which you and your spouse can communicate better and, in doing so, strengthen your marriage. As I've said throughout Path Five and elsewhere in this book, communication is truly one of the most crucial elements in a good relationship—one of the capabilities that can help a couple deal with life "for better or for worse."

What if your communication is already good? I urge you to keep working at it. Communication takes continual practice. Even if you and your spouse have always communicated well, you have to keep on working at it to avoid the risk of complacency.

And what if your communication isn't so great? Well, then I encourage you to face the issues we've considered in Path Five, work at the skills I've described, and do everything possible to improve the communication within your marriage.

This point brings us to a difficult aspect in our discussion. What if there's a complete breakdown in your marital communication? What if one spouse totally refuses to listen to the other? What if the differences in communication styles are so great that interaction breaks down completely? What if every discussion turns into an argument? If one or more of these problems occurs in your relationship, what should you do?

I believe that when a couple's communication breaks down completely, it's best for the partners to seek help from a third party. The couple needs someone who can be their sounding board or who can help them communicate. It's interesting to me how often spouses will speak openly with a therapist or pastoral counselor present, and later they'll tell me, "Father, she never told me that before," or "Oh, he never told me that before." Then I ask, "So how come you're saying it now?" It's almost as if they need somebody else there to be their referee or communication coach to help them talk about these issues. The presence of a counselor helps them keep their bearings.

Is this a problem? My opinion is, no, it's not a problem at all. It's helpful if a couple can benefit from a trained outsider's guidance.

So if you're "stuck" and can't communicate constructively, I recommend that you find outside help. If your communication is so hostile that insulting or violent behavior is a risk, I urge you in the strongest possible terms to seek assistance before you make your problems even worse. (See the appendix of this book for referral services to marital counselors.)

Whatever else, your marriage is built on effective communication. By following Path Five, you can keep your relationship strong and vibrant. You can stay in close emotional touch no matter what you're going through as a couple. You can maintain your strongest possible connection with real life and real love.

LEARN TO ACCEPT YOUR DIFFERENCES

"My husband and I come from different countries, so we grew up with different ways of doing things. When we were engaged, that was something we both felt was exciting—that we weren't the same. I still feel that it's fine that he is who he is, and I don't feel it's my job to change him. But he doesn't seem to like me for who I am anymore. He makes fun of my accent, he makes fun of the food I like, and he makes fun of other things about me."

—Elisa, twenty-five

"Sometimes she treats me like sort of a home-improvement project. Like I'm not her husband, I'm a fixer-upper. She wants me to dress differently or act differently. She tells me I look sloppy or I don't speak right or I need to do things more like she does."

—Alex, twenty-eight

"There are things about Carlo that I think are absolutely wonderful. There are some other things that are just sort of regular-guy things that are okay but don't exactly impress me. And there are some

things about him that drive me crazy. But I have to say this: overall the balance is good. He's a good man. I love him. He has far more good features than bad features. And after twenty-eight years of marriage, I can guarantee this guy isn't going to change, so I don't even bother trying."

—Martha, fifty-seven

"Nancy and I don't actually see eye-to-eye on everything, and we disagree on a lot of stuff. But we decided years ago to put all our cards on the table and play fair. If we disagree, we say so. We talk it out. If we're upset about something, we say so. We're not going to yank each other around and play games and stuff like that."

—Tony, thirty-one

The task of living with differences in a marriage presents couples with a mix of delight and difficulty. *Delight* because variety is the spice of life, right? Marriage would be tedious if a husband and a wife shared exactly the same interests, habits, preferences, mannerisms, and beliefs. But there's difficulty, too, since differences within a couple often create challenges and conflicts. Many spouses knock heads over relatively minor matters—taste in music, verbal tics, and harmless habits. Other spouses tolerate overbearing or even destructive behavior. As the two men and two women quoted above may indicate, couples often struggle with issues of how to cope with their differences, and this situation overall raises some important, potentially difficult questions:

- ❧ How can spouses distinguish between important and unimportant differences?

- ❧ Can (or should) one spouse attempt to change the other's beliefs or behavior?

∽ Can spouses live in peace when they see the world in totally different ways from each other?

Path Six is about the process of understanding which differences matter, which don't, and what you should—or shouldn't—do about them.

Chapter 12

Why Dealing with Differences Is So Crucial

More and more couples nowadays come from totally different backgrounds. Many others get married following such a rushed courtship or relationship that the partners don't really know each other. Following this hasty process, it's almost inevitable that conflicts will arise. A lot of couples I meet with lament their differences. They say things like, "You see, Father, he doesn't understand that I do things this way because of how I was raised." Or, "Father, she doesn't accept my background and my preferences." Well, you can accept your partner's differences if you've already gotten to know each other fully and have worked through various issues open-mindedly. But many couples haven't taken these steps. They've rushed their courtship, and they may even have skimped on exploring the issues they do or don't have in common. A likely result: conflicts over differences.

The truth is, all couples have differences, and these differences often show up when a man and a woman give themselves fully to each other in a long-term relationship. Coping with differences is part of being radically open to each other. Do you truly grasp that your partner is different from you? Do you understand that he or she may have a set of values, morals, and perspectives that you may or may not share? And as you build your life together, do you realize that some of your values, morals, and perspectives may even have to be modified?

Well, I have some bad news and some good news.

The bad news: understanding and coping with differences in marriage takes time, patience, and lots of hard work.

The good news: when you begin to comprehend and accept these differences, you can attain a great sense of strength, confidence, and serenity as a couple. You don't have to accept every last detail of your spouse's worldview or interests or habits. You don't have to agree with each other on everything. But when you truly accept each other as human beings—and when you "agree to disagree"—you'll reach a remarkable state of calm.

DIFFERENCES, DIFFERENCES . . .

In marriage, two completely different human beings come together to form a relationship in varying degrees of closeness. It's amazing, in fact, how varied the outcome may be when people pair off. Some couples seem so perfectly matched they inspire great amazement and admiration, so we exclaim, "They're perfect soul mates," or "They're made for each other." When couples seem mismatched, however, we ask, "How did these two people ever get together?" or "How have they stayed together so long?" This is one of the great mysteries: how and why some couples "work out" while others are constantly in conflict.

Sometimes we explain the situation by saying, "Opposites attract." And sometimes differences *do* balance the couple. For example, Aldo and Louise own a photography studio that specializes in taking pictures for commercial catalogues. Aldo runs the technical side of the business: he interacts with various clients' artistic directors, helps set up displays of products, and supervises a small team of photographers who take pictures of the merchandise. Meanwhile, Louise runs the company's business operations. She courts potential clients, negotiates deals, sets up appointments for the photo shoots, keeps the books, and handles all the other financial tasks. This couple's company wouldn't function if the spouses didn't have such well-balanced talents and temperaments. Their marriage, too, is balanced: Aldo is a dreamer, while Louise is more practical and down-to-earth. You've probably known people like Aldo and Louise, spouses who seem different from each other but somehow "just right"— capable of complementing each other's strengths and weaknesses.

But in some marriages, the best motto isn't "Opposites attract," but rather "Birds of a feather flock together." These are couples who are so much alike that they seem (except for one being male and the other being female) as if they're a perfectly matched set. Such spouses seem to agree on everything, and they often have the same likes and dislikes, the same habits and attitudes, even the same personalities. Jessie and Ernesto are a couple of this sort. Calm, detail-oriented, and cheerful, both spouses work as accountants in the same company; both are fully involved as parents of their three kids; and both enjoy playing competitive bridge. Friends tease Jessie and Ernesto by calling them Tweedledum and Tweedledee.

But even when couples seem so similar, there will be differences. Each human being is fundamentally different from everyone else. God made each of us unique. And that's what makes the world an interesting place. Still, the situation is unpredictable. Sometimes differences between spouses create a marvelous sense of variety within the relationship; sometimes differences make the partners miserable; and sometimes differences have consequences that fall on a spectrum between these two extremes. When we speak of partners complementing each other, that's when we perceive their differences as a blessing and a source of richness. When people truly complement each other, problems tend to diminish.

So what does complementing each other mean, anyway? It doesn't mean that the spouses are as alike as a pair of saltshakers, that's for sure. A better comparison would be that they're like pieces of a puzzle. They're not the same; rather, they fit together in harmony.

DIFFERENCES IN MARRIAGE—A SPECIAL SITUATION?

Our goal in Path Six is to understand how we deal with differences in relationships—especially differences that become problematic—and how to confront and solve the difficulties that these differences can create. Let's consider a few important questions:

- ～ What is it that aggravates us about other people—and can we change them so that we feel less aggravated?

- ～ Is there a secret formula to making people think more as we do—or even getting them to conduct themselves in a manner that is acceptable to us?

- ～ Can you live in peace with someone who sees the world differently from how you do?

The truth is, differences don't always create the perfectly matched set I referred to earlier, and couples with differences don't always fit together harmoniously, either. Differences can certainly lead to problems—and sometimes a lot of them. Sometimes the problems are minor issues that become a source of annoyance and aggravation. Sometimes the problems are bigger issues that grow until they loom like major barriers in the relationship. Most of the couples I know (whether as acquaintances, friends, or parishioners) refer in one way or another to differences between them. And it's not uncommon for such differences to be a source of friction within the marriage.

In fact, I've noticed that the same differences we tolerate in other relationships may cause more friction within a marriage. Here's a trivial but telling example. Steven, a gifted and accomplished schoolteacher, has a lot of random energy that often prompts him to drum his fingers absentmindedly. This behavior isn't exactly a huge character flaw, but his wife, Beth, finds this habit so annoying that she often berates her husband—sometimes in public—for this nervous tic. When I pointed out to Beth that her brother, Julian, also has a habit of drumming his fingers, she shrugged off my comment. "Well, yeah, they both do it," she said. "But, first of all, I can't exactly change my brother. It's just not that kind of a relationship. Also, I don't *live* with my brother! But I live with Steven, and his twitchiness really gets on my nerves."

Perhaps differences—in this case, a difference in physical self-expression—causes more tension in a marriage because the spouses spend so much time together. Or perhaps the issue is what Beth suggests: that marriage is a volitional arrangement, a matter of choice, whereas her relationship with her brother doesn't contain that element of choice. I'm not sure. (Plenty of brothers and sisters get on each other's nerves, too, even during adulthood.)

Here's a more extreme example that may further illuminate the issues.

Miranda and Ricardo have been married about ten years. Their marriage has been happy in many ways, but a significant difference between them is causing progressively more tension within the marriage. It's a rather classic situation of how the spouses express their feelings. Miranda is open to her own emotions and expresses them without apology. If she's amused, she laughs. If she's sad, she cries. If she's angry, she shouts and hollers. You always know what this woman is feeling! By contrast, Ricardo is reserved and, frankly, rather repressed. He himself admits that certain experiences please, frustrate, anger, amuse, or sadden him, but he doesn't feel comfortable expressing any of the emotions that go along with what he's experiencing. "That's just not how I learned to behave in my family," Ricardo explains. "I guess you could say I'm pretty buttoned-down. Okay, so I'm buttoned-down. That's just the way I am. What am I supposed to do, get a personality transplant?"

It's true that Ricardo has a right to be who he is and to feel what he feels. Miranda does, too. Neither of them should feel a necessity to be the other person—or even to act like the other person. However, the situation I'm describing still comes at a price. Miranda tells Ricardo, "I'm not saying, 'Get a personality transplant.' But if you feel something, then feel it. Otherwise I feel like you're not there. I feel like I'm married to some kind of robot. Or maybe to Mr. Spock—all brain, no heart. Your feelings aren't just about you. They're also about me."

I'm not sure how this couple will resolve the problem they're facing. I feel that their situation is interesting, however, because (as I suggested earlier) it helps to illuminate the issue of why differences sometimes cause more tension in a marriage than in other relationships.

Doesn't it always seem that the closer you feel to someone, the more you can feel hurt by his or her actions? This certainly happens in many relationships. When this type of situation occurs within a marriage, the resulting pain seems worse, and the partners' ability to forgive and move on tends to diminish. "Why does this hurtfulness take place? I believe it's partly because the "wounds" hit closer to the sacred center. You don't hurt "out there"—at the edge of your life. You hurt at the core, which is always more delicate. When an acquaintance or a distant friend offends us, we usually move on and brush off the offense with greater ease—it's no big deal. But we expect close relationships to be the source of love and support, not the source of rejection and insults. In the case of Ricardo and Miranda, the husband's inability to reveal his emotions is especially hurtful to the wife precisely because Ricardo's inexpressiveness hurts Miranda in her sacred center ("I feel like I'm married to a robot"). The same lack of emotion in many other people probably wouldn't affect her so much. But a difference of this magnitude is significant in a married couple.

WHEN SMALL DIFFERENCES CAUSE BIG PROBLEMS

It's common wisdom that spouses often knock heads over "the little things." Would a couple really split up because one partner wants the toilet paper to come off the back of the roll while the other wants it to come off the front? I don't know—but sometimes I wonder. Here's a very short list of complaints that I've heard couples state cause big problems:

- "She always leaves the cap off the toothpaste tube."

- "He never puts the toilet seat back down."

- "She leaves her lingerie hanging in the shower stall to dry."

- "He insists on reading at the dinner table instead of talking with me."

- "She vacuums around me while I'm trying to watch the ball game."

- "He can't talk about anything without using sports terminology."

- "She says 'like' about every other word."

- "He never cleans under his fingernails."

- "She takes an hour just to put on her makeup."

- "He never says 'excuse me' when he burps."

Trivial concerns? Of course. But their triviality doesn't mean that they don't reflect real differences or do real damage. The complaints I've quoted reflect small habits, tics, mannerisms, and preferences that are harmless in their own right. They seem insignificant, even silly. Yet somehow they still register on the marital seismograph; they can rattle a marriage in their own right; and they can sometimes predict a major earthquake if the spouses simply ignore the warning signs.

Here's an example of a couple who found that a small difference caused big problems—and how the spouses decided to resolve the issue.

Jane and Hiroshi have dinner together at least three or four nights a week. Both enjoy this time together at the end of the day, but they have different views of how to use it. Jane prefers to "downshift" and set aside everything that has occurred during the workday. By contrast, Hiroshi wants to discuss every last detail of what happened at the office. "The last thing I want to talk about over dinner is who said what to whom back at the office," Jane says. "I want to leave that all behind." Hiroshi has a different take on the situation: "I'm still processing the day. Talking with Jane is my way of deprogramming my brain." Tensions over this situation have led to several arguments. The dinner hour became a source of conflict, not relaxation. Eventually, the couple reached a compromise: they would talk about office politics only while fixing dinner; then, once they sat down to eat, they'd shift to non-work-related topics.

WHAT ABOUT BIGGER DIFFERENCES?

Although many couples squabble over minor issues, it's true that marriages run greater risks of conflict over truly major differences. I'm referring to issues such as:

- ∾ Personal and family priorities

- ∾ Preferences on where to live

- ∾ Career plans

- ∾ Decisions about whether to start a family and, if so, how many children to have

- ∾ Approaches to parenting tasks

- ∾ Financial goals

- ∾ Political orientation

- ∾ Philosophy of life

- ∾ The role of faith and spirituality in the marriage

These are the issues that create the bedrock of your relationship. If you and your spouse have significant differences over any of these issues, the foundation that supports your marriage will be unstable. It's no wonder that disagreement over these big issues can lead to conflict.

Some of our beliefs and values are so central to who we are that we need to make sure that you discuss them with a potential spouse early on in the relationship. I'm referring to fundamental beliefs, morals, and religious practices. Some of these issues may be open to compromise: career goals, attitudes about parenting practices, and life-stage priorities. Other issues may allow no room for compromise: religious beliefs, insistence on fidelity, and central tenets of morality. If you and your partner have core values that clash, can you work things out? Maybe, maybe not. But in any case, I sincerely hope that you discuss these topics and get to know where your partner stands on them before you make a long-term commitment to each other.

Do these issues indicate irreconcilable differences for you or not? Well, that depends. I've known couples who have found these sorts of issues impossible to resolve. I've also known couples who have managed to resolve their differences on exactly the same issues and reach a compromise. The fact that some do and some don't should be a tip-off. The outcome really depends on the individual couple—what the partners believe most fervently, how capable they are of discussing the relevant questions open-mindedly, how willing they are to meet each other halfway. I'm not saying that any one approach is right or wrong. I do feel, however, that every couple needs to explore the issues rather than pretend that they don't exist.

I recently received a letter from a man who married a very fundamentalist evangelical. The spouses had two different faiths and two different backgrounds. They'd dealt pretty well with their interfaith issues until their children started to ask questions: "Why does Mommy believe this?" and "Why does Daddy believe that?" and "Why do we do this with Mommy and that with Daddy?" These differences were now becoming a point of tension in their marriage; the couple was starting to realize that their different world perspectives were prompting their children to raise some basic questions. And when Mommy and Daddy provided different answers, there was conflict.

Is there true acceptance in this relationship? Is there true flexibility? Probably not. The spouses have probably been shoving a lot of issues under the carpet. Now that the children are bringing up these issues, the husband and the wife are having to deal with them. But they should have dealt with them a long time ago.

Every couple needs to consider the big picture. If you can stay open-minded but also stay true to your own beliefs, you and your partner have a good chance to balance what matters to you and reach an understanding. That may mean that you compromise and proceed to share your life together. It may mean that you admit that certain preferences or principles are so fundamental to your beliefs that you can't compromise. Some commitments *do* take precedence over marriage. But no one can reach the right conclusion for you. This is a quest that the two of you have to undertake alone.

I want to add, however, that sometimes having a guide along for the quest is a wonderful thing. By this I mean that even though you have to proceed on your own, you and your partner may want to find someone who understands the path. A thoughtful, impartial, well-trained therapist, pastoral counselor, or other mentor can make the journey easier and less exhausting.

START THE PROCESS EARLY

My hope is that if you're not married yet—or if you're still in the early years of your marriage—you'll start the process of discussing these major issues and resolve any differences as early as possible. Shoving disagreements out of sight won't help. On the contrary, this out-of-sight-out-of-mind approach will come to grief eventually. There's really no way around acknowledging the importance of these topics, discussing them, and working toward resolution. These are fundamental issues that provide the basis of how you'll live your life together. I strongly urge you to examine any differences between you *now* and resolve them before they cause any damage.

If you're married already, it's not too late to examine your differences. Here again, ignoring the situation won't work to your advantage; a head-in-the-sand approach will cause long-term problems. It's true as well that even couples who have resolved initial differences sometimes have to face new issues down the road. You and your spouse may find your beliefs changing over time; you may develop new interests and perspectives; or you may reach insights about yourself that alter your behavior. As a result, coping with major differences may be an issue you'll face in the future even if you've already addressed it in the past. Marriage involves constant change. Both you and your spouse will constantly grow and develop, so you'll have to accommodate each other's growth and development as the years come and go.

Lila and William are an example of a couple who never bothered to discuss their beliefs, attitudes, or preferences. Madly in love, they married after a six-month courtship. Now they're finding that they aren't "on the same page" regarding a wide range of issues. Religious issues, especially, are troubling them. Lila is Catholic; William is Southern Baptist. Although they agree that they have much in common as Christians, they now find the differences in their beliefs and practices a source of frequent misunderstandings. Will they manage to overcome these differences? I hope so. But they would have felt less stressed by the situation if they'd started earlier, when they were exploring their expectations about married life.

Another example of major differences: Kay and Barry. Unlike the previous couple I mentioned, Kay and Barry engaged in lots of discussions—both before they got married and after the wedding—to help them understand any issues that might cause tension in the future. They did a great job finding common ground and resolving potential conflicts. However, they couldn't anticipate everything, since life often presents surprises and challenges. What happened? Well, after the couple had lived and worked in the Chicago area for some time, Barry got a job offer from a company in California. This was an opportunity he'd dreamed about for years. He didn't care for Chicago; he didn't like the Midwestern weather; and he thought moving to the West Coast would be exciting. But Kay wasn't keen on this move. Having grown up near Chicago, she liked being geographically close to her family, and she felt that California would challenge the couple with much higher expenses, a new culture, and all the uncertainties of living in an unfamiliar community. The decision came down to differences in the spouses' priorities. Did Barry's career or Kay's family ties have precedence? To put it bluntly: their dreams collided.

After sorting through the issues, the couple made a joint decision to stay in Chicago. Barry's career *did* matter—something that Kay acknowledged without hesitance. But Barry himself admitted that the move to California was a gamble, one that might or might not lead to secure career advancement. The thought of living in a new place was what tempted him most. Yet this unpredictable goal wasn't good enough to justify relocating the whole family, especially when Kay's many Chicago-area relatives provided such a warm, supportive network for Barry, Kay, and their kids. In the meantime, Kay acknowledged that as the family's sole wage-earner, Barry seemed stressed out and needed some "safety valves" to help him cope with work-related stress. So when they decided against moving, Kay suggested that they make sure to factor in some R & R that would ease the pressures on her husband—including, if he wanted, a vacation in California.

DEALING WITH DIFFERENCES

How do you deal with the differences that you find between you and your partner? How do you abandon some of your own fixed ways of understanding reality and accept some of your spouse's perceptions?

Sometimes the answer to these questions will focus on little things that will prompt you to make specific changes to habits or expectations. Here's what Ben, married twenty years, says about a simmering domestic issue in his marriage: "We do the laundry every Saturday morning. I help out with that task, which is fine. But I have a tendency to put a whole bunch of stuff in the hamper *after* Jessie has already taken the rest of it down. I just forget about rounding up the last few items. And that drives her nuts, since she feels that she's never quite done. There are always those last few socks, pairs of underpants, whatever. So I've decided that because this issue really matters to her, but it doesn't matter to me, I'll just take the extra three minutes to gather up any clothes that are lying around—from the kids' room, from my room—and I'll take them down. Then we're done once and for all. It seems like a trivial issue, but it really bothers her, and it's no sweat off my back to do it. That's how I try to go along with her preferences. I've adjusted my attitude. If it matters that much to her and it doesn't matter to me, it's a no-brainer. It really helps her, and it hasn't caused me any difficulty."

But sometimes the response requires something more substantial or complex than just making little adjustments. You may have to open up to a different way of doing things. Maybe you don't clean up the kitchen the way your husband does, but you're better off accepting his method than alienating him and prompting him to think you're too demanding.

THE IMPORTANCE OF COMPROMISE

In the final analysis, what we're talking about is *compromise*—the willingness to admit that if you're going to overcome your differences, both parties will have to give in a little. You can't both have everything you want. I mentioned earlier that complementing each other doesn't mean that you should be the same; instead, it means that you fit together like the pieces of a puzzle. Sometimes the pieces don't fit just right, but they're not completely incompatible, either. Maybe you need to change your shape a little. Maybe your spouse needs to change, too. If you can smooth your edges somewhat, the differences between you will ultimately fit just right. But you have to change to make that possible.

What if you feel you can't compromise? What if the differences between you are so severe that you can't meet each other halfway?

Sometimes that happens. Hans and Ellie, for instance, struggled throughout their courtship with the issue of whether to have children. Hans felt—perhaps correctly—that he wasn't suited to become a father. Ellie had a longstanding desire to start a family. To their credit, this couple discussed the question of parenthood openly and in great detail. They even decided that they shouldn't get married until they could reach a decision about this crucial issue. Surely they could reach some sort of compromise . . . but ultimately they didn't. Ellie and Hans concluded that they couldn't find any middle ground about parenthood. Ellie wanted to have kids. Hans didn't. No matter how much they loved each other, marriage didn't make sense if they had mutually exclusive goals on this issue. Proceeding in any other way would severely stress the marriage in the long run, since one or the other of the partners would end up frustrated by the outcome; and the situation would be fundamentally unfair to any children they brought into the world. So they split up. An unhappy ending to this romance? Maybe—but less unhappy than many possible outcomes. I applaud this couple's honesty and clearheadedness.

But sometimes the situation seems to rule out compromise but isn't so clear-cut. An example of this situation is what happened to Marilynne and Manuel. This couple's quandary resembles Hans and Ellie's at the start of their story: Marilynne wanted to have kids; Manuel didn't. Similarly, the partners discussed the issue in great detail. Their decision took a somewhat different course, though, because Manuel reluctantly decided to go along with Marilynne's intense interest in parenthood. This flexibility might have ended up a problem, but it didn't. Marilynne not only gave birth: she gave birth to fraternal twins! But instead of finding fatherhood a burden, Manuel discovered that he loved being a dad. He's now heavily involved with raising the babies—so much so that he often bores his male friends going on and on about the glories of fatherhood. If Manuel hadn't compromised with his wife on this issue, he never would have had this experience.

THE POWER OF ACCEPTANCE

I believe that one of the most beneficial things you can do as you deal with your differences is to harness the power of acceptance. If you can learn to accept your spouse as he or she really is—without falling into the trap of trying to change the other person—you'll give both of you a great gift.

Do you possess this power? You do. Everyone does. Unfortunately, though, you may not be choosing to activate the power of acceptance. But I assure you that when you discover and put acceptance into practice, you'll find a higher level of inner peace in your life. Acceptance helps to give you a greater degree of harmony within yourself, and this internal harmony spreads to your relations with others. This is especially true within a marriage. Most of the problems that occur in a marriage originate in a lack of real acceptance of the other person. This lack of acceptance often brings great suffering and anxiety. That's why acceptance is such a powerful "tool" for all of us. I urge you to learn this skill and practice it.

How do you work toward acceptance? How do you abandon some of your own fixed ways of understanding reality and accept some of your spouse's perceptions? Overall, here's the answer: acceptance generally means opening yourself to the other person so that you can share your feelings and beliefs and really hear your spouse's viewpoints. Sometimes this means changing some of your attitudes. Sometimes it's a question of changing your priorities. If you can open yourself to your spouse's ideas and needs and understand where he or she is coming from, you're more likely to reach a higher level of acceptance.

KNOW YOURSELF FIRST

To reach a higher level of acceptance in your relationship, though, you need to know yourself first. You need to know what your own perceptions are. You need to be able to articulate why you feel or behave in certain ways. (No, saying "Because it's the right way," or "It's just the way I am," isn't good enough.) As we have discussed, you and your partner have different backgrounds and experiences that have shaped you. To negotiate successfully with your partner, you need to know why you feel and behave the way you do. And not only do you need to *know* yourself—you need to *accept* yourself. This means accepting both your strengths and weaknesses. You have talents, abilities, and gifts. At the same time, you have shortcomings, limits, and failings. Welcome to the human race. It's crucial for you to accept both what you have going for you and where you fall short. Doing so isn't easy, but it's a necessary step toward wisdom.

KNOW AND ACCEPT YOUR SPOUSE

Now, here's a hard task—perhaps the task that most people find the hardest one of all. Just as you should accept yourself for your strengths and weaknesses alike, I urge you to accept your spouse in the same way. Does

he or she have talents, abilities, and gifts? No doubt. Do you acknowledge and even celebrate these positive attributes? I hope so! (If
not, you might want to consider being a bit more generous with your
praise and appreciation. Nobody likes to be taken for granted.) And
does your spouse have shortcomings, limits, and failings? That's a
given—he or she is a human being, too, and therefore flawed and fallible. So here's the bottom line: can you acknowledge yet also forgive
and accept your spouse for being human and fallible? If so, you're giving your spouse a great gift. If not, it's going to be a stumbling block
for both of you.

KNOW YOUR PERCEPTIONS AND VALUES

Another aspect of acceptance concerns the importance of knowing your
own perceptions and values—and where they come from. For instance,
Chris and Gil had struggled for years with a conflict over parenting. Chris
felt that her husband overindulged the couple's three school-age boys.
"He buys them too much stuff," she said. "Whatever they ask for, they
get. He's not good at discipline. He's really spoiling the kids." Gil de-
fended himself in these words: "Well, it's a father's job to take care of his
kids, and this is how I do it. I want them to feel appreciated." As the conflict between Chris and Gil intensified, they decided to seek help from a
marital therapist. The counseling sessions revealed some interesting aspects of the situation, including how Gil's family background had influenced his parenting style. Raised by a single mother, Gil had endured
financial hardship during boyhood, and he'd never benefited from a father's presence, guidance, or affection. His tendency to overindulge his
own kids was partly an effort "to make sure they're never deprived like I
was." By understanding and accepting this aspect of his personal history,
Gil now realizes what motivates his behavior, and he can better compromise with his spouse on this issue. He realizes that he is present for his
kids in all the important ways that his father wasn't there for him; and he

realizes that he doesn't have to give the boys so much "stuff" to compensate for his father's failings.

FLEXIBILITY—THE KEY TO ACCEPTANCE

Living in South Florida and the Caribbean most of my life, I've been exposed to countless hurricanes. There are many benefits to living in the tropics—the sun, the beaches, the warm weather. But we do have those hurricanes, and they can be scary, fierce, and destructive.

Hurricane Andrew, which hit Florida in 1996, was one of the worst ever, and it's still considered one of the greatest natural disasters in U.S. history. The day after this storm ended, I went out to view the damage. Our family home wasn't too far from where the hurricane hit hardest. Fortunately, though, we all survived it, and there weren't many deaths in the region overall, given the storm's great impact.

As I wandered through the neighborhood and observed the enormous destruction all around, one thing that struck me hard was the number of massive trees that had been totally uprooted or torn to pieces by the hurricane-force winds. I'd grown accustomed to seeing these trees for many years as I'd grown up. These were the trees I'd climbed as a child—the ones I considered strongest and most permanent. Now they were gone! Interestingly, though, most of the palm trees had survived, even though the bigger, stronger-looking trees had taken a real beating. If you had looked at them the day before the storm, you would never have thought that these bigger trees would have been so severely affected. The flimsy-looking palm trees, however, had come through the storm much better. At first this situation seems like a contradiction, but this natural phenomenon makes a lot of sense. Palm trees are flexible; they adapt much better to strong winds. Palm trees sway and bend, while thick, solid trees break or get uprooted. So which trees are truly stronger? Which are more likely to thrive and flourish over a long lifetime?

When it comes to relationships, we can learn a lot from the palm tree.

The more flexible we are, the more easily we can accept changes and differences. Whoever practices the power of flexibility in his or her relationships is like the palm tree, and such people will more easily make it through the storms of life.

In a relationship, flexibility is a key ingredient to living with others. If you're flexible, you're able to adapt better to others' needs and withstand the pressures that family life exerts on you. Without that flexibility, harmony is difficult and life becomes more stressful.

Flexibility requires that you put yourself in the other person's shoes, to understand that things aren't black and white. You can't say, "It's my way or the highway." To some degree, you have to adapt your life to your spouse.

LONG-TERM FLEXIBILITY

Is there room for flexibility in relationships that have already lasted ten, twenty, even thirty years or more? I'd say that if a husband and a wife have been together for that long, they must have been practicing flexibility all along. There's probably been a lot of give-and-take over the years. People often learn to be more flexible as life presents them with challenges and opportunities. Many couples change almost without conscious awareness of the changes. Parenthood certainly presents a couple with a continuous series of circumstances that demand change: the birth of children, their growth through many stages, and their eventual departure from the household. Then comes retirement, aging, health issues, and changes in housing arrangements. These and many other situations prompt most people to reconsider their convictions and perspectives. The cliché is that people get "set in their ways" as they age. I disagree. I think people get more *flexible* as they get older. Why? I'm not sure. Maybe people learn from experience that flexibility works better than rigidity. Maybe there are changes in the human personality that occur naturally in most people over time. All I can say is that in my experience, young couples often seem *less* flexible than older couples do.

But during midlife, the task that many couples face is to avoid taking each other for granted. You may be more flexible—more willing to go with the flow as marriage carries you onward—but there's a risk of paying less attention to your spouse, giving him or her less credit, and tuning out the other person. Often this isn't the result of any actively negative feelings; it's just a kind of laziness. But that carries its own risks. If you don't give your spouse enough evidence that you care, there's a definite danger of drifting apart. Some midlife spouses say, "Oh, I do my thing and my wife does hers," or "My husband and I just go about our own business." When I hear these words, I often wonder if the couple has a relationship at all—or are they just two people living different lives?

Bruno and Victoria take this scenario to an extreme. Now in their early sixties, they are "empty nesters" just a few years from retirement. Bruno has a part-time law practice and is gradually phasing out his client work. After spending a few hours at the office, he often heads off to play golf. Victoria is a real estate agent who spends most of her time at the office, which she finds more congenial than her own home. She also goes shopping or out to movies with her girlfriends. What about husband-wife time? Bruno and Victoria don't even eat dinner together anymore. They go about their own business and rarely pay much attention to each other. They have no common interests or activities. On the rare occasions when they end up across from each other at the dinner table, they have nothing much to say. This isn't flexibility—it's mutual indifference.

HOW DOES IT ALL ADD UP?

I think we'd now agree that it's fine to have differences in your relationship. You can cope with many differences if you're accepting and flexible. But how, specifically, do you achieve acceptance and flexibility?

Here are some suggestions for how you can make these several issues add up. In Chapter 13, I'll offer some specific tasks that will help foster these goals.

ACCEPT THE INEVITABILITY OF DIFFERENCES

If you at least accept the inevitability of differences, you can start to sort through them, and this process can lead to achieving a greater degree of flexibility within your marriage. Again, it's not an issue of resolving all differences or of convincing each other to change your beliefs. Rather, it's a question of understanding where you stand and how to deal with the situation. You may disagree, for instance, about how to discipline a child. This issue involves a major aspect of parenting, and it can have real impact on your child's healthy development. Ignoring the issue doesn't serve anyone well. At the same time, attempting to sort out every aspect of the situation—your past experiences, your grasp of child psychology, your parenting strategies—can be a complex task.

PICK THE RIGHT TIME TO ARGUE

Half the battle of sorting out differences is timing. If you realize that an argument is brewing or a big problem needs solving, pick the right time to sort out the issues. Sometimes that means talking things over right away; sometimes it means postponing the discussion. If you can't talk things over immediately, reach a temporary agreement with your spouse: "Okay, let's drop the subject for now and get back to it later." You're more likely to be flexible in sorting out the issues if you're not feeling stressed.

Some suggestions:

∾ If possible, avoid arguing when you're exhausted, hungry, or in public.

∾ Make sure your kids are being safely looked after by another adult or else are sound asleep, since overhearing a parental argument may upset them.

∾ Make sure you have enough time to cover the subject and resolve your disagreements—don't rush the process.

∾ Discuss the situation openly, without rancor or efforts to "score points."

∾ Put to use what you've learned about listening to your spouse.

∾ Also, put to use what you've learned about how to argue constructively (by listening carefully and not interrupting).

∾ Try to see things from your spouse's perspective.

CHOOSE YOUR BATTLES

You also need to learn how to choose your battles. Some couples squabble over every difference of opinion; others are more selective. If you can, ignore issues that are insignificant. Is it really important if the spoons, forks, and knives get mixed together instead of segregated in the dishwasher's cutlery compartment? Does it really matter if you clean up the kitchen after every meal or only at day's end? Try to size up the basic substance of what you're discussing. If it's not of major consequence, compromise. If the complaint is truly trivial, drop it altogether. Save your energy for the big issues in life.

MAKE DECISIONS TOGETHER

Another important aspect of dealing with your differences has to do with decision-making. There's no question that making decisions as a couple requires a lot of flexibility and open-mindedness by both spouses. Sure, it's easier to make a decision on your own—there's no one to disagree with you! But solo decision-making is a recipe for resentment. If one spouse makes all the decisions, the other may not feel "invested" in the outcome. He or she may either feel resentful of being left out of the process, or, if something goes wrong, that spouse may feel tempted to say "I told you so." Making decisions together is a crucial skill in any marriage. The perfect decision may not always be the one you reach right away—you have to leave more time to consider all aspects of the problem, and you have to leave room for trial and error as you experiment with the possibilities. But generally speaking, a decision you reach together—one that both of you find acceptable—will serve you better in the long run than decisions that one partner makes and then "hands down" to the other. If you share responsibility for a decision, you're more likely to feel committed to following it.

WHEN YOU CAN'T RESOLVE YOUR DIFFERENCES

Unfortunately, some couples find every issue beyond compromise. They can't seem to be flexible about anything. In marriages where everything causes conflict, the problems you face may be more serious than just the day-to-day issues. If you and your spouse experience frequent, protracted conflicts, you should take time to uncover the root causes. What couples often fight about may involve complex, high-stakes issues that lie beneath the surface.

For instance, Tammy and Marv often argue with such intensity and hostility that it scares this otherwise loving couple. The situation grew worse and worse until the spouses finally went to a marital counselor for help. Through a process of therapy, Marv and Tammy realized that their wild arguments mirrored what each of them had witnessed in his or her family of origin. They were essentially mimicking dysfunctional arguments decades past. Once they reached some realizations about this situation, they started to learn better ways to resolve their differences.

Ask yourselves what you're really fighting over. Is the conflict what it seems—or is something else bothering you? Is the problem an issue within your relationship with your spouse, or could it even have its source in your own childhood experiences? Try to determine the real cause of the problem rather than just squabble over its manifestations in daily life.

I've mentioned this issue elsewhere in the book, and I'll mention it again: sometimes there's no substitute for good counseling. Deciding to get marital guidance or therapy isn't a failure. On the contrary, it's a great success when you can step beyond your worries and fears, seek help, and benefit from the insights of a well-trained, impartial third party.

". . . AND THE WISDOM TO KNOW THE DIFFERENCE"

All couples experience differences in their relationship. Every marriage has its limitations, contradictions, and flaws. It's important to realize that this side of Heaven, the perfect family doesn't exist. Everyone talks about dysfunctional families these days. Hearing these comments, I often respond, "Get serious! Show me a family that isn't dysfunctional!" Our imperfect human families are exactly where we need to practice the power of acceptance—and we all possess it; it is just a matter of learning to apply it to our reality.

There is a nondenominational and ecumenical prayer that Alcoholics Anonymous and other organizations often use, a prayer that I find to be helpful in implementing the power of acceptance in my daily life. I offer it to you now in the hope that you'll feel inspired by it as a way of practicing true acceptance in your own life:

Lord, grant me
the serenity to accept the things I cannot change,
the courage to change the things I can,
and the wisdom to know the difference.

If you apply these words to the difficulties you encounter in all your relationships, I believe you'll find the courage, strength, and wisdom you need to deal with the challenges you face in your marriage and in life more generally. There are things you can change and things you can't, and it's important to accept this truth—or at least to know the difference.

Chapter 13

How to Deal with
Your Differences

It's true that some people seem more accepting than others, so it's possible that acceptance is partly a character trait. However, I believe that acceptance isn't *only* a character trait—it's also a skill that you can acquire, practice, and perfect. This skill is first and foremost one of flexibility. And flexibility includes practical dimensions as well as psychological attitudes. It's a set of tasks as well as a state of mind.

What follows are six specific tasks that will help you and your spouse accept your differences and gain flexibility in responding to each other.

Task #1
Practice Self-Examination

The Greek philosopher Pythagoras had a great idea six centuries before the Christian Era. This ancient philosopher taught his students to spend at least ten minutes every night contemplating the errors and mistakes they'd made on that particular day. This effort wasn't intended simply as an empty analysis of what had gone wrong. Rather, it was a review session designed to help his students correct their behavior for the future. This practice later became the examination of conscience that's prominent within the Christian tradition.

By working to break bad habits and avoid mistakes, you can learn from your limitations. This process can be especially healthy if you practice it in the context of your relationships. The fact is, we all make mistakes. That's fair enough—we're only human. But why not embrace (rather than avoid) the possibility of repairing whatever damage we've done as a result of our fallibility? This is why I suggest that you take a good look at yourself before you demand change from your spouse. If you skip this important step, you risk getting into all kinds of relationship trouble.

Here's how I recommend that you adapt this ancient but valuable process to your busy modern life:

- Set aside ten minutes each evening to review what your day has been like.

- You can undertake this review either by thinking over the day's events in your own mind, or else by "thinking on paper"—that is, by jotting notes in a journal, in a diary, or on a notepad.

- Consider what has happened, especially interactions with other people—your spouse, your children, other members of your family, coworkers, friends, acquaintances, even total strangers.

- Note what has seemed satisfying or dissatisfying.

- Note also the actions you've taken that produced a *positive* outcome, such as helping someone, advancing toward an important goal, solving a problem, preventing a problem, and so forth.

- Note the actions you've taken that produced a *negative* outcome, such as accidentally or intentionally making someone's life more difficult, hurting someone's feelings, causing a problem, and so forth.

∞ Consider what you could have done better as you dealt with the day's tasks and challenges.

∞ Try to avoid passing judgment on yourself, but be honest and clearheaded about what you could have done or avoided doing.

∞ Consider what you might do in the future to make better choices; work harder to make a positive difference to people, solve problems, or resolve issues that remain unresolved.

∞ If prayer is part of your life, pray to God for insight and strength to deal with these issues in the future.

The process I'm describing won't necessarily be easy. We live in a culture that discourages self-reflection, so it's an unfamiliar task to many people. Some people find it daunting, even overwhelming. Some ignore their faults or weaknesses and resist acknowledging them, much less examining and learning from them. ("Well, it wasn't my fault. If only X hadn't happened [fill in the blank with a handy excuse], I wouldn't have done Y [fill in the blank with an undesirable outcome].") Others exaggerate what they've done and engage in vigorous self-criticism. ("I'm so terrible! I'm so sinful! No one is more awful than I am!") My recommendation: start this process of self-examination slowly. Take your time learning how to review your experiences and explore the implications of what you've done. Don't rake yourself over the coals. The intention here isn't self-mortification—it's learning from your mistakes. If you can get used to this process gradually and practice it gently, you'll benefit from it over time. The goal is progress, not perfection.

There's one last phase to self-examination. At the end of the week, review what you've written or thought about over the preceding seven days. What pattern do you see in the issues you've identified? For each strength and weakness you've noted, reflect on where the relevant trait comes from. Is it innate? Did you learn it from someone else? Did you acquire it from your own experience? Over a period of time, consider the ways in which you're growing (or not growing) as a human being.

Task #2
Assess Your Spouse

What I'm going to suggest now is a similar form of examination, but this one focuses not inwardly but outwardly—on your spouse. As such, this is a somewhat risky exercise. You have to proceed thoughtfully to perform it in a productive way. Why? Because—as I'm sure you can imagine—it's often easier to notice and criticize your spouse's shortcomings than your own. I am not advocating a marital "gripe fest" with your husband or wife as the victim! Rather, I'm suggesting that you consider your spouse's mistakes or shortcomings as the basis of compassion, not judgment. And I urge you to focus as much on his or her strengths as on his or her weaknesses.

Here's how I suggest you proceed:

- Again, set aside ten minutes each evening to review the day.

- Consider what has happened, especially your spouse's interactions with other people—you, your children, other members of your family, coworkers, friends, acquaintances, even total strangers.

- Note what has seemed satisfying or dissatisfying in his or her behavior.

- Note also the actions that he or she took that may have produced a positive outcome, such as helping someone, advancing toward an important goal, solving a problem, preventing a problem, and so forth.

∾ Note the actions that he or she took that may have produced a negative outcome, such as accidentally or intentionally making someone's life more difficult, hurting someone's feelings, causing a problem, and so forth.

∾ Consider what your spouse could have done better in dealing with the day's tasks and challenges.

∾ Try to avoid passing judgment on him or her, but be honest and clearheaded about what your spouse could have done or avoided doing.

∾ Consider what he or she might do in the future to make better choices, work harder to make a positive difference to people, solve problems, or resolve issues that remain unresolved.

∾ If prayer is part of your life, pray to God that your husband or wife may gain insight and strength to deal with these issues in the future.

I'd like to stress once again that the goal is *not* to find fault. You aren't in a position to pass judgment. Rather, you're trying to understand what has happened and—especially—why your spouse may have done what he or she did at various points of the week. Your goal is, in short, compassion—to *feel with* your spouse as the day's and the week's events come and go. If you undertake this task with an open mind and an open heart, you're likely to feel more love rather than less. If you end up feeling angry, hurt, frustrated, sad, or confused, you've gained an understanding of issues that you and your spouse now need to face and cope with together.

Task #3
Share Your Lists

Building on the previous two tasks, the next one allows you to share insights and gain understanding about your strengths and weaknesses.

What I recommend is that you select a time for this exercise that allows privacy, a period of calm, and a good chance of not being interrupted. (If you can't feel confident that the time is right, consider postponing the effort until the conditions are better.) Then follow this sequence of steps:

- ❧ Take turns reading out loud from the lists about yourselves.

- ❧ Alternate between a strength ("I helped the kids with their homework and didn't get impatient with them") and a weakness ("I wasn't quite so patient with you when you arrived home late for dinner").

- ❧ For each statement that you read, discuss the full situation. ("I wasn't really ticked off because you came home late—it was because you didn't even apologize.")

- ❧ Ask each other questions about the situations you raise. ("Would it help if I call you from the car when I'm stuck in traffic, or is that just another interruption when you're coping with the kids?" or "If you want me to cook more meals, could you please not criticize what I fix so often?")

- ❧ Now work through your list of comments about each other.

- ❧ State your comments as nonjudgmentally as possible; your goal isn't to attack the other person's character, but to identify issues that you can solve together.

- ❧ As you work your way through the lists, try to avoid getting defensive, angry, or judgmental about what the other person wrote.

- ❧ Remember that the perspectives you're hearing from your spouse aren't foolproof, but other people sometimes see us more clearly than we see ourselves.

- ❧ Work hard to balance the criticism you provide with praise for your spouse.

∾ Also, try to balance the amount of criticism and praise that each spouse is receiving—that is, make sure that you don't end up focusing on just one of you.

∾ Factor in time for a "cooling-off" period following your discussion—a chance to share a cup of coffee or a glass of wine, time to listen to music or give each other backrubs, or some other sort of relaxing activity.

One final note: I recommend that you not perform this exercise as an occasional marathon. If you make it part of a shorter but more frequent routine—perhaps each week, as I've suggested—it's less likely to be a big deal. Instead, it's likely to become a "quality control session" that allows you to address relatively small issues before they accumulate into bigger, more numerous ones.

Task #4
Identify Common Ground and Obvious Differences

Sit down with your spouse and consider the issues you face in an open-minded way. I'm not saying that you should try to analyze every aspect of married life; however, you're likely to be more flexible with each other if you examine the beliefs, values, and attitudes that may be helping or hindering your interactions as a couple. This task is a means of identifying both common ground and obvious differences. Ask yourself and discuss these questions together:

∾ What are your goals for yourself, your marriage, and your family?

∾ How can you balance the demands that you face individually, as a couple, and as a family?

∾ How can you more effectively balance *work life* and *family life*?

∽ What are your expectations about your social life?

∽ What are your expectations about your educational and vocational goals?

∽ What are your expectations about ideal family life?

∽ What do you believe is essential for the optimal growth and development of your marriage?

∽ What lifestyle do you feel is healthy for nurturing your marriage and family?

∽ What aspects of your current lifestyle would you like change?

∽ For couples with children: What do you find favorable or unfavorable about your own parenting skills?

∽ Also for couples with children: What do you find favorable or unfavorable about your spouse's parenting skills?

∽ If you could look back at the present from the viewpoint of the future, what would you like to remember as being the most wonderful times of your marriage and family life?

∽ From this same viewpoint in the future, what aspects of your family life would you like to avoid in the future?

∽ How can you and your spouse prevent marital arguments or conflicts?

Keep in mind that when answering these questions that there are no right or wrong answers—only differences of opinion. What matters most is that you consider the issues together in an open-minded spirit. If you and your spouse can accept each other's differences and work to find more common ground, you can make a great contribution to your present and future relationships.

Task #5
Walk in Each Other's Shoes

Even in a marriage where the spouses are supportive of each other, it's not uncommon for the husband and the wife to lose track of what each other faces on a day-to-day basis. This situation is especially common when the spouses have distinct roles, such as a homemaker wife and a wage-earner husband (or, for that matter, a homemaker husband and a wage-earner wife). It's difficult to grasp what your spouse is facing if his or her activities are a lot different from yours. One classic scenario of this situation: the husband who comes home after a hard day at the office, finds his wife slouched on the sofa, and doesn't think about the domestic and parenting tasks she's been tackling since he left the house that morning, but rather mistakes her exhaustion for laziness and asks, "So what have you done all day—just goof off?" But this sort of insensitivity isn't the sole cause of the problem. Even more sympathetic husbands and wives often fail to understand the stresses and complexities that their spouses face.

For this reason, I suggest a task I call "Walk in Each Other's Shoes." You can perform this exercise (like some of the others I've proposed) either on paper or as a nonwritten commentary. The goal is simply to imagine what your spouse faces in the course of his or her day. You do this task together almost as a guessing game. Here are the rules and steps:

- ∽ You take turns (perhaps flipping a coin to decide who goes first).

- ∽ The person who starts either lists the hours of the day on a piece of paper or keeps them in mind as he or she proceeds.

- ∽ Starting at your first hour apart, imagine (in detail) what your spouse is doing.

- ∽ Proceed to the next hour, the next, and the next.

- ❧ Continue in this way until you've worked your way through your spouse's entire day.

- ❧ Then allow your spouse to set the record straight about what really happens.

- ❧ Alternatively, you could allow yourself to be corrected on an hour-by-hour basis.

Sound easy? Maybe so—provided that you've already "walked in each other's shoes." In this day and age, when many couples share both wage-earning duties and parental duties, there may well be a higher percentage of husbands and wives than formerly who understand what each other's life is like. But this exercise is useful even for such people, and it's absolutely critical for spouses whose activities and obligations are significantly different. You may be amazed by what it reveals.

Working through the hours of his stay-at-home wife's day, for instance, a husband named Howard discovered that his wife, Allie, had a more daunting set of tasks that what he'd imagined:

HOWARD (TRYING TO VISUALIZE ALLIE'S TYPICAL DAY): Okay, so it's seven o'clock now and the kids are getting up. You're getting them ready for school. And now they're dressed, so they start eating breakfast—

ALLIE: Wait a sec. Marie wouldn't wake up even though I went into her room three times and shook her. And Beth dropped her barrette in the toilet but wouldn't use it even after I washed it three separate times with antibacterial soap. Then Marie finally got up. But then she wouldn't eat breakfast because the milk you bought was 2 percent, not skim, and she thinks she's gonna get fat drinking it.

HOWARD: So it's eight o'clock now.

ALLIE: No, not yet—more like 7:23. I'm having a big argument with Marie about lunch, which she says she won't pack *or* buy at school.

HOWARD: Al, do you think maybe she's got an eating disorder?

ALLIE: This is what I've been trying to tell you for weeks. I'm concerned that maybe she does, and I've told you that—but you haven't been listening!

HOWARD: Okay, I hear you. So we'll discuss it. But first—is it eight o'clock?

ALLIE: We'll say it's eight o'clock.

HOWARD: And you've dropped off the kids at school.

ALLIE: No, Howard, we're stuck in traffic while I'm *trying* to drop the kids off at school. It took me half an hour just to get there.

You get the idea. Everyone else's life seems easier than yours until you try to live it. Even couples who have been married for years often don't understand the moment-by-moment demands of each other. Walking in your spouse's shoes won't take you the whole distance, but it'll certainly give you a better glimpse of the journey. And that's often what husbands and wives need more than anything else as they try to understand their differences.

"SO DIFFERENT FROM ME . . ."

Differences challenge even the most loving couples. Differences strain many marriages until the spouses back off from each other to gain relief. Differences strain some marriages to the breaking point.

Yet differences between husbands and wives are also a source of delight, of good-hearted amusement, even of exhilaration. I can't tell you how many spouses I've spoken with who have told me, "My husband [or wife] is so different from me that it's like we're from different planets," or "We see the world in totally different ways"—yet many of these same people immediately state that they wouldn't want it any other way. "Why would I want my wife to be just like me?" one man asked during our recent conversation. "Why would I want her to agree with me on everything? If we weren't so different, our life together wouldn't be so interesting. She sees things that I've missed. She feels things that I don't feel. She understands things that I haven't figured out yet. And the reverse is true, too. Each of us is smarter and better and more alive than we would be if we weren't together, or if we were more alike."

"More alive than we would be otherwise. . . ." What a wonderful testament to differences in marriage!

So here's what I say: Acknowledge your differences. Clarify your differences. Struggle with your differences, if it comes to that. But work to understand your differences, compromise over your differences, and make something creative out of your differences. It won't be easy, but it's one of the most important paths to real life and real love.

And—if at all possible—celebrate your differences.

MAKE A COMMITMENT TO GROWTH AND MATURITY

One day Julia, a high-powered, ambitious businesswoman, received a beautiful and exotic flowering plant from her father, Abel. This plant was a Valentine's Day gift that Abel intended to express the love he felt for his only daughter. Julia was, in fact, the light of his life. She had a wonderful husband, three healthy children, and a thriving practice as a corporate manager.

But for some years now, Abel had been increasingly concerned about his daughter. Julia didn't do such a great job at balancing the various aspects of her life. She tended to take many things for granted, and Abel felt that she had begun to develop some odd priorities about her commitments and her responsibilities. She concentrated too much on her work, for instance, and her workaholic tendencies prompted her to neglect her husband and her children. She also focused too much on job-related socializing, which meant that she often spent less time with her family, her relatives, her friends, and other people she was close to. Julia's troubling priorities were part of what prompted her father to give her that particular plant for Valentine's Day.

Abel, who is a wise old man, asked his daughter one day about the plant several weeks after he'd presented it to her. It's true that Julia had enjoyed the fragrance and beauty of the exotic bloom for the first several days, but then she'd forgotten about it—and she'd even forgotten where she'd put it in her huge house. Now, prompted by her father's question, she remembered the plant with the beautiful flower and wondered what had happened to it. "Hang on, Dad," she told him, and she put him on hold to go look for it. After a while she located her father's gift somewhere upstairs. But to her dismay she discovered that the flower had withered and died and the plant was limp and dying.

"I found it," she told Abel when she got back on the line.

"Wonderful," her father responded. "How's it doing?"

"Not so great, actually."

"No?"

"It sort of—*wilted*."

"I see." Abel's voice couldn't help but reveal his disappointment.

But then Julia offered this solution to the problem: "Well, you know what? I liked that plant so much, maybe I'll go to the florist and buy another one."

The truth is that Abel is a generous man, and he wouldn't have minded giving his daughter another plant, but he wanted her to understand something about the plant—something that went far beyond the specifics of a single tropical bloom. "Maybe so," he told her. "But I'd like you to think about something. Maybe your life is a lot like that flower, Julia. There isn't another one exactly like it in the world."

"What are you telling me, Dad?" Julia asked.

"See if you can guess."

Julia was confused. "I don't get it."

"Your husband and your children need you to nurture and love them," said Abel. "Just as there will never be another plant exactly like that one, you'll never have another family like the one you have now."

Maybe these words weren't what Julia expected to hear—or even wanted to hear. But what a great lesson her father decided to offer her!

*   *   *

Here's the truth. If you don't nurture love, it can't grow. You can't just set your love on a shelf and expect it to blossom and thrive on its own. You have to feed it, tend it, and protect it. The more attention you give to the relationships that matter to you most, the more they will flourish. In this sense, our relationships are like exotic flowers—each a living organism, each a unique bloom. Unfortunately many relationships wither and even die simply because they aren't nurtured, fed, and cared for. Love thrives on tender loving care. You can't realistically expect relationships to grow if you don't pay attention to the significant people in your life and what they need from you.

I sense that many people in our society have time for everything *except* deeply valued, carefully nurtured relationships. Ambitious careers, material possessions, fancy gadgets, extravagant clothes, amusing forms of entertainment—there's almost no end to the external "stuff" that people want and spend enormous amounts of time and energy chasing after. But what about family and relationships? Well, those aspects of life certainly get some attention, but—at least in my opinion—not as much as they deserve. If they did, I bet we wouldn't hear so much about wives who feel neglected, husbands who feel they aren't respected, and children who feel starved for attention and love. The divorce statistics alone tell a sad story about how much attention people are (or aren't) putting into their relationships. The truth of the matter is that if you don't nurture love, it simply won't grow and mature.

Dr. Thomas Moore, in his book *Care of the Soul*, describes the relationship of love with the sacred center when he says, "Love is not only about relationship, it is also an affair with the soul." Love not only deepens our relationships; love also enriches us and makes us more fully human. That's why Mother Teresa's famous words—"Human beings have been created to love and to be loved"—are so eloquent. We are nourished by the love we feel and express as well as by the love we receive from others.

For this reason, I recommend that you nurture a deeper, more substantial form of love than what our society ordinarily encourages. Real love isn't just romance and good times. Real love is fundamentally what you discover about yourself and your spouse in the deep, indescribable oasis of the sacred center. Real love is the process of you and your spouse dreaming together to create a life that fulfills you both. I urge you to work with your partner—over the long term—to nurture your relationship as selflessly as possible. To do so, I recommend that you follow Path Seven: Make a Commitment to Growth and Maturity.

Let's now explore what that means.

Chapter 14

Growing on Your Own, Growing as a Couple

Married life is complex and sometimes difficult, and it involves ongoing compromise between the spouses. It often requires both the husband and the wife to set aside their own individual preferences in favor of their common good. Working toward the long-term goals of a happy marriage mean that you accept the reality of sharing day-to-day life with another human being rather than clinging to romantic fantasies and Hollywood images of perfect love.

At the same time, making a commitment to growth and maturity in marriage requires a husband and a wife to dream together. What I'm saying now may seem to contradict what I said a moment earlier. How can you focus on realism and yet also dream together? The reason you can do both—in fact, the reason you *must* do both—is that dreaming together is a crucial part of a couple's commitment to growth and maturity. When I say "dreaming together," I don't mean that you should reject reality. Rather, I mean that you should use your imaginations, speculate, and consider options for how your shared life will change, develop, and deepen as the years pass.

Why is dreaming together so important? There are a multitude of reasons:

- ❧ Dreaming together helps you stay open to your own individual needs and capacities for insight and growth.

- ❧ Dreaming together also helps you to stay open and responsive to your spouse's practical, emotional, and spiritual needs.

- ❧ Dreaming together encourages closeness in the here-and-now.

- ❧ Dreaming together also helps you create a sense of where you want to be as a couple in the future—ten, twenty, thirty years down the line.

- ❧ Dreaming together let's you speculate about possibilities, imagine scenarios, and experiment with ideas about activities and commitments that matter to you.

- ❧ Dreaming together helps you create a unified vision of your future as a couple.

In short, dreaming together helps you simultaneously advance your own development as an individual and also strengthen your marriage as a long-term commitment. When you dream together, you grow together, because you're both moving toward the same future.

By contrast, couples who don't dream together—or who develop significantly different life perspectives or visions for their future—may tend to grow apart rather than together. Sheila and David are a pretty typical example of this situation. At one time in their marriage fifteen years ago, both spouses were lawyers. Sheila resigned from her legal practice at the point that the couple started a family a few years later. She intended to resume client work after three to five years of full-time parenthood. But as she raised the couple's children—flying solo, I might add, since her husband spent most of his time at the office or in court—she found that she enjoyed the company of children far more than the company of lawyers and clients. Meanwhile, David's career as a litigator continued to expand and thrive during that time, and he got more and more involved in his legal practice. Sheila and David eventually found that their interests and commitments had dramatically diverged. Sheila wanted to shift her professional energies over to education, and she eventually obtained certification as an elementary schoolteacher. David got more and more ambitious as a litigator. The spouses didn't discuss their differing goals or their consequences for the marriage. Unfortunately, they grew apart until they had little in common, and they recently got divorced.

I often see couples like this in my office. One or the other spouse may lament, "Father, I'm married to a stranger." The spouses haven't necessarily changed, but their vision and goals have drifted apart. They may still love each other deeply, but they don't have a common future in mind. This is a difficult and potentially damaging situation for a couple—one that can lead to severe stress even among otherwise well-intentioned partners.

KNOW YOUR OWN DREAMS

A woman named Jackie had a terrible accident while crossing the street. A truck hit her, and she died almost immediately. When she got to Heaven, she arrived at the pearly gates and told Saint Peter, "This isn't fair! I was just beginning to enjoy my life, and then that stupid accident just ruined everything! Can't I have a little more time back on earth? I promise to come back in, say, six months. Please?"

Saint Peter rarely got requests of this sort—most people were happy simply to discover they'd made it into Heaven—but he decided to consider what this woman wanted. He had a talk with the Lord, the Lord agreed, and so it came about. Before she even knew what had happened,

Jackie found herself back on earth—right there on the street with the paramedics working on her! And, after just a few weeks in the hospital, she recovered and was released.

So what did she do? She decided to go visit her plastic surgeon for a total overhaul. She got augmentations and reductions, a tummy tuck, a nose job, and Botox all over the place. When the plastic surgery was complete, she looked twenty years younger. Then Jackie saw herself in a totally new light, and that inspired her to start a totally new existence. She began to live a fast, flashy life. She left her husband for a man ten years younger than she was. She started to do everything she'd ever dreamed of—a truly happy-go-lucky life. Why worry about the values and principles of her past life when she was having so much fun?

Then one afternoon about six months later, while she walked in the same neighborhood where she'd had her accident, Jackie crossed the street so carelessly that she got hit all over again.

Immediately she found herself in a very hot place with a huge red man holding a black pitchfork upside down.

"There must be some mistake!" cried Jackie. "I was supposed to go to Heaven after six months—that was the deal!"

To which the Devil replied, "Well, maybe so. But listen, honey, you changed so much that they didn't even recognize you up there!"

Let's admit it—there's a kernel of truth in this tall tale about Jackie. All of us know that our society puts a huge amount of emphasis on what's on the surface: physical beauty, classy clothes, and fancy accessories that make us look sexy and cool. Unfortunately, we can't really grow, mature, and flourish if we put all of our attention onto these exterior aspects of our lives. But I believe that even this fixation with the *outside* can teach us something about the *inside*.

Here's how. When we get up in the morning, each of us has a unique routine for getting ready, but all of them eventually lead to the bathroom.

Have you ever noticed what happens when you take that first good look in the mirror? Maybe I should speak only for myself. During that first glance in the mirror, when I'm just barely awake, I feel shocked and startled by the bright bathroom light and by how I look after a full night's sleep. I usually feel that there's a lot that needs "fixing" before I'm ready to face the world. I suspect that most people feel the same way. Most women have their makeup ritual. Most men shave and comb their hair (or at least they ought to). In any case, we realize that something isn't right, and we want to *make* it right. We don't want to be seen in public in a disheveled state. Decency and self-respect won't allow it. So we do what we can to look good for the world.

But there's another mirror we don't pay much attention to—the mirror that reflects the interior rather than the exterior. This is the mirror that perceives our inner state, the state of the heart and soul. This is the mirror that sees the sacred center and all its activity. We don't pay enough attention to this mirror because it requires an inner search, a deep look into our sacred center to find those things we sometimes don't want to face. We often shy away from this interior mirror, certainly more so than we shy away from the early morning mirror in our bathrooms. Why? Because we feel more comfortable staying on the outside and paying little attention to the inside. The inner mirror shows us images caused by our lack of inner peace and by the great dilemmas of life, including past resentments, envy, stored-up anger, and other troubling states of mind. So we prefer to ignore it. No one else sees what's there, and it tends to make us uncomfortable, so it's easy to shelve the whole matter.

However, we really should do everything possible to discover what this inner mirror can show us. We should give it some good, focused attention. Why? Because it's crucial for each of us to discover what's inside us. There are so many distractions all around us, and focusing on them to the exclusion of our interior state can mean we'll miss our true calling and our deepest longings in the process. And what is our true calling? What are our deepest longings? Early on in this chapter, I quoted the words of Mother Teresa, who defined our common human vocation: "to love and to be loved."

To love and to be loved . . .

These words provide one of the best, simplest, and most eloquent definitions of human nature. *To love and to be loved* is the very core of who we are. We must do everything we can to discover our ability to love—to see and understand what we are ultimately capable of doing. This is the key to our true growth and development. It's also the key to our satisfaction in relationships, especially the relationships that matter most, such as marriage.

In response to this situation, one of the most important steps you can take is to know your own dreams. Please note that by "dreams," I'm not referring to the superficial situations we crave or the objects we covet—a fancier car, a classier house, a higher-status job. I'm not talking about the external changes we imagine may alter our lives (much as Jackie thought plastic surgery would fulfill her goals). I'm referring to the deeper, more subtle, more creative aspirations. Consider this list of questions:

- What are the most important things in your life?

- What are your fundamental values?

- What pursuits or interests make you happy?

- Which of your life goals remain unfulfilled?

- What as-yet-unaccomplished tasks would you like to do with or for the people you're closest to?

- If you had only six months to live, what would you spend that time doing?

- Do you feel that your life has meaning beyond your present, mortal existence?

- Do you have a sense of spiritual connection?

As you attempt to answer these questions, you'll begin to understand aspects of your inner self that include your deepest values, aspirations, and goals. The process I'm advocating here isn't easy, but it's a crucial step to understanding your dreams.

SEEK PSYCHOLOGICAL GUIDANCE

I'm continually amazed that in the twenty-first century, some people still think that counselors and therapists are only intended for the mentally ill. Some people even reject the mental health profession in general. Why? I just can't explain it. Perhaps this attitude against psychologists, psychiatrists, and other therapists is a legacy of age-old biases. Perhaps it's a side effect of a few irresponsible "pop-psychologists" out there who dispense eccentric theories and practices. But the general resistance to psychological counseling still doesn't make sense. Worse yet, it means that many people who would benefit from counseling never get it.

Here's the truth. If you broke your leg, you wouldn't hesitate to get help from an orthopedist. If you suffered a heart attack, you'd be happy to get good treatment from a cardiologist. If you broke out in a bad rash, you wouldn't rant and rave about how crazy dermatologists are—you'd eagerly seek their help. So if we're willing to accept good treatment for our bodies, why are so many people resistant to the psychotherapy that's often so beneficial when we have emotional troubles?

I especially see resistance among many men. Women are often far more insightful about the benefits of marital counseling, yet their husbands won't accept even the notion. This is frustrating at best and often tragic. Many issues in a marriage can benefit from a counselor's insights, and rejecting that option can burden and sometimes permanently damage an otherwise promising relationship. In reality, getting psychological guidance on personal or marital issues can help you understand your problems, think up better solutions than you'd think up on your own, redirect your life in a more creative direction, and more easily find the happiness you deserve. But taking this step starts by acknowledging that you need help. That's nothing to be ashamed of. If we only paid as much attention to our emotional well-being as we tend to pay to our physical fitness, we'd all be much more likely to attain growth and maturity.

SEEK SPIRITUAL GUIDANCE

One of the best ways to work on your inner self is to seek spiritual guidance. Guidance of this sort may mean a conversation with your priest, minister, or rabbi about issues you face at your stage of life. It may mean something more organized, such as a seminar or retreat sponsored by your church or temple. There are other options as well in most religious traditions. In any case, spiritual guidance can help you to maintain clarity about many decisions and life transitions.

HOW TO DREAM TOGETHER

Once you better understand your own dreams, you can take the crucial step of dreaming together as a couple. Do you share the same life issues and values? Perhaps you do. If so, then you've won half the battle. There will be abundant and fundamental ways in which you can share what matters most to you. If not, you have a challenge to face, but that doesn't mean it's a huge problem—only that you need to work harder to build common ground that you can "inhabit" together.

No matter what stage you're in as a couple—whether you're committed to each other and heading toward marriage or you're already married—dreaming together is an essential ingredient in nurturing your relationship. This process can be deeply fulfilling and, for many couples, a lot of fun. But it can also be challenging in some respects and require a lot of consideration and forethought. Here's why:

One of the main challenges today for any couple is our culture's great emphasis on "being yourself." We put a high premium on individualism, and there are, in fact, many positive aspects of that emphasis. However, it's important for people to work together for the common good, too, both within the wider community and within the private "community" of a marriage. Men and women who focus too intensely on their own well-being and their own development don't necessarily contribute as much as they should to a mutually supportive relationship. I believe that one of the reasons that so many young men and women are delaying marriage is that they're reluctant to answer to anyone else for their actions. They want to be *free*. Well, freedom to do whatever you want is great in some respects, but it's also limiting in others. Many happily married couples I know state that building a life together offers satisfactions and delights that they never even imagined would be possible back when they were single. Ultimately, we all grow most profoundly in relation to other human beings, not just as individuals.

Here's how I see this issue. There's a big difference between *individuality* and *individualism*. Individuality means developing fully as a unique human being. Attaining your individuality means that you reach your highest potential and fulfill the promise of whatever talents you have to offer. It's entirely possible to achieve your individuality while contributing your time and effort generously to other people—to your spouse, your children, your community, even all of humanity. By contrast, individualism means putting yourself first—above other people, perhaps above your community, perhaps even above God. Individualism tends to isolate you rather than to connect you with others.

What are the implications for marriage? I think it's clear that a husband and wife can have a strong sense of individuality and still be thoroughly focused on each other and on their relationship. Some of the happiest couples I know consist of spouses with strong personalities—sometimes great eccentricities!—who are nonetheless devoted and attentive to each other. But a husband and wife who are obsessed with their individualism aren't likely to have much energy for each other. Each will be too concerned with himself or herself. If each spouse's motto is "I'll do my own thing," neither will be likely to put enough value on "doing *our* own thing."

My recommendation: emphasize your *collective* needs over your *individual* needs. Ironically, striving to be better as a spouse will almost certainly be the best way to become better, happier, more fulfilled human beings as individuals, too. Why? Because individual development most often comes directly from focusing on your development together. If you truly want to gain a good understanding of yourself, and if you truly want to be the best person you can be—to live to the best of their ability, and to discover your own gifts and talents—then helping your spouse to develop and grow will be a central part of what makes your own development possible.

At the same time, it's also true that you need to avoid shortchanging yourself. You *do* need to make sure that you change and grow in your own right. If your personal growth somehow ends up stunted or frustrated, and if you feel unhappy with yourself—whether physically, spiritually, or emotionally—you'll probably end up being a boring, frustrated person. The situation will damage your marriage. So you need to strive for balance between developing yourself and attending to your spouse's well-being and happiness.

This need for balance is crucial for all couples—early on, in a "settled" marriage, during midlife, and later in life.

DREAMING TOGETHER FOR COUPLES EARLY ON

For couples who are just starting out—either as prospective marital partners or as spouses in the early years of a marriage—dreaming together is crucial. It's a must-do aspect of exploring your present and future relationship. Why is it so important? Because dreaming together helps you in two critical ways.

First, it contributes to the process of your getting to know each other.

It assists you in showing where your separate visions of life overlap. During the premarital counseling I provide to couples, I can always tell if the partners have shared their goals and vision for life as they prepare for marriage. The future spouses sometimes express very different visions of life—of work issues, of parenting, of domestic arrangements, of financial issues, on and on. At times the differences are so great that I can't help but wonder what these two see in each other! If the future groom dreams of raising horses in Wyoming and the bride-to-be dreams of a career in the fashion industry, they have a problem.

Second, dreaming together is one of the ways that a new couple creates a vision of where they're heading together. They're making a plan for their future. I don't mean to say that everything they dream about will come true. Obviously there's an enormous amount of work necessary for any couple to make their dreams a reality. But dreaming together is certainly a way of "sketching" what they want to have happen. Examples include:

- What kind of work each of them wants to do

- What sort of further education they plan to acquire

- How affluent a life they intend to live, and what their long-term financial goals are

- Whether they intend to have children—and, if so, how many, and how soon

- Where they want to live and under what circumstances—in an apartment, in a house; in a city, in a town, or in a rural setting; near their families or off on their own

- What sort of social life they want to have

- What sort of hobbies, recreational activities, and other pastimes they find important

ॐ What kinds of commitments they want to make to their wider community (such as attending church, volunteering in their town or neighborhood, taking part in local politics, and so forth)

I urge you and your partner to explore all of these topics before marriage, as you settle down together after your wedding, and on an ongoing basis. The dialogue you undertake is important in its own right; that is, simply the recurrent act of discussing these issues will help draw you close and keep you close. In addition, your discussions will provide important insights about where you agree, where you disagree, and how you need to compromise.

DREAMING TOGETHER FOR SPOUSES IN A "SETTLED" MARRIAGE

What if you've been married for a while—let's say two, three, five years or so? What if you and your spouse have settled in together, you know each other pretty well, and you're now comfortable with married life? Does this mean that you don't need to dream together?

On the contrary, dreaming together is just as important for a "settled" couple as for prospective spouses or newlyweds. Marriage is a long-term journey, and dreaming together is one of the ways that you "navigate" as the years pass and your relationship changes and develops. If you don't dream together, there's a risk that you'll lose touch with each other. You may cease to discover or define goals you hold in common. You may, in fact, diverge from each other and head off in different directions, perhaps so much that you no longer feel emotionally close. In addition, dreaming together is an important part of the ongoing process of getting to know each other as you mature, deepen, and learn from experience. The process of dreaming together also helps your relationship evolve. As the two of you change and have new experiences, your relationship should change as well, to accommodate your growth and development.

Here's an example. One of the most crucial issues for a couple to dream about is whether or not they plan to have children. Few aspects of their life together can be more fulfilling, but probably none will be more demanding and challenging. So the husband and wife should think through on many levels (practical, emotional, financial) how they plan to raise a family. Dreaming together in this sense is both a way of deciding what the couple prefers and a way of visualizing what the reality of parenthood will be like.

Jake, currently in his fifties, found this process a huge help in preparing himself to be a father. "I didn't even want to have kids until I met Arie," he explains. "I was thirty years old and had never really spent much time around children. But when Arie and I were engaged, we talked a lot about parenthood and what we wanted. I was pretty up front with Arie about my attitude, and she was blunt with me, too. For a while our difference of opinion seemed like a big obstacle between us. But as we talked, I got more and more curious about having kids and what that would be like. I'd say things like, 'It's not that I don't like children—it's that I'm afraid I'll be a terrible dad.' And Arie would say, 'No, you'll be great. You just don't know that yet.' So we'd discuss what the day-to-day tasks are like, and that reassured me. Sometimes I'd raise issues that she hadn't thought about, like saving for college costs, so that helped her figure things out, too. And little by little we made the decisions that led to our having a family." Jake and Arie have now raised two sons almost through their high school years—an experience that Jake eagerly offers as one of the most fulfilling of his entire life.

I should state outright that I feel that child-rearing should never be the exclusive responsibility of the mother. The old division of labor— Mom takes care of the children, Dad brings home the bacon—is pretty much obsolete nowadays. A much healthier perception of marriage and parenting is when the spouses share responsibilities, jobs, and parental duties. That way, at every stage of life, when life throws its curveballs, both spouses are there to catch them together. They're able to adapt more flexibly and help each other more supportively. They're more capable of dealing with each set of challenges.

But here's the bottom line: you need to figure out your own priorities and chart your own path. Dreaming together doesn't mean only a vague exercise in wishful thinking. It's also a practical, useful way to figure out complex decisions like parenthood—or, for that matter, educational or vocational issues.

DREAMING TOGETHER FOR SPOUSES IN A MIDLIFE MARRIAGE

After many years of married life, many couples feel that they know everything about each other and can predict everything the future will bring. This sense of familiarity and stability isn't necessarily a bad thing. In fact, the calm of a midlife marriage can be a wonderful thing.

However, I suggest that couples still dream together. Midlife marriage may be pleasantly calm, but there's always a risk that calm will turn into stagnation. It's easy for spouses to take each other for granted. It's also easy for the comforting routines of married life to wear a clear path in the ground that starts to look remarkably like a rut.

Janice is a typical example of a woman who fell into a rut. An accountant by training, she has worked the same job for twenty years, and she's been married to Stewart for almost that long. The couple's two daughters are now both getting ready to go to college. Everything about her work, her marriage, and every other aspect of Janice's life is stable. Not a bad thing. Overall, she is content. But she feels restless and jittery in ways that she can't quite describe, much less explain. At times she feels twinges of something like despair. "Is this it?" she asks. "Is this what the rest of my life will be like? That would be the worst thing in the world— and I feel bad about complaining. But sometimes I just can't imagine going on like this. It's like I've got the 'Seven-Year Itch'—but it's not really my husband I want to divorce—it's my own life!"

I believe that part of what ails Janice is a lack of ongoing dreams. She and her husband haven't put in the time to look down the road and imagine what to do with their lives. I'm not advocating that they chuck everything, run away, and do something radically different. But I sense that they've let their horizons narrow, and that's not healthy. Among other things, I feel that they don't really know each other anymore, which eventually will lead to a sense of estrangement or resentment.

The first thing that's necessary for a midlife couple is enough freedom to let each spouse develop in different areas, but in ways that won't draw them apart. Growing together doesn't mean doing exactly the same things together. However, it does mean allowing each other's ambitions or dreams to develop. As years pass, you need to have mutual agreements to let each other develop in different areas, and you need to support each other in your dreams. Here are some examples of one spouse's dream and what the other spouse can do to be supportive:

- ∾ After decades of responsibilities as a stay-at-home parent, Maya wants to go back to college and get a degree. Her husband, Nick, can be supportive by encouraging her studies, accepting her absence several nights a week, and taking her aspirations seriously.

- ∾ Ken is sick of life in the fast lane. At sixty years of age, he now hopes to "downshift" to a part-time schedule and devote ten hours a week to volunteer activities at his church. Melinda, Ken's wife, can support him by anticipating the couple's reduced income in the future and limiting expenses accordingly.

- ∾ Nancy, who has always wanted to pursue her musical interests but has never had time for this pursuit, started piano lessons some months ago. At first her husband, Liam, teased her about her aspiration: "Next stop, Carnegie Hall!" But he should support Nancy's musical avocation in its own right, not because it will lead to a career.

∞ Marcus and Annette have always spent their vacations at the beach. But Marcus, who loves to travel, wishes the couple to range farther afield and see different historical sites in the U.S. now that they're retired. Annette enjoys the unstructured weeks by the sea, but she wants to support her history-buff husband by agreeing to road trips every other year.

Be sure that there's *mutual* support in the relationship. In a lot of marriages, there's a tendency for the woman to get shortchanged. There's a tendency for the men to have more leeway in exploring their options and undertaking exciting opportunities; in the meantime, the women are expected to hold the family together single-handedly, which probably means suppressing their ambitions. This situation isn't fair to the wife, because she doesn't get as many chances to explore her own talents and interests. It isn't really fair to the husband, either, because it gives him a "blank check" that may lead to selfishness or self-indulgence. My recommendation: find a middle ground in which each spouse can change, grow, and develop. Dream together in a way that lets each of you contribute generously to the other's development.

In addition to supporting each other's dreams, middle-aged spouses need to rediscover each other *as a couple*. Relationships often change when kids grow up and leave the family. In many marriages, the "empty-nest syndrome" can prove challenging. The spouses now have more time available and long-delayed opportunities to focus on each other. Some couples find this transition delightful, but others find it confusing, even stressful. Spouses sometimes discover that they've forgotten how to see each other as husband and wife, not just as coparents. They may need months—even years—to explore their relationship anew, get acquainted again, and learn new ways of relating.

Among other things, couples may experience changes in one or both spouse's sexual appetite. Such changes are often normal, but they can lead to misunderstandings if not discussed openly. It's crucial for the partners to discuss their own and each other's emotional and physical needs. Many spouses have a tendency to withdraw into their own little worlds. Sexually speaking, this approach can lead to efforts to avoid each other physically, whether by going to sleep earlier, dozing in front of the TV, or disengaging from shared activities and interests.

Some couples even convince themselves that they don't need sexual intimacy in their marriage. They may say, "Oh, we're beyond that." I believe that this attitude is usually a sign of dysfunction. The frequency of sexual intimacy may change, and that's fair enough, but there still needs to be some sort of physical sharing. When there's no physical intimacy at all, there's a problem. The exception, of course, is when one or both partners have some sort of physical disability. But otherwise, a rejection of sexual interaction usually means that the spouses have disassociated themselves from each other. Sometimes (though rarely) both partners feel this way. Usually it's one person imposing his or her own problem on the other.

Sometimes the couple simply gets out of the habit of intimacy. The spouses forget to give each other any physical or emotional affection, and they lose a sense of intimacy as a central to their relationship. When this happens, it's often difficult to reconnect. It's unfortunate in its own right, since intimacy can be so fulfilling and reassuring; but in addition, a fading of mutual desire and delight is also risky. Why? Because one partner may continue to crave affection even though the other doesn't, and this imbalance can tempt that partner to fill the emotional void outside the marriage. In my experience working with couples, this situation is often what prompts infidelity. A spouse who feels sexually neglected is often much more prone to look for a nonmarital partner for physical and emotional affection.

If any of these scenarios sound familiar, it's time for you and your spouse to rediscover each other. And midlife marriage is the perfect time to do this. With your children grown up and leaving home, you'll find that parenthood is no longer the focus of your marriage. This situation gives you an opportunity to focus on each other instead. This is an absolutely crucial transition. From the time you and your partner meet to the time you're elderly, you'll have many stages of discovering and rediscovering each other. The demands on your time and energy will energize some of this process of discovery. However, it's crucial that you take responsibility for the process. If you just hope for the best and "go with the flow," you're likely to drift apart. But if you stay active in the process—dreaming together even as you enter your fifties and sixties—you're more likely to rediscover each other and redefine your marriage on an ongoing basis.

DREAMING TOGETHER FOR SPOUSES LATER IN LIFE

The process of dreaming together can occur even in couples who have been together for a very long time. Let's say we're talking about a couple who have been together twenty-five years or more. They've been loyal. They've been supportive. They've seen each other through stages of professional growth and childrearing. They're approaching retirement. What now?

Well, some people want a new stage in life. I see this in a lot of women. They want to get a college degree or maybe try out a new job. They want to reinvent themselves. Others just want to kick back and play. Some men go out and buy a sports car—or a motorcycle! Still others want to do volunteer work. These are all legitimate options. As the saying goes, "Different strokes for different folks."

What if one spouse lacks a desire to change and grow? Sometimes there's a sense that this person has just fallen into a rut. He or she has given up on ongoing development. There's a sense of indifference, of apathy about life. Sometimes this may even involve health issues, such as when this person isn't taking care of him- or herself. Maybe the man becomes a couch potato, or the woman becomes overweight. The attitude is "I don't care about myself." They let themselves run down physically or emotionally. Then the other spouse feels, "Hey, wait a minute. I'm married to somebody different now—totally different." This is a bad situation for both partners. It's important for people to grow together with a positive self-image, to have a sense that they can always be better and do everything possible to grow and change in positive ways.

When you lose a healthy sense of ambition, you lose a zest for life. That affects more than you as an individual; it also affects your marriage. If you start to coast, you enter a stage of apathy and indifference. Nothing really matters. It's possible that this state of mind may indicate some form of depression or some other health- or mental health–related issue. It's important to take that possibility into account. But it's also possible that the you have just disengaged from life—gotten into a "whatever" state of mind that's essentially a form of emotional or spiritual laziness.

Actually, this can happen in different ways at different stages. But in any case, it usually means that one spouse has lost a certain zest for doing things, for participating fully in their activities or even in their marriage. That can certainly be a problem. It's not even that people have given up; they haven't made a willful choice to disengage from life. They're just exhausted. Emotional and spiritual fatigue settles in after a while. People get tired of the job they're working. They get physically tired. This is all understandable. Life is demanding, and people's obligations over the years take a toll. But it seems to me that there's a volitional aspect to the situation. You may rightly decide that you're not going to go out and run any marathons, and that's fine, but you still need to maintain your health. You may not keep the same schedule you did when you were twenty-five, but you still need to stay active. You may not participate in fifteen different activities, but you still need to maintain some interests and do more than just watch TV or stare out the window. This holds true for your marriage, too. You may not be the frisky husband or wife you were during your early years together, but you still need to pay attention to your spouse, be affectionate, and make sure that your spouse is the center of your life.

NURTURE YOUR RELATIONSHIP

My hope is that the preceding discussions will give you some good ideas about how you and your spouse can dream together. Some couples undertake this task almost without planning—they speculate about the future, compare notes about their needs and interests, and compromise as they work toward shared goals. Other couples need to focus on dreaming together with more forethought. Either way, I believe that this issue is a central aspect of making a commitment to growth and maturity.

I also believe that you and your spouse can take some other important steps toward this goal. Elsewhere in this book, we've discussed the importance of foundations, of respect, of honesty, and other subjects. All of those issues are crucial. But in addition, I recommend that you work toward growth and maturity by nurturing your relationship on the deepest psychological and spiritual levels.

Those need to be part of your fundamental intentions as a couple over the long term. Four approaches that I strongly suggest are that you seek psychological guidance, seek spiritual guidance, leave the past behind, and keep hope alive. Let's explore each of those approaches in turn.

SEEK PSYCHOLOGICAL GUIDANCE TOGETHER

I've stated throughout this book that I regard psychological guidance as helpful—even crucial—in attempting to understand complex life issues. Earlier in this chapter, I described how seeking individual guidance on psychological issues can help you know your own dreams, understand your past, and make decisions about your future. I also believe that psychological guidance can help a couple with these issues, and many more, including issues that concern communication, sex, parenting, careers, and retirement. Unfortunately, many couples are reluctant to seek help from a psychologist or other mental health professional. Why? I guess they hold the same views—erroneous preconceptions, in my opinion—that make people reluctant to speak with a counselor under other circumstances. Rest easy. Seeking psychological guidance for marital issues is a sign of strength, not a sign of weakness. It shows that you're open to the insights that a counselor or therapist can share with you—insights that can help foster your growth and maturity as a couple.

It's true that some spouses seek psychological guidance because of stresses and misunderstandings within the marriage. These are excellent reasons to work with a counselor. Other husbands and wives, however, start marital therapy (also called couples counseling) as part of a more open-ended quest to understand their relationship and how they can improve it. Couples counseling is an excellent way to consider some questions that can have a big impact on your marriage:

- How do you nurture your relationship?

- If you're close, how can you maintain and strengthen your closeness?

- If you're not close, how can you become closer?

- How do you grow and mature in your love for your spouse?

- How can a couple build a strong and meaningful life together?

- What are goals or decisions that can make your marriage stronger?

If the possibility of couples counseling interests you, there are many options to choose from. Secular (nonreligious) counseling is available in most communities through neighborhood mental health centers and private practices. Your best bet for locating a suitable counselor is to request a referral from a trusted friend, physician, or pastor. Some communities also have regional referral services. In addition, most Christian churches and Jewish temples will provide services for (or referrals to) couples counseling.

Some denominations actually require counseling for couples prior to marriage. Marriage in the Catholic Church requires premarital counseling. If the prospective bride and groom are both Catholic, the couple goes through a *pre-Cana*—up to four months of classes in preparation for marriage. If either the bride or groom isn't Catholic, the couple attends a weekend *engagement encounter*—a retreat in which the couple attends group sessions as well as taking on individual assignments. Protestant ministers may also require premarital counseling before the wedding. Four meetings between the minister and the couple is typical. Other engaged Christian couples may attend weekend Family Life Conferences, which a branch of Campus Crusade for Christ sponsors and organizes throughout the United States.

For young couples, psychological guidance of this sort can offer assistance as they face decisions about sexuality, about whether to have children, or about family/spousal roles. More established couples may concentrate on the challenges of marital change, child-rearing, educating the children, finances, and family logistics. Still later in life, couples may benefit from guidance about preretirement and retirement issues: taking stock of life accomplishments and shortcomings, charging values, plans for old age, and so on. I believe that couples counseling can be a huge help in addressing issues that spouses can't ignore—not just "problems" (in any sense of the word), but also the potential that you have as husband and wife but haven't yet entirely fulfilled.

SEEK SPIRITUAL GUIDANCE AS A COUPLE

Just as I recommended spiritual guidance to you earlier for your own individual quest, I also recommend that you and your spouse seek spiritual guidance together. I believe that all couples can benefit from spiritual advice or a religious retreat now and then. For young couples, guidance of this sort can provide a compass to help guide them through the complex decisions and events that life will present throughout their marriage. For spouses who have been together for many years and are already on a path of growth, spiritual guidance can strengthen them as they deepen in insight and maturity.

I should add that psychological guidance and spiritual guidance aren't necessarily separate agendas. The issues you face (and perhaps struggle with) in each may overlap. In fact, certain kinds of counseling may address both sets of issues. An example: Jerry, a corporate lawyer, felt stagnant and depressed despite his success in the business world. He feared at times that his life had become meaningless, and he worried about his tendency to drink heavily as a way of relieving the stress and anxiety he felt. On seeking advice from his minister, Jerry realized that the *focus* of his work was a large part of what troubled him. Spiritual counseling helped to clarify his personal values and goals; he discussed his career options with his wife; and he eventually quit his corporate job, found work with a local not-for-profit foundation, and now devotes his legal expertise to helping homeless families in his city. Jerry's sense of meaninglessness was partly a practical problem and partly a spiritual dilemma, and counseling helped to resolve both.

LEAVE THE PAST BEHIND

A real impediment to growth and maturity in couples' relationships is constant references to the past. Many people live chiefly in the past and pay little attention to the present or the future, even though the here-and-now and what's to come are really what matter. Living in the past is a big mistake. Unfortunately, it can stunt your development. Why? Because it prevents you from enjoying the people right in front of you—perhaps even including your spouse—and it can prevent you from creating a future together.

I'm constantly amazed by how many people base their sense of reality on obsessing about the past. Such obsessions may focus on good things that have happened long ago, or they may focus on bad experiences. Either way, it's a problem.

For instance, Shelley, now in her early fifties, struggled for years with a haunting sense of loss. She had fallen in love with Allan two decades earlier, and the couple had been engaged to be married. Then Allan fell in love with another woman and broke off his engagement with Shelley. The collapse of what had been a genuinely close relationship jolted Shelley severely, led to a long period of depression, and damaged her ability to trust other men or to feel confident about making commitments. A number of later love affairs suggested the possibility of relationships, perhaps even marriage, but in Shelley's mind, none of her prospective husbands measured up to Allan. Shelley shied away from committing herself to anyone. In short, she fixated on the past in ways that damaged both her present and future happiness. She felt "painted into a corner" (to use Shelley's own words) by her obsession with the past. But she couldn't seem to overcome this state of mind. She seemed more intent on focusing on long-past regrets than on devoting her time and attention to a new, vibrant relationship in the here-and-now.

Unfortunately, many men and women spend way too much energy dwelling on the past. Sometimes people rehash old events over and over. I'm constantly amazed by how many people walk into a confessional to tell me things that they've confessed time after time. I often have to remind them, "I'm sure God has already forgiven you. Will you please forgive yourself?" (Or, as the venerable Catholic wisecrack puts it: "Get off the cross—we need the wood.") For some reason people can be very hard on themselves by accentuating past errors or negative experiences. It's as if they can't accept their own fallibility, concentrate on learning from their mistakes, and make the best of the time and opportunities before them. This is a big mistake!

The greatest problem with living in the past is that it keeps you from growing toward the future and improving the overall state of your life. In short, it limits your potential for growth and maturity. Wouldn't it be healthier and more constructive to move on and get down to work on the tasks at hand? Can you change what happened long ago? Not at all.

Trying to do so will expend energy on a task you can't possibly accomplish. Can you make different choices, explore new opportunities, or develop talents and gifts in the present? Yes, indeed. The present is, in fact, the arena where you can accomplish something. So I say, yes, learn from your mistakes, grow from your experiences, and don't fall into negative behaviors in the future. But then move ahead. Accept your potential for development and creativity.

KEEP HOPE ALIVE

The virtues of faith, hope, and love are among the strongest pillars of Christianity—essential qualities for anyone who wants to understand the mysteries of God and life. I've always felt puzzled, though, that we Christians talk a lot about faith and love, yet hope is a virtue we don't discuss much. I'm not sure why. Hope is certainly one of the most powerful and important psychological and spiritual attributes as we move through life. The experiences of people who have overcome challenging and even tragic events provide us with inspiring examples of how the power of hope can strengthen us and change our lives. Hope teaches us that growth is possible despite pain and struggle.

Of all the virtues that we can talk about, hope is one of the most necessary. When you have hope, you have a vision. When you have hope, you have a perspective. Hope allows you to move beyond the pain you experience, the confusions you feel, and the struggles you encounter. When you don't have hope, your horizon narrows. You close yourself into a much smaller space, and your problems and difficulties become obstacles that you'll find difficult, even impossible, to overcome. But when you have hope, you have an open vision of the world. You gain an almost limitless horizon.

What does hope have to do with relationships and married life? Everything. It's not a well-kept secret that marriage is challenging. Every couple faces difficulties—difficulties that the partners face together in coping with life's challenges, but also difficulties that they encounter in living together as husband and wife. I don't mean this comment as a negative assessment of marriage. On the contrary, I believe that marriage offers one of the greatest sources of happiness in our earthly life. But even the happiest couple will face difficulties. As we've discussed throughout this book, marriage assumes a radical openness by each spouse toward the other, which in itself is a daunting challenge. Both day-to-day tasks and the long-term confront couples with demands that require abundant patience, imagination, and hard work. To complicate matters, every marriage will face its share of hardships, uncertainties, disappointments, emotional ups and downs, practical demands, and tragedies. Even the most blissfully wedded husband and wife will eventually face the reality of death. As you can imagine, one of the abilities that a couple should add to its "repertoire" is hope.

If you really want to grow and mature—and if you want your relationship to grow and mature—hope is crucial. Hope is, in fact, a kind of "fuel" that helps to energize love. You already possess the solutions to many issues in your relationship, but hope is an ingredient that will provide stamina and strength as you and your spouse deal with life's challenges. Even partners who love each other may, if they lack hope, tend to feel depleted and overwhelmed by what they encounter over the years. It's not that they don't have good intentions or don't try hard; rather, the risk is that they'll give up too easily. They'll tend to feel that life should be easier—that God or fate or reality should give them fewer obstacles or complications. They'll be tempted to despair when hit by setbacks, disappointments, or tragedies. In short, they may feel entitled to a better set of circumstances than seems likely, given the tough times that most human beings face sooner or later. The attitudes I'm describing suggest a less than fully mature perception of life. By contrast, a couple with hope will probably maintain a more flexible, accepting vision of human experience, and the spouses will respond with greater imagination, energy, and stamina as they cope with whatever they face. They will, in short, be more mature.

Here's my deepest belief about this situation. We begin to grow and mature in our relationships—each in our own way—when we discover our own inner God-given capacities for hope, faith, and love, and when we're open to others' capacities for the same virtues. This statement is true regardless of the nature of our relationships; it applies to our ties to family members, to friends, to spouses, and to everyone else we encounter. It's certainly relevant to what couples face as they build their lives together. When we put aside minor matters—material possessions, petty whims, and selfish impulses—and when we pay attention to love and allow ourselves to be motivated by it, then we can truly begin to find happiness and fulfillment in our relationships. I assure you that your relationships will grow and mature best if you base them on lasting commitments and selfless love. Good relationships and good marriages stand the test of time when they are based on hope, faith, and love. Through these virtues, we all tap into our deepest capacities to give and to receive. Through these virtues we attain our greatest abilities to help fulfill the people we love. Through these virtues we also fulfill our own greatest potential for true freedom and happiness.

Chapter 15

How to Make a Commitment to Growth and Maturity

There's no way to quantify emotional and spiritual growth. I'd never claim that a specific set of exercises will guarantee that you achieve maturity, either on your own or in your marriage. I do believe, however, that certain steps you take can foster growth and maturity, or else help you understand the progress you're making—and the progress you need to make. What follows are seven tasks that I hope will facilitate this process.

Task #1
Dream Together

I stated in the previous chapter that spouses need to know their own individual dreams but must also dream together. Here's an exercise that will start the process of doing both. (You can undertake this task at any stage of marriage.)

Part One involves knowing your own dreams. Working separately at first, you and your spouse should explore your individual aspirations, hopes, and wishes for the future.

- ∾ Write the current date in a notebook or on a blank sheet of paper.

- ∾ Write a brief summary of your life—your work, your marriage, your immediate family situation (kids, no kids), your extended family situation (elderly parents, etc.), your state of health, and any other core issues.

- ∾ Write a one- or two-sentence comment about what you find satisfying or dissatisfying about these aspects of your life.

- ∾ Now write the date five years hence. Below that date, write what you wish or dream you could do, have, or be in five years. List anything that seems important or appealing to you.

- ∾ Below this "wish list," write what you would have to plan, do, and accomplish to make each wish or dream a reality.

- ∾ Now write the date ten years hence. Below that date, write what you wish or dream you could do, have, or be in five years. Once again, list anything that seems important or appealing to you.

- ∾ If you want to expand the exercise, write the date fifteen or twenty years hence. Follow the same procedure for listing what you wish or dream you could do at that point in your life.

- ∾ Below this "wish list," write what you would have to plan, do, and accomplish to make each wish or dream a reality.

As you respond to this first phase of the exercise, you can list any dream that appeals to you. Keep in mind, however, that the more extravagant or fanciful your dreams are, the more difficult a task you'll face in achieving them. But there's no reason not to dream big. The goal of this task isn't to organize a battle plan guaranteed to change your life; rather, it's a kind of brainstorming session and reality check.

Part Two is a process of dreaming together. Since your spouse will have written down his or her own dreams, you should now compare notes. Read to each other what you've written. Discuss what each of you would need from the other to make your dreams possible. Consider what the consequences of different scenarios would be—benefits and drawbacks, expenses, time commitments, and impact on other members of your family.

This task isn't an exercise in logistical planning. It doesn't solve the many issues that arise when spouses start to change the status quo. Long-term planning isn't the goal here. Rather, the goal is to put a spotlight on hopes and aspirations that usually remain unspoken within a marriage. The goal is also to prompt discussion of how you can transform individual dreams into dreams you share as couple.

Task #2
Discuss Childbearing and Parenthood Early

Discussions about childbearing and parenthood need to start as early as possible in your relationship. In fact, they should precede by many years actual decisions about having kids.

Here are some general issues to consider:

- **Accept that when you have children, your life will change radically**—much more so, in fact, than you can possibly imagine. Most couples are surprised by how numerous and extensive these changes are. Can you figure out these changes in advance? Probably not. But if you discuss what's coming up before the baby arrives, you'll at least be more realistic about what's happening.

∾ **Think about how you and your spouse will balance your affection for each other** with your affection for the new life that will be part of your household. Many couples make the mistake of putting all their emphasis and all their energy on the child, which can leave your marital relationship hungry—even starved—for affection.

∾ **Consider ways to ration your energy among the various tasks you face as a spouse and as a parent.** If you're not careful, you may intensify the fatigue that's an inevitable part of parenting. You need to allot time both to your children and to your spouse. Don't risk malnourishing your marriage!

∾ **Figure out ways to set aside time for sex.** Many couples end up so busy and so tired that they forgo any (or enough) sexual activity. This is not a good situation! Yes, family life is incredibly busy. But your sexual relationship is so important and so energizing for your body, mind, and soul that it's risky to imagine that it's somehow a low-priority aspect of your marriage.

∾ **Avoid spending time on less important or even trivial pastimes, when the time could be more creatively devoted to your marriage.** Many couples pay more attention to TV or computer games than they do to each other. Does that really reflect your priorities?

To advance the discussion, ask yourselves (and each other) these questions:

∾ How many children do you plan to have?

∾ What sort of arrangements will be necessary (maternity leave, paternity leave, childcare for other kids in the family) before and after the baby's arrival?

∾ In what ways will other family members (grandparents, adult siblings, others) help you once the baby is born?

- What are your plans for parenting arrangements—Mom only at home, Dad only at home, Mom and Dad trading off, or something else?

- What are your plans for how parenting will affect your work obligations?

- What arrangements have you made to cover increased financial expenses as you start your family?

- What arrangements have you made for additional health-related issues (obtaining insurance coverage for the children, finding a pediatrician, and so forth)?

- How will you and your spouse factor in time for each other as husband and wife during the parenting years?

- What kinds of emotional and spiritual resources (including friends, relatives, counselors, parenting support groups, and pastors) are available to you to provide support during the parenting years?

Task #3
Husbands, Get Involved in Parenting

I see a remarkable changes taking place throughout our culture. The more husbands get involved in parenting tasks, the more respect and understanding they have for what's involved in parenthood. These changes may seem obvious, but the consequences in many marriages are revolutionary. It's not just that men are contributing more time and energy to daily tasks of raising children than they did even a few decades ago; they're also gaining greater insights into the decisions that a couple should share about how many children they can handle and how the spouses will go about raising them. Husbands also now have to sacrifice more of their own time and energy for the good of the whole family. It's no longer enough for Dad to arrive home from work and expect his wife to take care of everything. He has to pitch in and help out, too.

However, I feel that many fathers can reach out and contribute even more within the domestic arena. Here's what I recommend:

Be there for your kids. The most important action a father can take is to be there on his children's behalf. In stating these words, I'm not invoking the cliché that "simply showing up is half the job." A cruel or abusive father is usually worse than none at all. What I mean is hidden in the words *on his children's behalf.* Dads, be present in your children's lives. Look after them. Give them all the emotional and spiritual gifts you have to offer. Being part of your kids' lives through all the day-to-day, often tiny events of family life—dressing the children, fixing their meals, playing their games, listening to their stories, helping them with their homework—matters more than any material gifts you can offer them.

I realize that being present for the day-to-day events isn't always possible. Work obligations can also keep fathers away from their children far more than they'd like. Divorce often separates fathers from their kids. How can you deal with the limits that work schedules demand or that custody arrangements impose? Just do the best you can. Kid-centered activities often make more of a difference than grandiose gestures intended to "make it up to the kids" for time away from them. Frequent, relatively brief occasions of hanging out, playing games, or helping with homework may prove more satisfying than rare, protracted fancy outings and special occasions.

Get savvy. Learn everything you can about kids. Perhaps you already have some experience dealing with younger siblings, cousins, or nieces and nephews; if so, you're ahead of the game. But don't feel concerned if you're a first-time father. Many men haven't taken care of children before they become fathers, yet they learn fast and do fine once their own kids arrive on the scene. The key is to open your mind and get savvy. Some sources of information:

- **Your wife.** If your wife is experienced in caring for children, she's your best source of information. Best of all, you are parenting together, so you have the ideal situation for sharing her accumulated lore and advice. Keep an open mind and learn as much as you can.

- **Friends and relatives.** One of the best ways to learn about kids is simply to spend time with them. Since no one has established a rent-a-kid service yet, I recommend hanging out with your own siblings, other relatives, or friends who already have children. Your own kin may be ideal; close pals can be as good or better. The goal: gain direct experience from old hands. You can acquire skills on feeding, diapering, childproofing, and playing. Most good friends will be pleased to offer their opinions and will probably give you an earful.

- **Books.** This country is awash in parenting books. You can find hundreds about babyhood and scores on other subjects. Take your pick. One caveat: here, as with other subjects, don't assume that book learning equals true knowledge. I recommend focusing on good overviews of child development rather than "cramming for the final" through specific care-and-feeding manuals.

- **Videos and CDs.** Some good materials are available that focus on parenting skills.

- **Classes.** Especially for first-time parents, good parenting classes can be invaluable. Your local adult school or community college may have offerings. Classes may offer specific focus on babies, toddlers, preschoolers, and adolescents. Information from instructors can be valuable; the companionship and accumulated advice of other parents can be still more so.

Take it as it comes. All parents encounter rough patches during the parenting years. Rest easy—it all goes with the terrain. One of the things that children do best (and often!) is to confound your expectations. If you want everything to go according to your plans, you're certain to feel frustrated. A wiser strategy: don't push the river.

One man described his experience to me as follows: "Before I had kids, I told a friend of mine—the mother of three teenagers—that I questioned my ability to go with the flow. She said, 'Well, if you don't know how to do that yet, your kids will teach you.' And they have."

So by all means learn everything you can ahead of time, plan well, and do what you can to keep family life organized. At the same time, be ready to scrap your assumptions and improvise. This advice holds true on everything from weekend plans to vacations to the whole of life itself. Parenthood is nothing if not unpredictable. Don't expect otherwise.

Accept imperfection. There isn't a parent alive who doesn't mess up. You'll mess up, too. Like most American men, you'll feel terrible about it simply because our culture teaches you that guys should be cool, competent, and always in control. Rest easy. Everyone's parenting years are full of mistakes. Your children will survive, forgive you, and go on unfolding regardless. Forget about cultural expectations of mastery and finesse. Just love your kids, do the best job you can, accept the imperfections of everyday life, and proceed.

Lighten up! Last but definitely not least, don't forget to laugh. Parenting your kids may well be the most important thing you ever do, but it doesn't have to be serious. Accept the silliness and unpredictability of raising kids—*they* will, certainly. Maintaining your sense of humor will help you survive any number of crises.

Task #4
Wives, Give Your Husbands Time and Room to Grow

If you're like many women, you may find that one of the hardest tasks of marriage and parenthood is watching your husband grow into his role as father. Most American men have only minimal experience caring for kids until the birth of their own children; as a result, their wives often feel frustrated by their husbands' uncertainty and awkwardness. In other instances, women simply disagree with their husbands on how to perform certain parenting chores. Fair enough. If you find yourself dealing with these issues, however, it's worth thinking through the situation and stepping carefully to avoid undercutting your husband's good intentions and growing abilities.

Give your husband time to grow. Fatherhood, like motherhood, creates enormous change. If your husband feels confused or ambivalent, it's entirely understandable. Confusion and ambivalence don't necessarily mean that he's not committed to being a good father. Give your husband time to sort through his feelings. Talk things out. Stay open to the emotions that each of you will experience during the course of your years as parents.

Many men end up passionately devoted to their children. One man I know expressed his feelings this way: "I wanted to get married but never really wanted to have kids. Over the years, Sandy and I talked over the possibility and went around and around. I just couldn't imagine that kids would be more than a burden, and I didn't think I'd be a good father. Eventually I decided, okay, we'll have a kid, but only one. And I wouldn't guarantee how good I'd be as a parent. But the moment Sandy gave birth, everything changed. The baby came out and stared and me and I just melted. I fell madly in love. I knew right then that I'd do anything I could for my daughter. And I will. And the same goes for our son, who was born three years later. I've had to learn while doing the job, but that's fine. My kids are great teachers."

These last two points are crucial.

First, much of parenting involves on-the-job training. Many men I know find this surprising. In a culture where men often feel that they ought to know everything, it's a shock—and in some ways a relief—when they discover it's fine to learn as they go.

Second, many men (not to mention women!) are surprised by how frequently they gain crucial hints or directions from children themselves. Kids often tip parents off about what they need—yet another reason why you don't need to know everything. Both of these issues underscore the fact that many parenting tasks are acquired skills. If men haven't had early opportunities to acquire knowledge about childcare, it doesn't mean they won't pick up what's necessary. Even the most self-doubting new dad can be a quick study.

Give your husband *room* to grow. Your husband and your child will have their own relationship, one that is inevitably different from what you have with the child. Whether your husband is familiar with childcare or totally inexperienced, give him enough space to figure out his own ways of performing childcare tasks. If you persistently criticize his methods or style, you may undercut his willingness to take part in what needs to be done. A dad named Jake told me, "I take care of our kids a lot, but every time I dress our daughter or fix her a meal, my wife steps in and does it over. She puts Samantha in a different outfit or fixes her a different meal. I end up feeling like I'm not doing things right—my work isn't up to her standards. It's depressing when I'm trying so hard." There's a risk in such cases that the husband will simply give up. This is a regrettable development for everyone concerned, but it's not entirely surprising. Since mothers and fathers often parent differently, it's important that spouses provide each other with enough space to do things in their own individual ways.

Take the long view. Becoming a skilled parent is a long process for fathers and mothers alike. Many men struggle with contradictory cultural messages before deciding the kind and level of involvement they want as the father of their children. In addition, practical considerations (such as being the family's primary wage earner, if that's the case) may complicate your husband's ability to be as involved with the kids as he'd like to be. All of these issues put both of you under pressure. How should you respond? That's a question that no one outside of your marriage can answer. But my recommendation applies to most couples: take the time you can—and offer each other the time you both need—to grow into the tasks and roles of parenthood. Working together can only serve you well in the long run.

Task #5
Cultivate Your Relationship

The foundation of family life is the parents' marriage. If that foundation is shaky or tense, its instability can jeopardize the children's well-being. This situation leads to a quandary: on the one hand, the parents need to focus on their children, but focusing on kids *to the exclusion of the marriage* can undercut everyone's best efforts. The level of intimacy, cooperation, love, and respect that the partners share will greatly influence their satisfaction in all things. The relative stability and warmth of your marriage will also influence how your children establish intimate relationships in the future. In short, nurturing yourselves as husband and wife is one of the best ways for you to nurture your children.

During the parenting years, it's easy to forget that you're not just a mommy or a daddy. Sometimes a woman can get so involved in raising children that she ignores her husband's needs. Sometimes a man can become so engrossed in playing the breadwinner role that he neglects his wife. In this age of complex work-family roles, the spouses may both be involved in work and parenting, which is good, but they may ignore each other all the same.

My recommendation: don't ignore each other as husband and wife. Yes, it's essential to care your children fully and lovingly, but don't make them so completely the center of your life that you lose sight of your marriage.

Take time to be a couple. Your husband-wife relationship is the foundation of your family. Everything else grows out of that relationship. Making a living and raising your children demand most of your energy, but you should set aside at least a little time to nurture each other as partners. Pay attention to each other. Listen to each other closely. Read your spouse's body language. (One man I know told me, "I didn't even realize my wife was unhappy in our marriage until she said she wanted a divorce.") Unfortunately, the little things add up. If your spouse is complaining about some of these important but little things, consider how they may be adding up into something bigger. Everyone needs to feel important, nurtured, and appreciated.

Try to set some time aside for fun. You may feel that you can't afford a baby-sitter or an evening on the town, but you can't afford to burn out, either. Share some good times as well as the meaningful but exhausting tasks of parenthood. And if you're having trouble spending time together, you need to talk about that. Why is it hard to spend time with each other? What are the problems you're having either individually or as a couple that prevent you from relaxing and enjoying each other's company? Is the problem external—something economic or career-oriented, perhaps—or is it emotional or spiritual? Try to sort out what's causing the problem. Address those issues before the stresses involved do any damage to your relationship.

Don't become *only* a parent. When a child is born—especially the first child—some women tend to pay much less attention to their husbands, and they may forget that their husbands need time and affection, too. This is understandable in some ways, since a new mother is under a lot of stress as she copes with the tasks of caring for a new baby. But ignoring or neglecting her husband is unfortunate. It can lead to neglecting the marriage—always a big mistake. There's also the risk of jealousy at times, for the husband may start to feel that the child is the only thing that matters in his wife's world. It's almost as if there's a romantic triangle in which the kid is the other party.

My advice on this situation: I recommend that the husband be considerate of his wife's situation and all the tasks that she must now perform; at the same time, the wife should be considerate of her husband's role. Both spouses need to maintain a sense of balance.

Find time for physical intimacy. Many couples complain that once they're parents, romance and passion fade out of their life. One or both spouses may be too tired to make love. During the early months of parenthood, especially, when many mothers are nursing, some women just don't feel interested in sex. Such disinterest and fatigue are common, normal, and often temporary. However, many couples also find that even when parenthood seems less stressful and the demands on them ease, an active love life simply ends up far down on the list of priorities. If so, the couple should at least discuss the situation openly. Partners may or may not be able to change anything right away, but most people will feel more comfortable if their thoughts and feelings are out in the open. Discussions can help avoid misunderstandings. Some partners may worry, for instance, that the decline in lovemaking shows that their spouse no longer feels any sexual attraction, so it's often reassuring to learn that the situation is solely a matter of physical fatigue. In addition, it's possible that discussions will lead to planning more time together. Get organized. Find time away from your children. Plan times together that are relaxing and special. Celebrate your relationship as a couple.

Indulge yourselves—together. Finally, here are some other, more specific suggestions for taking care of yourselves—admittedly small things that can make a difference:

- Steal time together for a late-night snack or glass of wine and some spouses-only conversation.

- Take a walk in the park together.

- Give each other back rubs.

- Join a parenting support group so you can compare notes and exchange ideas with other parents.

- Listen to music together after the kids have gone to bed.

- Treat yourselves to a take-out meal so that neither of you has to cook.

- Hire a mother's/father's helper to take some pressure off your shoulders.

- Trade child care with a parent in the neighborhood so that the two of you can have more time off together.

- Go on a date—not necessarily a night out, but special time together when the kids are looked after by a grandparent or a babysitter. (Ideally, this should be a romantic occasion, such as a candlelit dinner together.)

Task #6
Nurture Your Own Growth and Maturity

Many spiritual traditions teach directly or indirectly that the earthy nature of family life doesn't rule out profound growth and maturity; on the contrary, the here-and-now aspects of marriage and parenthood contribute to what make them powerful forces of spiritual development. This concept appears in Christianity, Judaism, Hinduism, and Buddhism, among other traditions. Hinduism is especially explicit about how family life is essentially a spiritual practice.

Some traditions call this "the path of the householder." The householder rejects both the path of worldly pursuits (wealth, fame, and sensual delights as ends in themselves) and the path of renunciation (asceticism, rejection of all material goods). Instead, the householder takes a middle way that accepts both the reality of the flesh (sex, childbearing, child-rearing, and the nature of ordinary earthly life) and the reality of the spirit (prayer, meditation, and other disciplines). The day-to-day tasks and rhythms of marriage and parenthood are central to the householder's path. This path is simultaneously an end in itself—the task of giving your spouse and your children what they need to thrive— and a means of undertaking a personal quest—the pursuit of selflessness. By focusing on your family's needs, you move beyond your own personal desires, which opens your heart and mind to higher states of understanding. It's precisely by serving others that you grow toward wisdom and maturity.

Whether or not you choose to view parenthood as the householder's path, what are some ways in which you can combine child rearing tasks and spirituality? I can't think of many topics with a more personal set of answers, but here are some suggestions:

Formal religious practices. Many people find that participation in formal religious practices are the core of family spirituality. Membership in a church or temple becomes the hub that family life revolves around. If this situation suits your purposes, I urge you to pursue it in the ways that truly serve your family's needs. Church or synagogue activities can provide support, resources, companionship, and solace like little else in our earthly life.

Other paths. Here are some other activities that may contain spiritual dimensions you'll find helpful in overcoming stress and tension:

- Practicing t'ai chi, hatha yoga, or other forms of physical relaxation

- Dancing, singing, playing a musical instrument, painting, or practicing some other art

- Hiking, swimming, running, or engaging in other sports

- Prayer and meditation

Find an ally. You don't have to go it alone. No matter how much you're convinced that you can tackle family life unassisted, you'll almost certainly do better if you have an ally for the voyage. This ally is, ideally, your spouse. If a husband and wife are emotionally close, they will provide each other with invaluable sustenance as they attend to their family. But of course this alliance isn't always feasible. In addition, even spouses who are close friends and reliable partners may need other allies as they face the rigors of parenthood. Such an ally can be a friend, a relative, a counselor, a psychotherapist, or a member of the clergy. Whoever it is, though, it's important that this person be someone who will listen nonjudgmentally. Find someone you really trust.

Keep a journal. You can also write down your feelings about family life and explore them in a journal. The only rule in this method is not to censor what you write. Your feelings aren't right or wrong, good or bad. They just *are*. It's important to have an uncensored way of getting those feelings out, and a journal is an excellent means to this end.

How should you proceed? Just get started. The particular kind of journal doesn't matter: whether plain or fancy, the style is irrelevant; it's the process of writing that matters. Simply write what you're feeling—

daily, if possible. Be open and honest with yourself. You may have feelings that you find shameful, scary, or embarrassing. If so, that's okay. For instance, many parents feel angry with or frustrated by their children. You aren't hurting anyone by setting these feelings down on paper, and the release of these feelings will help to heal you. Allow yourself to feel what you're feeling. The act of writing itself will help you, since it's a safe, helpful way to vent your frustrations, and in the long run it may also help you gain a sense of perspective about your experiences.

One caveat: *make sure this journal is private.* Although "negative" emotions about family life are common, what you write may still hurt your spouse's or your children's feelings if they discover your journal. Make sure you keep it in a safe place that no one else can reach.

The goal of journal keeping is to get in touch with your feelings. One suggestion: try to tune out all the "shoulds." Ask yourself these questions:

- What do I *really* feel?

- What do I *really* fear?

- What do I *really* need?

- What do I *really* want?

If you keep saying to yourself, "I should . . . I should . . . ," it's a red flag. Because when you act only on all the *shoulds,* you're often out of touch with what you really feel and need. If you can be perfectly honest with yourself, you're more likely to get in touch with what you're really feeling.

Support groups. Many support groups exist for parents. Check your local newspaper for listings of groups, seminars, and workshops. Likely sponsors are Parents Without Partners, Jewish Children and Family Services, the United Way, and Catholic Family Services. Your local community college may also suggest good support groups.

Should you consider joining a support group? That's a question only you can answer. Many people shy away from this option; they feel uneasy about talking about family issues in a group. In general, however, most support groups are nonthreatening; participants are usually nonjudgmental. The goal is simply to discuss family issues, to share personal stories that others may find relevant, and to consider options or acquire skills that may make the parenting years easier and less stressful.

Task #7
Consider a Marriage Renewal Encounter

Many couples reach a stage where they feel their relationship has become stale or uninspired. Neither partner really wants to work on their marriage anymore. This is a regrettable, avoidable state of emotional stagnation. In fact, couples can make a decision to renew their commitment. When there's an element of faith in a marriage—when a couple is faithful and loving toward each other because they've made a lifelong commitment—there's usually an openness to making the relationship work. They've made that promise, that covenant before God, to be true to each other.

The commitment and faith I'm describing is the fundamental core of what happens at marriage renewal encounters. People who go through the encounter process are encouraged to do everything possible in this mode of renewal—to use whatever tools they have available to make the spark reignite. What was once meaningful in the relationship can become meaningful once again. I find that the people who participate in these marriage encounters all tell you pretty much the same thing: "We had lost our way in our marriage, and we weren't paying attention to each other." And most of them say that the encounter or retreat helps them to start paying attention to each other again.

These encounters go through all the basic issues that we've been considering in this book. The couples need to ask each other and themselves some central, sometimes difficult questions:

- ∾ Do I respect my spouse?

- ∾ Do I communicate with my spouse?

- ∾ Do I spend time with my spouse?

- ∾ Do I nourish my spouse?

- ∾ How do I treat my spouse sexually?

- ∾ Do we have other problems—such as in-laws, money problems, and so forth—that interfere with our relationship?

None of these problems exists all by itself. All relationship problems tend to be interrelated. Couples that have financial problems usually have sexual problems, too. Communication affects sexual satisfaction and vice versa. Couples who are having problems with their in-laws usually have communication problems or sexual problems or other problems, too. Intimacy affects everything in our lives, and very few couples are able to separate one issue from another. Very few couples can say, "Our relationship in bed is great, but everything else is terrible." The problems are usually widespread.

What is a marriage renewal encounter like? Since there are many dozens of encounters organized by many different denominations, it's hard to generalize. But here's a quick overview:

Most encounters start with one or more talks given by trained professionals—psychologists, marriage therapists, or others. And these talks give a "center" to the process. But there's also a dialogue that takes place within each couple and also sometimes among a group of couples. There may be five, six, or more couples together in a room with the mediator, and they discuss the issues they're facing.

The details of the programs vary, but almost every denomination now offers marriage retreats and encounters. Benefits of the encounters include improved communication skills, an awareness that other couples face similar issues as those you face, and greater closeness with your spouse.

For a listing of organizations that sponsor marriage encounters, see the Resource Guide at the end of this book.

WITHIN ONE'S REACH

"To mature is in part to realize that while complete intimacy and omniscience and power cannot be had," writes the American scholar Sisela Bok, "self-transcendence, growth, and closeness to others are nevertheless within one's reach" [*Secrets*, 1983]. This statement comes close to summarizing what I've tried to state throughout Path Seven. Growth and maturity aren't a destination you'll reach; they are a process you'll undergo, a journey you'll take. Complete intimacy, omniscience, and power are not human capacities. But something remarkable is within our reach: self-transcendence, growth, and closeness to others.

Although men and women can choose many paths as they take the journey toward growth and maturity, I believe that the most commonly chosen and most accessible path is that of marriage and parenthood. An easy path? No, of course not. Sharing your life with a spouse and children is complex, challenging, and often difficult. But family life is one of the most remarkable and beautiful gifts that God has granted us—a voyage that allows you simultaneously to devote yourself to others, and, in so doing, to become most fully yourself.

Conclusion

At the start of this book, I mentioned that in my various roles as a priest, radio and television show host, and columnist, many people come to me with concerns and questions about the expectations, habits, roles, changes, decisions, and daily events that constitute their relationships. Men and women struggle with these issues because they are genuine, recurrent aspects of real life and real love. Although Hollywood may claim otherwise, good relationships aren't fundamentally made of romance and sexiness; rather, they're the long-term result of mutual generosity, patience, and compromise. My hope is that this book has helped you better understand the Seven Paths that I consider the fundamental approaches to good relationships.

I'd like to conclude with some thoughts and affirmations about each of these Paths.

THE FIRST PATH: BUILD SOLID FOUNDATIONS

Real life presents all couples with a multitude of tasks and challenges to face as the partners share their years together. It's easy to feel daunted, even overwhelmed, by all the changes that occur when a man and a woman learn to live with (and for) each other. But if you can build solid foundations from the start, you can construct the rest of the relationship with greater confidence in the future. In my view, the most important step you can take toward attaining real love is to allow each other fully and openheartedly into your sacred center—the innermost core of your being.

THE SECOND PATH: RESPECT EACH OTHER

How can partners truly love each other if they feel no respect? It simply can't be done. Yet respect, like so many dimensions of a good relationship, is a long-term process, not a one-shot event. Respect in a relationship is your willingness to understand each other, your ability to accept the balance between good and bad in each other's personal qualities, and your commitment to compromising over day-to-day differences between you.

THE THIRD PATH: CLARIFY YOUR EXPECTATIONS

As an old wisecrack puts it: "Reality is overrated." Maybe; maybe not. But reality is what we have on here on earth. If you expect something different—something easier, something glitzier—you're likely to be disappointed. We are all flawed, limited human beings. If a man and a woman expect perfection when they form a relationship, their expectations may become a burden that weighs down both partners. A better approach: clarify your expectations—ideally, by communicating closely with each other—so that you can strive for real love through shared insights rather than through separate illusions.

THE FOURTH PATH: BE HONEST

Like respect, honesty is a must-have, must-do for solid relationships. How can your relationship be true if it's based on falsehoods? How can you trust the complex process of building a life together if what you say and what you do aren't worthy of trust? Although I believe that the greatest violation of honesty within relationships occurs when the partners resort to infidelity, other betrayals of trust can damage otherwise strong bonds. Honesty must honor the sacred center: a commitment to be fully who you are and to speak your heart and mind to the person you love most.

THE FIFTH PATH: COMMUNICATE

Communication is in many ways the "nuts and bolts" of real love. It's the moment-by-moment, specific ways in which you cope with life together, solve the problems you face, find common ground, and express the love you feel for each other. Marital counselors often state that most problems in relationships center on communication issues. No wonder—a relationship brings two completely different human beings together! You are reaching across an unimaginable gap of separateness. Yet if you can speak carefully, if you can listen closely, if you can think open-mindedly, you and your partner can bridge that gap in ways that few other kinds of relationships can attain.

THE SIXTH PATH: LEARN TO ACCEPT YOUR DIFFERENCES

This brings us to the question of differences. Relationships—and marriage above all others—are acts of radical trust. Trust that the partners can accept each other, flaws and all. Trust that they will *inspire* change in each other without *demanding* change. Trust that they will live as two individuals yet also live as one in a holy union. Real life means that there will inevitably be differences between you and your spouse; real love means that you will find ways to share, grow, and dream together.

THE SEVENTH PATH: MAKE A COMMITMENT TO GROWTH AND MATURITY

In one of the most famous and beautiful passages in the Bible, Saint Paul writes: "There are in the end three things that last: faith, hope, love, and the greatest of these is love." Marital love is in turn one of the deepest, truest expressions of faith, hope, and love. A couple's years together on earth should be cause for great celebration. You don't have to attain perfection in your marriage. But growth and maturity as you share faith, hope, and love—those are worthy goals for your time together.

I wish you health, peace, and God's light in your life together!

Appendix: Resource Guide

A common source of frustration in many relationships is the partners' belief that they have to solve all their problems by themselves. In fact, many resources exist specifically to help couples cope with the problems they face. My recommendation: If you're having difficulties in your relationship, find help. Locating resources may take a few phone calls or a few sessions at your computer, but the effort will be a lot easier and more productive than just suffering in silence.

To address these issues, I've written this section of *Seven Paths* to bring possible resources to your attention. I've categorized the listings carefully; please note, however, that some organizations' services overlap, so check the whole list to make sure you aren't missing a good source of help. Also, note that some resources are clearinghouses or umbrella organizations, not direct providers of services; they can, however, direct you to specific agencies or groups that offer services in your community.

The Resource Guide contains three sections:

- Organizations and associations
- Online information
- Further reading

ORGANIZATIONS AND ASSOCIATIONS

Many organizations provide useful information on specific issues and problems that may affect couples and families. Here's a sampling, presented in alphabetical order by category:

Alcohol and Drug Abuse

American Council for Drug Education
164 West 74th Street
New York, NY 10023
212.758.8060
800.488.DRUG

National Council on Alcoholism, Inc.
12 West 21st Street
New York, NY 10010
212.206.6770
800.NCA.CALL (hotline)

Narcotics Anonymous
P.O. Box 9999
Van Nuys, CA 91409
818.773.9999

National Clearinghouse for Alcohol and Drug Information
P.O. Box 2345
Rockville, MD 20847-2345
301.468.2600 or 800.729.6686

National Council on Alcoholism and Drug Dependence
12 West 21st Street, 7th Floor
New York, NY 10010
800.622.2255

Center for Substance Abuse Treatment
Information and Treatment Referral Hotline
11426-28 Rockville Pike, Suite 410
Rockville, MD 20852
800.662.HELP

Child Abuse

American Professional Society on the Abuse of Children
407 South Dearborn Street, Suite 1300
Chicago, IL 60605-1111
312.554.0166

National Committee for the Prevention of Child Abuse
P.O. Box 2866
Chicago, IL 60690
312.663.3520

Child Care

National Association of Child Care Resource and Referral Agencies
1319 F Street, N.W., Suite 810
Washington, DC 20004-1106
202.393-5501

National Child Care Association
1029 Railroad Street, N.W.
Conyers, GA 30207-5275
800.543.7161

Health Issues

American Academy of Pediatrics
141 Northwest Point Boulevard
P.O. Box 927
Elkgrove Village, IL 60009-0927
847.228.5005 or 800.433.9016

American Cancer Society
1599 Clifton Road, N.E.
Atlanta, GA 30329
800.ACS.2345

American Heart Association
7272 Greenville Avenue
Dallas, TX 75231-4596
214.373.6300 or 800.242.1793

Cancer Care, Inc.
1180 Avenue of the Americas
New York, NY 10036
800.813.4673

Cancer Information Service
Office of Cancer Communication
NCI, Bldg. 31, 10A07
9000 Rockville Pike
Bethesda, MD 20890
800.4.CANCER

Loss and Bereavement

Accord Aftercare Services
1930 Bishop Lane, Suite 947
Louisville, KY 40218
800.346.3087

Center for Death Education and Research
Department of Sociology
University of Minnesota
909 Social Science Building
267 19th Avenue South
Minneapolis, MN 55455-0412

The Compassionate Friends
P.O. Box 3696
Oak Brook, IL 60522-3696
708.990.0010

Marriage and Relationships

Academy of Family Mediators
4 Militia Drive
Lexington, MA 02173
617.674.2663

American Association for Marriage and Family Therapy
1133 15th Street, N.W., Suite 300
Washington, DC 20005
202.452.0109

Association for Marriage and Family Therapy
800.374.2638

Worldwide Marriage Encounter, Inc.
2210 East Highland Avenue, Suite 106
San Bernardino, CA 92404-4666
909.863.9963

LifePartners
6770 Eagle Ridge Road
Penngrove, CA 94951-9728
707.792.6700 or 800-DREAM-4-2

Counseling Catholics
Maria E. Camejo, MS, LMHC
13550 Kendall Drive Suite 130
Miami, Florida 33186
305.559-4546

Mental Health Issues

American Association of Psychiatric Services for Children
1200-C Scottsville Road, Suite 225
Rochester, NY 14624
585.236.6910

Sandwich Generation/Care of the Aging

American Senior Citizens Association
P.O. Box 41
Fayetteville, NC 28302
919.323.3641

Children of Aging Parents
Woodbourne Office Campus, Suite 302A
1609 Woodbourne Road
Levittown, PA 19057-1511
215.945.6900 or 800.CAPS.294

Self-Help

National Self-Help Clearinghouse
Graduate School and University Center
City University of New York
25 West 42nd Street, Suite 620
New York, NY 10036
212.642.2944

Single Parenthood

Parents Without Partners
401 North Michigan Avenue
Chicago, IL 60611-4267
800.637.7974

Stress

Parental Stress Line
800.632.8188

Violence

National Domestic Violence Hotline
800.799.SAFE or 800.787.3224

National Organization for Victim Assistance
1757 Park Road, N.W.
Washington, DC 20010
202.232.6682

ONLINE INFORMATION

As in other aspects of contemporary life, computer online services have increased your options for obtaining information on any of the issues listed above and others. That's the good news. The bad news is that the sources of information change often and unpredictably. Although what follows is a list of online resources that couples may find useful, keep in mind that any list of resources will change over time.

Fathers

www.fathersworld.com
A virtual community for men interested in fathers' issues, including balancing work and family.

www.slowlane.com
"The online resource for stay-at-home dads."

Financial Planning

http://lifenet.com/
A site with interactive calculators and other information to help guide you through major financial life events.

htp://update.wsj.com/
Continually updated information on markets, business, and investing from *The Wall Street Journal*.

www.wife.org
A financial-planning Web site for women, sponsored by the Women's Institute for Financial Education.

Health Issues

http://KidsHealth.org/
Tips on keeping children healthy or helping them when they're sick.

www.health.org
Information for children and adults about alcohol, drugs, and tobacco use and other health issues.

www.healthtouch.com/level1/bout.htm
Information on health, wellness, and illness.

www.kidsource.com
Information on education, health care, and products for parents and children.

www.menninger.edu
An educational Web site sponsored by the Menninger Child & Family Center with intent to spread useful information about psychiatric issues regarding children.

Loss and Bereavement

www.growthhouse.org
This site includes detailed information on family bereavement, helping children with illness and grief, the aftermath of miscarriage and stillbirth, and resources for the bereaved.

Marriage and Relationships

www.wwme.org
Worldwide Marriage Encounter, Inc., assists couples to live fully intimate and responsible relationships.

www.retrouvaille.org
A spiritual resource for couples who are serious about renewing their marriage.

www.lifepartners.com
A coaching experience for couples who need help in renewing their relationships.

www.counselingcatholics.com
A counseling service available on the Internet.

Parenting Issues

www.familyeducation.com
Established by the FamilyEducation Network, this site provides educational information, with specific focus on various issues as diverse as toddler behavior, home schooling, and learning disabilities.

www.parenthoodweb.com
A library of articles covering many issues, including pregnancy, children's products, and expert advice.

www.parent.net
Information for parents on a wide variety of topics.

www.parents.com
Parenting information from the publishers of *Parents*, *Child*, *Family Circle*, and *McCall's* magazines.

www.parentsplace.com
A "parents-helping-parents" community that offers advice, interactive tools, and firsthand wisdom from real parents; topics include infertility, illness, and bereavement.

FURTHER READING

Any big American bookstore now contains hundreds, if not thousands, of books about marriage and relationships. Here's a selection of classic and current books on relationships covering most of the topics discussed in this book:

Communication Between Spouses

Tannen. *You Just Don't Understand: Women and Men in Conversation.* New York: Ballantine, 1990.

Wallenstein, Judith. *The Good Marriage: How and Why Love Lasts.* New York: Houghton Mifflin, 1995.

Divorce

Blau, Melinda. *Families Apart, Ten Keys to Successful Co-Parenting.* New York: Putnam Books, 1993.

Fassel, Diane. *Growing Up Divorced.* New York: Pocket Books, Simon and Schuster, 1991.

Gardner, Richard. *Boys and Girls Book About Divorce.* New York: Bantam Young Readers, 1985.

Kaufman, Taube S. *The Combined Family: A Guide to Creating Successful Step Relationships.* New York: Plenum Publishing Corp., 1993.

Marguilis Sam. *Getting Divorced Without Ruining Your Life.* New York: Fireside, 1992.

Neuman, M. Gary. *Helping Your Kids Cope with Divorce: The Sandcastles Way.* New York: Times Books, 1998.

Wallerstein, Judith S., and Sandra Blakeslee. *Second Chances: Men, Women and Children a Decade after Divorce.* New York: Ticknor and Fields, 1989.

Drugs, Alcohol, and Tobacco

Garner, Alan. *It's O.K. to Say No to Drugs: A Parent/Child Manual for the Protection of Children.* New York: Tom Doherty Associates, 1987.

U.S. Department of Justice. *Drugs of Abuse*. Drug Enforcement Administration, 1988.

Family Life

Jones, Charles, Lauren Temperman, and Suzanne Wilson. *The Futures of the Family*. Englewood Cliffs, NJ: Prentice Hall/Simon & Schuster Co., 1995.

Spock, Benjamin. *Rebuilding American Family Values*. Chicago and New York: Contemporary Books, 1994.

Fathers

Lamb, Michael, ed. *The Role of the Father in Child Development*. New York: John Wiley & Sons, 1976.

Louv, Richard. *Father Love*. New York: Pocket Books, 1993.

Osherson, S. *Finding Our Fathers: The Unfinished Business of Manhood*. New York: Free Press, 1986.

Pruett, Kyle. *The Nurturing Father*. New York: Warner Books, 1987.

Scull, Charles. *Fathers, Sons and Daughters*. Los Angeles: Jeremy Tarcher, 1992.

Sullivan, S. Adams. The Father's Almanac. New York: Doubleday, 1992.

Williams, Gene B. *The New Father's Panic Book: Everything a Dad Needs to Know to Welcome His Bundle of Joy*. New York: Avon, 1997.

Juggling Work and Life

Hochschild, Arlie. *The Second Shift*. New York: Avon, 1997.

———. *The Time Bind: When Work Becomes Home and Home Becomes Work*. New York: Owl Books, 1998.

Houston, Victoria. *Making It Work*, Chicago and New York: Contemporary Books, 1990.

Middleman-Bowfin, Gene. *Mothers Who Work: Strategies For Coping*. New York: Ballantine Books, 1983.

Oldes, Sally. *The Working Parents' Survival Guide*. New York: Bantam Books, 1983.

Shreaves, Anita. *Remaking Motherhood*. New York: Ballantine Books, 1988.

Loss

Bowlby, John. *Attachment and Loss*. Vol. 3, *Loss*. New York: Basic Books, 1980.

Edelman, Hope. *Motherless Daughters: The Legacy of Loss.* Reading, Mass.: Addison-Wesley, 1994.

Grollman, Earl. *Living When a Loved One Has Died.* Boston: Beacon Press, 1974.

Krementz, Jill. *How It Feels When a Parent Dies.* New York: Alfred A. Knopf, 1981.

Kübler-Ross, Elisabeth. *On Death and Dying.* New York: Macmillan Publishing Co., 1969.

LeShan, Eda. *Learning to Say Good-By.* New York: Avon, 1976.

Myers, Edward. *When Parents Die: A Guide for Adults.* New York: Penguin Books, 1997.

Raphael, Beverley. *The Anatomy of Bereavement.* New York: Basic Books, 1983.

Mothers

Bassoff, Evelyn. *Between Mothers and Sons: The Making of Vital and Loving Men.* New York: Dutton, 1994.

Bernard, Jessie. *The Future of Motherhood.* New York: Penguin, 1974.

Kelly, Marguerite, et al. *The Mother's Almanac.* New York: Doubleday, 1975.

Towle, Alexandra. *Mothers.* New York: Simon & Schuster, 1998.

Parenting Styles

Brazelton, T. Berry. *On Becoming A Family.* New York: Delacorte Press/ Seymour Lawrence, 1981.

Galinsky, Ellen. *The Six Stages of Parenthood.* Reading, Mass.: Addison Wesley Press, 1987.

Satir, Virginia. *The New People Making.* Mountainview, Calif.: Science and Behavior Books, 1988.

Parents as Partners

Galinsky, Ellen. *Six Stages of Parenthood.* New York: Addison Wesley Publishing Company, 1987.

Samalin, Nancy. *Loving Your Child is Not Enough.* New York: Penguin, 1989.

———. *Love and Anger: The Parental Dilemma.* New York: Penguin, 1992.

Steinberg, Lawrence. *Crossing Paths: How Your Child's Adolescence Triggers Your Own Crises.* New York: Simon and Schuster, 1994.

Single Parenthood

Wayman, Anne. *Successful Single Parenting*. Deephaven, Minn.: Meadowbrook, 1987.

Stepparents

Burns, C. *Stepmotherhood*. New York: Times Books, 1985.

Diamond, Susan. *Helping Children of Divorce*. New York: Schocken, 1985.

Ecklcr, Jamcs. *Step-by-Stepparenting*. While Hall, Va.: Betterway, 1988.

Kaufman, Taube S. *The Combined Family: A Guide to Creating Successful Step-Relationships*. Ncw York: Plenum Press, 1993.

Rosen, M. *Stepfathering*. New York: Ballantine Books, 1987.

Stress

Carlson, Richard. *Don't Sweat the Small Stuff*. New York: Hyperion Books, 1997.

Covey, Stephen. *The Seven Habits of Highly Effective People*. New York: Fireside, Simon and Schuster, 1989.

Ginsberg, Susan. *Family Wisdom*. New York: Columbia University Press, 1996.

Houston, Victoria. *Making It Work*. Chicago and New York: Contemporary Books, 1990.

Saltzman, Amy. *Downshifting*. New York: Harper Collins, 1991.

Twenty-First-Century Parenting

Jones, Charles, Lorne Tepperman, and Suzanna Wilson. *The Futures of the Family*. New York: Prentice-Hall, Simon and Schuster, 1995.

Pipher, Mary. *The Shelter of Each Other: Rebuilding our Families*. New York: Grosset/Putnam Books, 1996.

Rank, Mark Robert, and Edward L. Kain. *Diversity and Change in Families: Patterns, Prospects and Policies*. New York: Prentice-Hall, 1995.

Wright-Edelman, Marion. *The Measure of Our Success: A Letter to My Children and Yours*. New York: HarperCollins, 1993.

Violence

Curran, Daniel et al. *Social Problems, Society in Crisis*. New York: Simon & Schuster and Co., 1996.

Miedzian, Myriam. *Boys Will Be Boys: Breaking the Link between Masculinity and Violence*. New York: Anchor, 1991.

Work-to-Home Transitions

Brazleton, T. Berry. *Working and Caring*. New York: Addison-Wesley, 1985.

Hewlitt, Sylvia Anne. *When the Bough Breaks: The Cost of Neglecting Our Children*. New York: Basic Books, 1991.

Hochschild, Arlie. *The Time Bind: When Work Becomes Home and Home Becomes Work*. New York: Owl Books, 1998.

Hochschild, Arlie, with Anne Machung. *The Second Shift: Working Parents and the Revolution at Home*. New York: Viking Penguin, 1989.